Pierre Jean Grosley, Thomas Nugent, Francisco de Macedo

New observations on Italy and its inhabitants

Pierre Jean Grosley, Thomas Nugent, Francisco de Macedo

New observations on Italy and its inhabitants

ISBN/EAN: 9783742828910

Manufactured in Europe, USA, Canada, Australia, Japa

Cover: Foto ©Suzi / pixelio.de

Manufactured and distributed by brebook publishing software
(www.brebook.com)

Pierre Jean Grosley, Thomas Nugent, Francisco de Macedo

New observations on Italy and its inhabitants

NEW OBSERVATIONS

ON

ITALY

AND ITS INHABITANTS.

WRITTEN IN FRENCH

BY TWO SWEDISH GENTLEMEN.

TRANSLATED INTO ENGLISH

BY THOMAS NUGENT, L. L. D.

AND FELLOW OF THE SOCIETY

OF ANTIQUARIES.

VOL. II.

LONDON:

PRINTED FOR L. DAVIS AND C. REYMERS,

PRINTERS TO THE ROYAL SOCIETY.

MDCCLXIX.

VELETRI

OBSERVATIONS

ON

ITALY.

ROME.

ANCIENT and modern Rome have been the object of so many disquisitions, investigations and surveys, that all farther discoveries seem to be at an end : the whole however is not yet exhausted. I shall hazard some considerations on certain objects, which have either escaped curiosity, or which I shall examine in a new light, and to avoid confusion shall distribute them under distinct titles. But these considerations, like all those in which I have indulged myself in the course of this work, are, to use the words of a French writer*, " Not the measure of the things, " but the measure of my sight."

* Montaigne, L. ii. c. 10.

ANTIQUITIES.

At every ftep in Rome, you meet with fome monuments, or fome ruins, relative to facts the more interefting, as on them it was that the eyes of the mind became opened in its earlieft ftudies.

Rome is the firft world that was known to us, and a world to the embellifhment of which hiftory, eloquence, poetry, and all the moft ornamental arts, have emuloufly exerted themfelves; *civitas, in qua nemo hofpes nifi Barbarus (a)*; a city, where they only are ftrangers who are ftrangers to literature, and to all knowledge either ferious or polite; and who never heard *di quelli Omaccioni che vi habitarono, di quei Republiconi liberi, finceri e d'animo veramente Romano**, of thofe great men, of thofe free honeft and bold republicans, whofe fouls were intirely Roman. *Movemur enim, nefcio quo patto,* faid Cicero, *locis ipfis in quibus eorum quos admiramur adfunt veftigia (b.)*

Indeed, where is that imagination which is not affected at the firft fight of that capital, fo long

(a) Cicero ufed to fay of Athens, *Quâcumque ingredimur, in aliquam hiftoriam veftigium ponimus.* De Fin. L. v.

* Annibal Caro Litter.

(b) " I have," faid Montaigne, " feen elfewhere edifices in
" ruins, and ftatues both of gods and men defaced; and yet
" I cannot without wonder and veneration behold the fepul-
" chre of this once fo large and potent a city. I was acquainted
" with the affairs of Rome long before I knew any thing
" of thofe of my own family. I had the Capitol and its
" whole figure in my mind, when the Louvre was quite un-
" known to me, and had heard of the Tiber before the Seine.
" My thoughts have run more on the condition and fortunes
" of

long the feat of univerfal empire, to which were
led in triumph the kings and the fpoils of thofe
nations who now think themfelves invincible,
and which ftill in many refpects is poffeffed
of the empire, and of the eternity, annexed
to the deftiny of Rome! The modern Capitol, in
its prefent appearance, has been erected on the
foundations of the ancient. Michael Angelo, the
author of the plan, has fpread all over the three
bodies of the ftructure, their accompaniments and
avenues, that grandeur and majefty, by which fuch
an edifice fhould be diftinguifhed.

The night which followed the *poffeffo*, I faw all the
outward parts of thefe buildings illuminated in the
Roman manner; that is, with flambeaux of white
wax. The halls, the fquare and its avenues,

" of Lucullus, Metellus, and Scipio, than of any of my own
" countrymen.——Finding myfelf ufelefs to this age, I recur
" to that other, and am fo taken with it, that this old Rome,
" in its free, juft, and flourifhing ftate, (for neither am I de-
" lighted with its infancy or old age) affects and warms me,
" fo that I cannot fee the fituation of their ftreets and houfes,
" and thofe ancient ruins reaching to the very antipodes,
" without all the powers of my foul being ftirred. I am
" charmed when I view the countenance of thofe Romans,
" their attitude, and their garb. I ruminate thofe great
" names to myfelf, and make my ears ring with them.

" *Ego illos veneror, et tantis nominibus affurgo.*

" —Of things in fome meafure great and admirable I ad-
" mire even what is common. I break out into wifhes that
" I could fee them converfe, walk and fup together. It would
" be ingratitude to overlook the remains and images of fo
" many perfons, fo eminent for virtue and courage, whom I
" have feen born and die, and who fet us fo many good ex-
" amples did we but mind them." B. iii. c. 9.

fwarmed

fwarmed with people from the city and the
neighbouring country, whom the ceremony had
drawn to Rome. The defcendants of the Sabines,
of the Equi, of the Volfci, &c. were there with
their children and wives, in all their finery and
peculiar dreffes, very becoming and fmart, and
in infinite variety ; all animated with that free
open hilarity, little of which is to be found among
the people of Rome, nor in general among the
inhabitants of cities ; and making up to thofe
whom they thought moft able to explain to them
the fine things which they faw, and moft of them
for the firft time ; almoft all of a fine ftature, well
fhaped, and in their air and carriage that pleafing
eafe and freedom, which in the Italian ladies is
generally ftifled by art, *tametfi bona eft Natura**.

By the illuminations, the two wings along the
fquare of the Capitol appeared to me not precifely perpendicular to the main body from which
they are detached : it feemed as if, at their extremities facing the town, they inclined towards the
fquare, thefe extremities intercepting the fight of
the illumination. This flight irregularity I had
not perceived by day light. The architect, to
be fure, was forced to it by the irregularity of the
ground ; or perhaps it might only be an optical
deception.

I had heard, and had even read in fome accounts, that the Capitoline mount is at prefent
almoft on a level with the ground of Rome; and
fo it is, as to that part which faces the Forum Romanum, or Campo Vaccino. This part, which

* Terent. *Eunuchus.*

was

was made of the *subſtructiones* attributed to Tarquin, has been lowered, and the ground of the Forum greatly raiſed, ſo that they now communicate by a very gentle ſlope. The true Tarpeian rock ſtill retains a great part of its ancient ſteepneſs : it forms the outlet from the ſquare between the right wing of the modern Capitol and the main body. This outlet leads to the banks of the Tiber by a rugged declivity, and ſo ſteep as ſcarce to be aſcended without the help of one's hands. In a word, though the ground at the bottom be raiſed, any one thrown down from it would have good luck to eſcape with his life.

AUGUSTUS's MAUSOLEUM.

That any part of Auguſtus's mauſoleum ſtill remains viſible, is owing to its ſolidity : *mole ſuâ ſtat*. In its circular form, and poſition with regard to the Tiber, it was like Adrian's mauſoleum, now the caſtle of St. Angelo. The pyramids of Egypt gave the Romans their firſt ideas of thoſe huge funeral monuments, in the greater part of which they had likewiſe adopted the pyramidical form : Auguſtus, we may ſuppoſe, thought the circular more analogous to the majeſty of the ſovereigns of the univerſe.

The *rudera* of this mauſoleum ſhew it to have been an edifice not leſs grand than ſolid. The whole carcaſs is ſtill exiſting in a round tower about forty feet diameter ; the walls of which, in a part of the external ſurface, are ſtill incruſted with thoſe ſtones, placed lozenge-wiſe, which the ancients called *Opus reticulatum*. The inſide of this tower is every where perpendicular and of a

piece ;

piece ; whereas the outfide is ftill divided into two ftories, the firft with a double wall of a prodigious thicknefs. The projecture of this wall was un-queftionably a foccle, or bafis to the columns appertaining to the fecond ftory, which perhaps was of a flighter conftruction, and only with pilaf-ters, of which no manner of veftiges are now remaining. The wall of this fecond ftory, which is ftill of a confiderable height, is crowned with a continual arbour, and fhaded by fome vines planted within the monument. The grapes of this vineyard, which was originally planted with the mufcadel vines of Alexandria *(c)*, were then completely ripe. On this terrace I ufed to go and entertain myfelf with the profpect of Rome, and the country under the cannon of St. Angelo, and whilft eating of this excellent fruit I meditated on the vanity of human grandeur.

It would be very difficult to decide from the prefent condition of the places, whether the infide of this monument was diftributed into niches for the urns in which were to be depofited the afhes of a family, which Auguftus, to be fure, flattered himfelf was to partake of the fuppofed eternity of his empire : if fo, its inward difpofition muft have been the fame as that of the Columbarium *(d)* in the Appian road, which was the receptacle for the afhes of all the freedmen of the Auguftan family. I have already faid that the inward wall is, throughout its whole circumference, perpen-

(c) Thefe produce a grape which the Italians highly prize, and call it *Uva*. . . . . . .

(d) It was difcovered in the beginning of this century, and M. Bianchini has given a learned defcription of it.

diculâr

dicular and fmooth; but at the foot of this wall, and under its double thicknefs, were vaults, ftill intire, and every where varnifhed with a kind of cement or red maftic, which has loft-nothing either in its folidity, or the glofs of its colour. Thefe vaults, once perhaps the dormitories of the Marcelli, the Germanici, the Agrippæ, the Drufi, the Liviæ, the Octaviæ, and the firft Cæfars, that is, of fome of the greateft perfonages ever known in the whole univerfe, now is a lay-ftall for the dung and all other filth ufed in manuring the garden which has been made within the monument.

The artifts in building the maufoleum had, by way of diftinction, a tomb for them in its neighbourhood, where has been found this infcription:

D. M.

Ulpio Martiàli,

Aug. Lib. a Marmoribus.

I am furprifed that fome antiquaries fhould have been fo far miftaken, as to make any other monument than this maufoleum the tomb intended by Virgil in thefe beautiful lines in the fixth book of the Æneid:

Quantos ille virûm magnam Mavortis ad urbem
Campus aget gemitus, vel quæ, Tiberine, videbis
Funera, cum tumulum præterlabere ruentem!

Firft, this maufoleum faced the Campus Martius, which in Auguftus's time was ftill without the circuit of Rome. Secondly, it was between the Tiber and the Flaminian road which croffed the

Campus Martius. Thirdly, Auguftus, according to Suetonius, had begun it in his fixth confulfhip; and Marcellus died in the eleventh confulfhip of his uncle, who reckoned his intermediate confulfhips by the years : now, fuppofing the building of this maufoleum to have taken up four or five years, it had been juft finifhed when Marcellus died.

On beholding thefe auguft ruins, the place of the Scipios tomb, the remains of the funeral monuments of fo many heroes who raifed Rome to fuch power and glory, it is natural for the mind to fall into that reflection, which they produced in Lucretius,

Tu verò dubitabis et indignabere obire,
Mortua cui vita eft jam vivo et pænè videnti*.

OBELISKS.

Near the entrance of Auguftus's maufoleum ftood two obelifks, of which Sixtus V, caufed one to be removed, and fet up facing the north front of Santa Maria Majore : the other is faid to be ftill buried under the rubbifh by which the ground of Rome has been fo prodigioufly raifed, efpecially in this part. They were without hieroglyphics, and doubtlefs the very fame which, as Pliny informs us, were by Auguftus's order cut in the quarries of Upper Egypt.

The many monuments of this kind brought from Egypt to Rome, but afterwards thrown down from their pedeftals, and the greater part of them fince fet up again by Sixtus V. are the

* Lucret. L. iii.

moft

moſt ſingular tokens of the grandeur of this ancient capital of the univerſe. I thought it very ſtrange that moſt of them ſhould have been placed in the lobbies of the largeſt edifices, the proximity of which buries them and deſtroys a great part of their effect. The only one retaining its proper place is that in the ſquare Del Popolo: the like advantages lay open to others; they ſhould have been diſtributed in the ſeveral ſquares of Rome.

I have had a very cloſe view of that obeliſk which Auguſtus, in the beginning of his reign, erected to the Sun in the centre of the Campus Martius. Being thrown down together with its baſe, it had for ſeveral ages lain buried under ruins, and afterwards under houſes built among thoſe ruins. To ſome it was part of the foundation; to others it was the cellar wall; and in ſeveral it had been a chimney back or hearth, by which laſt uſe, of courſe, all the parts expoſed to the fire for ages have been defaced. At laſt, Benedict XIV. clearing it of all theſe incumbrances, had a deſign of ſetting it up again: it is broken in four places; a common misfortune to thoſe which Sixtus V. reſtored to their honour. To repair the calcined part is a difficulty which Sixtus the Vth's architect had not to deal with: this however may perhaps be anſwered by a new poliſh and veneering.

The hieroglyphics ſtill viſible on all the found parts are in relievo, though at firſt ſight they ſeem *intagliatas*; the ſpace taken up by each figure being ſo grooved, that the moſt prominent parts of the relievo are lower than the ſurface of the block in which they ſeem enchaſed;

chafed; an expedient, no doubt, contrived for
fecuring thefe parts of the relievo from the
frictions which thofe enormous maffes muft
have ·undergone in the feveral operations for the
tranfportation of them, raifing them on the
pedeftals, &c. Thefe hieroglyphics, it muft be
obferved, are of a moft excellent workmanfhip.

Near the obelifk of the Campus Martius lies
its bafe, an enormous cube of the fame granite
as the obelifk; and on it an infcription in Roman letters, in the moft exact proportion; but
the infcription itfelf is quite plain and artlefs,
faying little more than that Auguftus, AIGUPTO
CAPTA, dedicated that monument to the Sun. I
felt a pleafure in viewing this bafis and its
infcription, from confidering that Virgil, Horace,
and all the great men and wits of Auguftus's
court, had once been taken up with the fame object.

EMPEROR's PALACE.

The palace which fo many emperors had
embellifhed and enriched is now totally buried
under its ruins, fo that the furface of it is
only a park planted with yews and cypreffes.
That it ftill covers ineftimable treafures, there is
the more reafon to believe, as it is the place
which of all others has been the leaft fearched.
This ground belongs to the houfe of Farnefe,
as a fief conferred by Paul III. on his fon
Peter Lewis Farnefe. This mine of riches,
whether from negligence or the jealoufy of
its proprietors, lay untouched till the year
1720. From the difcoveries then made, M. Bianchini formed his *Hiftory of the Palace of the*
Cæfars,

Cæfars, publifhed in 1738. The two coloffufes,
now in the gardens of Colorno, were part of thofe
difcoveries (*e.*)

I have heard at Rome, that it was among
thefe ruins M. Bianchini met with the unhappy
accident mentioned in the eulogium of that
gentleman by M. Fontenelle, who, it may be
prefumed, had not a true account of the following particulars of it. M. Bianchini, not lefs
eftimable for his piety than his extenfive knowlege,
had prefided over the works and difcoveries carried on in the year 1720. The ceffation of thefe
works only whetted his inclination for enlarging
thofe difcoveries; and prompted by his ardent
defire, he ufed to frequent thefe ruins, attended
by his fervant, who with a pick-axe explored fuch
places as feemed the moft promifing. Whilft
bufied in a fpot where the founding of the
furface denoted a large cavity, the ground
gave way under him, fo that he fell perpendicularly into a fubterraneous place; on the edges
of which he was kept up by his elbows without his feet reaching the ground: his age,
ftature, and repletenefs, allowing him but little
agility, his efforts, and thofe of his fervant to
get him up, only widened the aperture, and
broke away the fupport on which his elbows
refted. In this extremity, M. Bianchini, undaunted
at the apparent certainty of his fate, repeated the
prayers for thefe who are at the point of death;
and his fervant being at length quite fpent, he fell

(*e*) In an oblong fquare of one hundred and fifty feet to
one hundred, anfwering to the northern front of the palace,
were many fuch ftatues.

from the height of about thirty feet on a heap of rubbifh : here he called out that he was not hurt, afking for a light that he might improve this accident: accordingly he found himfelf in a vaft falon with frefco paintings. All his hurt feemed only a very flight contufion, but the confequences carried him to his grave within two years.

The imperial palace ftood on the fouth-weft fide of the Forum Romanum, which eaftward was terminated by Titus's triumphal arch, which to this day forms one of its outlets. On the interior face of one of the pillars of this arch is reprefented the candleftick with feven branches, which among other fpoils from Jerufalem had adorned Titus's triumph on that fignal occafion. The Jewifh quarter being near this monument, they, to fave themfelves the afflictive fight of fuch an object, have purchafed of the government the privilege of opening a narrow paffage, which fideways from the arch opens a communication between their quarter and the Forum Romanum, or Campo Vaccino. I have feen fome perfons fo void of fentiment and juftice, as to fneer at that unhappy people for a delicacy, arifing from thofe rare and fublime principles, which dictated the pfalm *Super flumina Babylonis.*

Oppofite to the ruins of the emperor's palace, and on the north-eaft fide of the Campo Vaccino, are thofe of the Temple of Peace. Some large roofs, which make the moft confiderable part of thefe ruins, have been walled in towards the Campo, and are now the receptacle

or

or staple for the horned cattle, of which the Campo is the market. Thus the Forum Romanum is returned exactly to the very same condition in which Æneas found it on his coming to Evander.

Passim armenta videntur
Romanoque foro & lautis mugire carinis.

All this part of Rome was, during its highest prosperity, the best inhabited, and now is taken up by churches and convents. Rome may be said to have removed into the Campus Martius and the plain along the Tiber, of which that field made a part. Cities not only become extinct, they likewise change their place. Among those which I have seen, Lyons, Marseilles, Ancona, &c. have like Rome come down from the mountains, where their founders had placed them, and which they had long occupied, to extend themselves along the levels.

CHRONOLOGICAL DISSERTATION on the COMMON SEWERS.

Ponimus cloacas inter magnifica, says Justus Lipsius, in his Considerations on the Roman Grandeur; *et sordes has inter illos splendores.* And in reality, perhaps never was work, intended for public service, carried to such a pitch of grandeur. Distributed among the vallies within the first inclosures of Rome, and continually refreshed by copious springs, they emptied themselves into the Tiber, through the valley which separates mount Aventine from the Palatine.

Such is the solidity of their construction, that
they

they have withstood the depredations of ages, and several both inward and outward causes of decay. I have seen the Cloaca maxima, at its issue into the Tiber; it is from twelve to fifteen feet in breadth, with the like height. I could not but admire the enormous blocks of which it is built, the stability of the arch, and the regularity of its form, which has not failed in any one part, though the stones are joined bare, without morter or cement.

Admiration increases on considering the depth of the excavations and the trenches which this kind of building required; and that, farther, it was the work of Rome's second century, that is, when Rome was only an irregular heap of cottages.

De canna staminibusque domos*.

Indeed, if ancient and modern historians are to be credited, the Cloaca maxima was only part of such undertakings in the time of Tarquin the elder, who according to those historians laid the foundations of the Capitol, lining the Tarpeian rock with a huge body of masonry (*substructio*) still existing (*a*); who confined the bed of the Tiber by a quay distinguished, even in the most polite ages of Rome, by the denomination of *Pulchrum littus*;

* Ovid. Fast. L. iii.

(*a*) Within this body of masonry was the Carcer Tullianus, of which the part now subsisting makes a chapel consecrated to St. Peter, who is said to have been confined in it. This part is built of blocks in the same manner like those of the Cloaca maxima.

who

who encompaffed Rome with a ftone wall; and, laftly, who began the great Circus which could hold one hundred and fifty thoufand fpectators. Yet at the firft *cenfus* in the following reign, the number of inhabitants, both of Rome and its territory, did not much exceed eighty thoufand; all hufbandmen living on the produce of their grounds and the work of their hands; all warriors without pay and engaged in continual wars; all handicrafts-men either by calling or neceffity.

In many countries the difficulties concerning works much inferior to thefe are cleared up at once, by attributing them to fairies, to forcerers, and even to the devil himfelf; and I own I fhould as foon be for giving to them the honour of all the edifices and conftructions attributed to Tarquin, efpecially the fewers in queftion, as to that very limited fovereign of an infant unfettled ftate, and which never fo much as thought of coining money till three hundred years after.

The Romans of the more enlightened ages could not but fee into this contradiction. Pliny was aware of it*; but, to avoid overthrowing one of the main foundations of the conceit entertained by the Romans, and the nations whom they had fubdued, relating to the grandeur of the *eternal city*, even in its infancy, he fuppofes that in building the Cloaca maxima Tarquin had fet all the people of Rome to work. And, to help out this fuppofition, he makes Tarquin treat them with a feverity of which moft defpotic ftates fcarce afford an inftance. " If any," fays he†,

* Plin. L. xxxiii. c. 2.   † L. xxxv. c. 15.

" were

" were difcouraged by the length and dangers of
" the work, fo as to give themfelves up to defpair,
" and deprive themfelves of life, Tarquin cau-
" fed their bodies to be nailed crofs-wife, and
" thus left unburied to the vultures and other
" birds of prey." *In quo,* adds Pliny, *pudor Romani nominis proprius, qui fæpe res perditas fer-
vavit in præliis, tunc quoque fubvenit.*

But this circumftance, fo little agreeable to
the conftitution of Rome even under its kings,
and of which no mention is made before Pliny,
cannot convince me of the main fact.

Some more clear particulars than thofe which
Dionyfius Halicarnaffæus* himfelf relates concerning the firft inhabitants of Latium, might difcover the real authors of this conftruction,
which bears fo near a refemblance to many
others erected in the moft remote times; times,
when that part of Italy between the two feas
was covered with towns, dwellings and inhabitants, before the Roman name was fo much
known.

At leaft it is certain from Livy, that before the
Trojans, according to the Roman notion, brought
their houfehold gods into Latium, a colony of
Arcadians had already fettled on the mount Palatine; a colony of the fame kind, and doubtlefs of
the fame date, as all thofe the conjunction of
which had formed Italic-Greece, which the Greeks
themfelves, by way of excellence, called *Great
Greece.* Philofophy, the arts and fciences, had
flourifhed in this fine country before Romulus
had made himfelf known there by his afylum
and the rape of the Sabines.

* Lib. i.

fc

It is even very probable, that colonies prior to the emigrations of the Greeks had taken care to difplay, in their public works, a grandeur expreffive of their power and profperity. The filence of hiftorians concerning thefe ancient foundations is amply compenfated by the public edifices of old Poeftum (*f*), which are exifting even to this day: and count Gazola, mafter of the ordnance in Spain, caufed plans and elevations to be taken of them; and in 1758 they were engraving at Naples under his infpection. The tafte and proportions of thefe edifices, and their refemblance to thofe which are ftill exifting in Upper Egypt, prove them anterior to the commencement of arts even among the Greeks.

To thefe primitive colonies, whofe work they are, perhaps fhould be attributed thofe monuments of fubterraneous architecture, which are common in Great Greece, Sicily, Phœnicia, and Egypt; I mean thofe caverns, wrought by human fkill, which hold the firft rank among the antiquities of Cumæ and Puzzolo; the catacombs of Naples, Meffina, and Syracufe; and the cryptæ along the coaft of Phœnicia, hewn in the rocks; together with thofe immenfe galleries which run to fuch an extent under ground in part of Egypt; and all the works of this kind, of which the firft men found the models in thofe wonderful caverns exhibited to them by nature, among the ruins out of which it has formed moft of the iflands of the Archipelago. The Myrmidons, who difplayed their valour at the fiege of Troy, and gave them-

(*f*) On the gulph of Tarentum.

felves out to be the defcendants of ants, wno lived under ground, might perhaps owe both their name, which, according to Pliny, was in the early times common to all the Greeks *(g)*, and this tradition concerning their origin, to their anceftors having been particularly noted for works of this kind.

Now in one or other of thofe early ages muft be placed the foundation of thofe edifices, the ruins of which Evander fhewed to Æneas, on the very fpot which Rome afterwards came to occupy.

Disjectis oppida muris,
Relliquias, veterumque vides monumenta virorum.

Accordingly, in the fifth century of the chriftian æra, Evander was commonly accounted the founder or reftorer of Rome *(h)*. Under the empire of paganifm Rome had not dared to relinquifh the opinion which referred its origin to Romulus, fuch opinion being connected with religion by a number of ceremonies implying that origin*.

To thefe indications may be added the dimnefs and uncertainty of what light appears in the firft ages of Rome; the chimeras of the Romans concerning their origin and its fuppofed epocha; their ftudious fondnefs of referring to themfelves and their anceftors whatever had an air of grandeur;

(g) Hos eofdem *(Græcos)* tribus nominibus appellavit ; Myrmidonas, et Hellenas, et Achæos. L. iv. c. 7.

(h) See Servius on the 10th verfe of Virgil's firft Eclogue : *Roma ante Romulum fuit, et ab ea Romulus nomen adquifivit.* See M. Boivin's Differtation on the Origin of Rome. *Mem. de l'Acad. des Infcr.*

* See Ovid. Faft. *paffim.*

their

their conftant admiration of thefe very fewers in queftion; their goddefs Cloacina*, to whom they attributed the fuperintendency of them, and whofe worfhip is dated from Tatius Romulus's collegue (i). After all, reducing the teftimony of the Roman hiftorians to their juft weight, we fhall only conclude that the conftruction of the Cloaca Maxima is not pofterior to the fecond century of Rome.

Againft the fuppofition of fuch an undertaking being formed, carried into execution, and completed, by a town in its infancy and perpetually embroiled in wars, I might object, at leaft as a reafon for doubting, the long patience of the Parifians in bearing, and in a quarter which was for a long time the beauty of Paris, and clofe by the walks of that quarter, the ftench and many inconveniences of an open fewer, without any water running into it, loft in dead grounds, and the infected atmofphere of which over-fpread no fmall part of the garden ground fupplying that great city. At length, M. Turgot was the man who contrived and made a ftone-work fewer, which by means of the water running through, and thus cooling and cleanfing it, fhould equal thofe at Rome; yet it

* Lact. de Falfa Relig. c. 20. Aug. de Civ. Dei, L. iv. c. 23.

(i) To the premiffes may be farther added the little agreement between the difpofitions of the ftreets of Rome with that of the fewers or drains; quæ, fays Livy, primò per publicum ductæ: nunc (in his time) privata paffim fubibant tecta, L. v. if Livy did not impute this irregularity to the hurry and tumult in which Rome was rebuilt after being laid in afhes by the Gauls: but if Rome, at that time no fmall place, was rebuilt on the former fites, Livy's teftimony makes for me, and confequences diametrically oppofite refult from the fame fact.

is but little above twenty years fince fuch a city
(thanks to that valuable citizen) has been provided
with a conveniency of fuch importance: *tantæ
molis erat, &c.!*

The reafons of neceffity, which called for
fuch an undertaking at Paris, did not exift in
Rome under Romulus and Tarquin. Its inhabitants may be fuppofed to have been none of the
moft delicate perfons : it ftood fcrambling along
the Tiber, on hills and eminences, the vallies of
which were natural drains for the waters and filth,
difcharging them into that river.

St. CONSTANTIA's CHAPEL.

The Roman antiquaries are divided concerning
the little church or chapel of St. Conftantia, without the Porta Pia, and facing that of St. Agnes ;
fome holding it to be a modern ftructure, whilft
to others it feems an antique. It is a rotondo
about twenty feet in diameter, furrounded with
collaterals, and at prefent disfigured by an ugly
roof over-fpreading both dome and collaterals.
The hollow in the collateral facing the door is
occupied by that fplendid porphyry monument,
embellifhed with a very prominent bas-relief of
vine-branches and bunches of grapes, draughts of
which are to be met with every where.

They who judge the chapel to be an ancient
temple prove it from this tomb ; whilft others take
it to be the baptiftery which Anaftafius the
librarian fays, in the Life of St. Silvefter, was
erected at Rome by Conftantine for baptizing the
two Conftantias, one his fifter, the other his
daughter: and this opinion feems to prevail againft
all the many marks of antiquity fo manifeft in the
edifice,

edifice, and though the baptiftery mentioned by Anaftafius is found to be Conftantine's baptiftery, which at prefent is that of St. John de Lateran.

On the other hand, to conclude from the porphyry tomb and its embellifhments, that the temple in which it now ftands was anciently confecrated to Bacchus, is going too far. Firft, The ornaments of tombs were left to the fculptor's choice, who ufually fuited them to the profeffion or inclinations of the perfons for whom they were intended, like the tomb in the Capitol, on which is reprefented Homer's apotheofis. Secondly, To place any monument of this kind in towns, and much lefs in temples, was quite contrary to the cuftom of antiquity. This was certainly removed to the place where it now ftands, as the intended fepulchre of fome chriftian of the firft diftinction, after having originally ferved for the fame purpofe to fome very eminent, or at leaft very rich pagan *(k)*; fo that this edifice is to be judged of by itfelf, abftractedly from the tomb within it.

It has in little all the proportions of that beautiful church which Juftinian built at Ravenna*: but what is to be inferred from this refemblance? The Greeks, having before them many ancient edifices of the rotondo form, adopted it for their firft churches, whilft the Latins took the model of their facred ftructures from the Roman bafilics.

(k) It is to this temple, as converted into an oratory, that perhaps fhould be applied this paffage of Ammianus Marcellinus, which has efcaped the Roman antiquarians : *Julianus,* fays that hiftorian, L. xxi. *initio, Helenæ conjugis defunctæ fuprema miferat Romam in furburbano viæ nomentanæ condenda, ubi uxor quoque Galli, quondam foror ejus, fepulta eft Conftantina.*

* See RAVENNA.

In

In order to a conclufive decifion of this point, plans and elevations of all the parts of the building both within and without, with exact copies of the mofaics with which part of the floor and the roof are ftill covered, fhould be laid before thofe connoiffeurs to whofe judgment the difpute was to be referred : likewife the adjacent ground fhould be fearched, whether it was not furrounded with a colonnade, as fome of its outward parts feem to indicate.

Farther, in this church are two chandeliers of the fineft Grecian marble, and the fafhion and workmanfhip anfwerable : the height of them is about four feet : their ornaments are in the tafte which Michael Angelo had formed to himfelf, in this kind, from antique pieces. A fmall head, in the manner of the fineft camaieus, projects from each of the triangular faces of the feet of thefe chandeliers. One of thefe heads had been newly broken off and carried away ; and according to the facriftan, the offender was a young French artift.

ANTIQUITIES in the VATICAN and CAPITOL.

The ruins with which the inhabited parts of ancient Rome are covered muft naturally affect the antiquarians, as reprefenting to their imagination various monuments of the magnificence and grandeur of ancient Rome. The Vatican and the Capitol, amidft the multitude of ftatues and bufts efcaped from the ravages of time and barbarifm, exhibit fome which every eye muft behold with pleafure. The Vatican antiques are as univerfally known as St. Peter's. The Mufæum Capitolinum,

tolinum, in giving the curious an idea of thofe which Benedict XIV. has affembled in the Capitol, at the fame time muft excite an eager defire of feeing fuch beauties. The intent of Leo X. and Benedict XIV. in forming thefe collections, was to fecure the enjoyment of them to the public: how different from that croud of rapacious popes and nephews, whofe leading view was to enrich their houfes with the fpoils of ancient Rome! It is however to be wifhed, that thefe collections were abfolutely public, and that they who are entrufted with the keeping of them did not fell the fight of them, and fcrew an income out of the artifts who are obliged to ftudy them : fuch a monopoly correfponds neither with the magnificence nor the intentions of a mafter, who has fo many ways of providing for perfons of this clafs.

The villas of Borghefe, Pamphili, Medicis, &c. the palaces of Farnefe, Barberini, Verofpi, Maffimi, Albani, &c. are likewife very rich in antiques ; but nothing equals, if not in choice at leaft in quantity, thofe of the Juftiniani palace. The apartments, the ftair-cafe, court, walls, every corner of this palace, are filled or covered with antiques : in a word, under a large fhed belonging to it, and where are piled up all thofe for which room could not be found, one fees at once more than are to be found in all Europe, Rome and Florence excepted. At the fight of fuch riches we admire the munificence of the prince which has thus provided for their confervation ; but the quantity rather aftonifhes than fatisfies.

Befides, all thefe pieces, though real antiques, are far from being equally valuable. Every artifan,

who had an hand in filling Rome *(l)* with monuments of this kind, was not a Phidias or an Apollo-
dorus; the majority of them only copying their
moſt celebrated pieces: every where one meets
with copies of the Venus of Medicis, ſome good,
ſome middling, and often very bad. I ſaw one at
Rome, which had been lately diſcovered, and
pretty well repaired, ſet out for ſale in a work-ſhop
near La Trinitá di Monte. The repair which
moſt of theſe antiques ſeem to require is a very
dangerous trial, in which they are always loſers:
it were perhaps to be wiſhed, that they were treated
after the example of Michael Angelo with the
celebrated Torſo of the Vatican, the repair of
which he modeſtly declined as above his ſkill,
great as it was. The tradition which had attributed to him the repairing of Laocoön is mani-
feſtly falſe, the ſecond-hand legs and arms bearing
no porportion to the bodies to which they have
been fitted.

CARDINAL ALBANI's PALACE.

Cardinal Alexander Albani is at preſent the
capital repairer of antiquity. With him the moſt
mutilated, moſt disfigured, moſt irremediable
pieces recover their original beauty: *nova facit
omnia:* the fragment of a buſt, which, even when
entire, all antiquaries would have diſregarded as
una teſta incognitiſſima, from him receives, with
new life, a name which irrevocably perpetuates
its rank.

As a repoſitory for thoſe pieces, he was building, without the Salara gate, a palace in the taſte

*(l) Statuas Thuſci primùm in Italia invenerunt, quas amplexa
poſteritas, pæne parcm populum urbi dedit, quàm natura procreavit.*
Caſſiodor.

of thofe of ancient Rome. Its front is covered with exquifite embellifhments, and interfected by a portico over which runs the firft ftory ; a difpofition which, if it cools the ground-floor apartments as fhaded by the portico, leaves them only a falfe light. This front faces a parterre with fine waterworks, and innumerable antiques, terminating in a vaft femi-circular portico, which is open towards the garden, furmounted with a continuous baluftrade, and the outward part mured. This portico puts one the more in mind of the *xyfti*, or covered walks, of the Romans, as being ftocked with thofe objects with which a learned luxury delighted to embellifh them ; that is, the ftatues and bufts of the moft eminent perfonages. To ftatues and bufts cardinal Albani has added altars, tombs, bas-reliefs, and monuments of all kinds, and all in part made whole by new work. It is in buftos that thefe renovations chiefly fhew themfelves, in the nofes, the ears, and whole parts fitted to thofe which time has fpared. Thus one fees there the Grecian poets, philofophers, and orators, with amendments and additions ; and the name of each newly engraved in Greek characters. We had feen cardinal Albani before feeing his palace ; and on our intimating a defire of admiring that ftructure and its ineftimable contents, he anfwered with fomething of a fneer, " It is not " made for eyes ufed to the wonders of French " architecture : to you the plan muft appear chime- " rical, and the performance execrable."

CARDINAL PASSIONEI's HERMITAGE.

With lefs expence and parade cardinal Paffionei had built and ornamented his Camalduli hermitage.

The

This hermitage, contrived on the fide of the mountain of Frefcati, had a profpect of Rome, part of the Campania and its fea, with an horizontal view of the Rufinella of the jefuits lying under it. The difpofition was modelled from the irregularity of the ground. The apartments formed as many infulated pavilions, difperfed among groves communicating along ferpentine paths : and thefe paths ended at the main walk, which itfelf was laid out only as the mountain would permit, being cut in it like a little bank. Along the borders of this walk, of thefe paths, and thefe groves, were placed funeral monuments which the cheerful verdure around them enlivened. Thefe monuments were ancient tombs of all dimenfions, urns of different figures, moftly very uncommon, and Greek and Latin epitaphs of all ages. The moft remarkable piece, at leaft in its bulk, was the tomb of an emperor of the lower ages. Cardinal Albani, to whom it belonged, had made an offer of it to cardinal Paffionei, with the exprefs provifo that he fhould hoift it into his hermitage, fuppofing this to be utterly impoffible ; however, cardinal Paffionei, by dint of machines and oxen, at length effected it.

Among the epitaphs, that on a Greek actrefs attracted particular notice, being of a great length, in characters of the beft times, and finely preferved. I was for copying thofe infcriptions which I thought moft affecting, or moft fingular ; but the cardinal faved me that trouble, informing me that he had fent a complete collection of them to the Royal Academy of *Belles Lettres* at Paris.

In the dining room ftood a ciftern taken out of the ruins of Adrian's villa at Tivoli. It was an oblong fquare of four feet to three, and one in depth, and pierced in its centre for a tube; which playing at meal time furnifhed water for drinking, and rinfing the glaffes: this water, equally excellent for its coolnefs and quality, is the very fame which watered Cicero's Tufculanum; the cardinal having alighted on the ancient pipes. I never faw any goldfmith's work comparable to this ciftern, either for elegancy of form, tafte of the ornaments, or delicacy of workmanfhip. The cardinal, in his pavilion, had a clofet of books rather choice than many. In the moft confpicuous part of this clofet hung a portrait of the celebrated M. Arnaud, a Sorbonne doctor; and near it was a large octavo bound in green, without a title: on opening it, there was the *Lettres Provinciales* in five languages.

But this hermitage had nothing fo extraordinary in it, as its founder: he was free, open, and juft, in his converfation, in his dealings, and all his actions; in a word, cardinal Paffionei was really a phænomenon in a country and a court, which are the very centre of intrigue and the moft artful practices. In his love of literature he had no equal: nobody ever fhewed more ardour in promoting it, and nobody ever more heartily detefted the jefuits: this love and this hatred were the two fprings of his views, his fchemes, and his whole conduct. An unexpected reftraint on his declared fentiments proved his death: though eighty years of age, his genius and conftitution retained all their vigour.

His

His deceafe was followed by the fpeedy deftruction of his hermitage: the people of Camalduli,
on whofe ground it was built, feconded by their
neighbours, immediately fell to pulling down a
place which he had formed, and was his fupreme delight. I have heard, that, to make the
quicker work in its demolition, his rancorous
enemies tumbled down from the mountain moft
of the monuments, which the cardinal had placed
there.

A few general obfervations on fome ruins of
ancient Rome fhall clofe this article.

PILLARS.

Befides the numberlefs pillars ftill ftanding, and
thofe daily difcovered, Rome is ftrewed with
fragments which ferve as borders and fhores to the
terraffes on each fide of the great ftreets. In a
ftreet near the Barberini palace I have feen half a
fluted pillar of tranfparent eaftern marble put to
that ufe. The very pavement of the ftreets and
fquares is interfperfed with granite and porphyry.

APERTURES in ANCIENT MONUMENTS.

I have clofely examined the apertures obfervable
in the triumphal arches and all the ancient monuments exifting at Rome. Thofe gaps, which are
exactly fquare, and always parallel to each other, in
the correfponding parts of the monuments, feem
to have been made only for admitting the extremity of the joifts of the ftories of dwellings contrived in thofe monuments, or which run up againft
them. During the inteftine wars with which Rome
and all the other cities of Italy had been rent, thefe
monu-

monuments ferved for citadels, and troops were placed in them. When ignorance and barbarifm came to prevail, thefe antique ftructures were looked on only as maffes fit for making lodgements in, or grafting houfes againft them, as is ftill done in the amphitheatres of Arles and Nîmes.

The little round temple, ftill exifting by the fide of the Tiber towards the mouth of the Cloaca Maxima, is by the antiquarians of Rome looked on as the temple of Vefta. Juftus Lipfius on the other hand maintains, that this temple, which was originally built by Numa in the valley between the Capitol and the Palatine mount, was afterwards inclofed by Auguftus within the precinct of his palace : yet Horace has faid,

> *Vidimus flavum Tiberim, retortis*
> *Littore Etrufco violenter undis,*
> *Ire dejeEtum monumenta regis*
> *Templaque Veftæ.*

If thefe *monumenta regis* be taken for the quay called *Pulchrum littus*, which was accounted to be the work of Tarquinius Prifcus, then the *templa Veftæ* will be the little temple ftill fubfifting, and which ftood at the head of that quay. It is at prefent dedicated to Santa Maria del Sole. According to the cuftom of the ages mentioned in the preceding article, a filthy houfe with a fmithy has been grafted againft it ; a ufe pretty analogous to the primitive confecration of this temple to the Goddefs of Fire.

ANTIQUE VASES.

Etrufcan vafes are now known and common all over Europe. Clement XII. and Benedict XIV.

have

have enriched the Vatican library with a collection of this kind, which, befides the prodigious quantity of the pieces, is equally admired for
the fine prefervation of them, and the elegancy and
variety of their forms. This elegancy, which the
ancient Romans firft borrowed from the Etrufci
and the Greeks, has been continued down to the
prefent time, even in the moft common veffels.
A country girl returning from the fpring with a
pitcher of water on her head, perfectly refembles
thofe figures which the moft exquifite antiques
reprefent in the fame attitude. How little of this
elegance is to be feen in the veffels of our northern
countries! Yet fome good patterns diftributed
among the workhoufes of our potters and porce-
lane makers might introduce it with little coft:
fome of thefe models might be had along the coaft
of Provence.

WINE-JARS.

In the fouthern provinces of France I had feen
a lefs elegant kind of antique veffels, very narrow
for their height, contracted at one third part from
their height, with two handles near the orifice,
and terminating in an inverted cone. From
finding afhes and calcined bones in fome of them,
all the veffels of this kind were concluded to be
cinerary urns. But at Rome, and in all the
country near it, fuch veffels are difcovered every
day; and their uniform figure declares them to be
the *amphora* fo often occurring in the Latin poets.
From their handles is derived their name *(m)*;
and the inverted cone at the bottom was for

(m) From ἀμφὶ and φέρω.

receiving

receiving the groffer parts of the fediment : on the orifice, which was thicker and fuller than the other part of the veffel, was fitted a cover to be fealed hermetically with maftic. In thefe veffels it was that the ancients kept their moft valuable wines for fuch a number of years.

The fhape of them was not the beft contrived for getting the wine out clear of all fediment; but we are unacquainted with the manner of the ancients making their wines, and how, in being kept forty, or fifty, or fixty years in lofts, thofe wines improved to that perfection fo much cried up by the Latin poets. Let modern poets in their turn celebrate the invention of cafks, to which the ancients were ftrangers, and which are fo very convenient and handy for all the feveral operations relating to the juice of the grape. The inverted cone at the bottom of the *amphora* would not allow of their ftanding; another inconveniency with which the moderns are not troubled *(n)*.

From thefe ancient inconveniences it appears, Firft, That in the ages when luxury was at its height, the Romans, ftill confining themfelves to the wines of their own growth, which were extremely rough, or to the Greek wines which were as lufcious, had made no improvement on the difcoveries of the primitive times for preparing and keeping wine *(o)*; Secondly, That in common life they were very fober as to liquor; and the debauches into which

(n) This explains the *jacere* in that fable of Phædrus: *Anus jacere videt epotam amphoram.* The *nobilis tefta* of the fame fable is cleared up by Horace's *Græca tefta.*

(o) See their very complicated manner of making wine, Columell. L. xii. c. 21. Plin. L. xiv. c. 20.

they

they fometimes gave, more from bravado than from liking, were never carried to any great excefs. Thirdly, That refinements in preparing wine, and the difcovery of the utenfils neceffary to fuch preparation, were referved to nations, who after planting vines fhould cultivate them in proportion as wine fhould agree with their climate and conftitution.

I think I have already taken notice, that the very populace of Italy ftill ufe wine very temperately, and that all the time we were in the country we did not fee fo much as one Italian intoxicated. The wine drank by the commonalty is generally heavy, thick, and turbid, and confequently not very inviting to indulge in: befides, the difeafes which excefs would infallibly produce, the quarrels to which it gives rife, the very indecency of appearing drunk among fober people, are a fufficient reftraint to a nation who in every thing go by rule.

Accordingly, wine is made in Italy as it was two thoufand years ago, and nearly with the fame utenfils. Of thefe the chief are a kind of bathing-tubs: the wine is ftirred about in them; then it is worked, and water mixed with it: this operation takes up the two months following the vintage.

Boiled wine is made more expeditioufly. It is brought from the vineyard to the proprietor's houfe, where it is boiled in large caldrons, and, when cool, is left to fettle. Terracina, and thofe towns of the Campania through which we paffed in going and returning from Naples, were bufied in this employment, and in the very ftreets, the walls ferving for chimnies. I never faw any
Neapolitan

Neapolitan wine made, but was told that to promote the fermentation, they throw into it live animals, and a great deal of quick lime, quenching the latter with water; whence this wine contracts a thickness, from which it never recovers. Of all these wines, that which pleased me the best, and which I could have drunk of during the whole remainder of my life, was Orvietto wine: it is of a pale amber colour, and, besides being extremely light, is rather a perfume than a liquor. Florence comes the nearest to the French wines, of which the Florentines certainly imitate the preparation: it is Bourdeaux wine, but lighter and warmer, besides a flavour which the French wines have not.

The Burgundy wines, which are brought into Italy, confirm the Italians in the way of preparing theirs, the former generally losing its colour, and not a little of its texture. By the way, Champagne is a better traveller; but its tartness and froth do not agree either with the taste or the smell of the Italians, who, between the qualities of this wine, and the cast of the people among whom it grows, find some resemblance, analogous to the opinion which they are pleased to harbour of that people.

St. PAUL's GATE.

Cestius's tomb, which was erected in Augustus's reign, and is now wedged in the body of the rampart intersected by St. Paul's gate, proves this gate to be more modern than the author of *Roma antica e moderna* imagines, who, copying some antiquaries, refers the construction of it to the reign of the emperor Claudius. Under the first emperors the ramparts and gates of Rome were rather matter

of ornament than neceffity. Thefe emperors, as
fovereign pontiffs, were the heads of a religion
which took cognifance of the walls, the gates, and
the *pomærium* of towns. The augural ritual*
prefcribed *quo ritu condantur urbes, quâ fanctitate
muri, quo jure portæ*; and the wedging a tomb in the
wall of a town would have been a moft flagrant infult
on thofe laws, efpecially as they annexed to tombs
and all funerary monuments, an idea of defilement
and impurity. When Aurelian furrounded Rome
with the inclofure now fubfifting, philofophy, and
afterwards chriftianity, had enlightened men's
minds with a fenfe of the futility of thefe antiquated
fuperftitions; and Ceftius's tomb was confidered
as an indifferent mafs, and accordingly incorporated with the new rampart.

Monfignor ASSEMANI's MUSEUM.

The Vatican library I often ufed to vifit: the
beauty of the place, the riches it contains, the
polite readinefs of the learned perfons who have
the keeping of it, every circumftance combines
to invite a foreigner's vifit. One day I met there,
pretty early, a cardinal not lefs eminent for his
extenfive erudition than his rational piety: he was
accompanied by fome bifhops of the *Propaganda*.
Every place was opened to him by monfignor
Affemani, patriarch of Antioch, and one of the
chief librarians. M. Affemani afterwards led us
into a cabinet, in which are lodged the curiofities
which he collected in Arabia, Egypt, and Judea.
Among thofe of art we particularly admired
fome intaglios and camaieus, efpecially a Cleo-

* Verrius Flaccus, verbo *Rituales*.

patra

patra in relief, on an exquifite agate-onyx. Among the natural curiofities we took notice of a pretty large piece of ftone, of a deep green, and tranfparent, though without polifh. M. Affemani affured us that this ftone was a fragment which he had caufed, in his prefence, to be broken from a mountain of Upper Arabia : the whole mafs was an emerald like that fpecimen, which had not been feparated from the reft without a great deal of trouble and labour. By the weight it feemed neither glafs, nor any compound fub-ftance. The cardinal tried it with a diamond cut point-wife ; but it did not feel it : yet I have fince feen fuch ftones, and was told that they are formed in the iron forges by the confluence of metallic parts vitrifying there.

M. Affemani having, during his long ftay in Judea, made himfelf particularly acquainted with that famous country, I took this opportunity to lay before him a queftion, which had been for-merly put to me by a countryman of mine. Its object was, firft, the Jordan, which to the Holy Land is what the Po is to Italy ; fecondly, the Dead fea, which receives this river, that is, re-ceives all the waters falling by rains, fogs, and dews, throughout all the extent of the Holy Land. The point was, to know, firft, whether thofe waters were abforbed into the Dead fea merely by evapo-ration, or by fome communication, either external or fubterraneous, between the Dead fea and the Mediterranean or the Red fea ? fecondly, where had thefe waters any receptacle or iffue before the ground funk fo as to form a bed for the Dead fea ?

The cardinal dwelled on thefe queftions, and

turned them on every fide, fo that M. Affemani frankly owned, concerning the firft, that he knew of no communication between the Dead and the neighbouring feas *(p)* : concerning the fecond, after ftruggling hard between the *poffe* and the *effe*, and labouring to explain one by the other, he acknowledged that thofe queftions were abfolutely new to him, and that he had no obfervations relating to fuch points, adding, that he would leave no ftone unturned to procure fome, either by himfelf, or thofe who were in the way of making them to the purpofe.

This difcuffion was followed by another, on the manner in which the church of Rome governs the churches in the Eaft Indies and the adjacent country. The patriarch and the bifhops maintained, with much warmth, that the fureft way of prefer-

(p) The maps of the Holy Land feem to point out this communication, in the Kifhon, a brook which they reprefent as connecting the fea of Galilee with that of Syria ; but accounts contradict this as an error. *La fuente,* fays P. Rodrigues de Yepes, in his Account of the Holy Land, fol. 27. *non mucho de alli corriendo al Septentrion topa y fe encuentra con el monte de Hermon, y fe abre y divide en dos rios : el uno que camina à la mano yfquierda, hafta defcargarfe en el Mar Syriaco entre el Promontorio de Carmelo y la Ciudad di Ptolemeida, donde el Propheta Helias mato los Prophetas de Baal. El otro rio va à la mano derecha, hafta llegar al lago de Genezareth, y entra en el entre el Pueblo & Caftillo di Magdalo, y la Ciudad de Tiberia,* i. e. " The brook Kifhon, in its courfe northward, not " far from thence meeting with mount Hermon, divides itfelf " into two ftreams ; one turning off to the left till it difcharges " itfelf into the fea of Syria, between the promontory of Car- " mel and the city of Ptolemais, where the prophet Elifha flew " the priefts of Baal : the other branch takes to the right as " far as the lake of Genezareth, into which it enters between " the town and caftle of Magdala, and the city of Tiberias.

ving

ving thofe churches in the purity of the faith was to keep them in an immediate dependance on the holy fee : this they proved from all the ancient herefies, which would not have been heard of had that dependancy been eftablifhed in the more early times. The cardinal objeted the conduct of the apoftles in fettling bifhops, the total extinction of the Japanefe church, which, had national bifhops been appointed there, would have been a church to this day ; laftly, the opinion of Benedict XIV. who, faid he concerning this important article, thought as the apoftles acted.

AQUEDUCTS.

The ruins of towns, which, throughout the whole extent of the Roman empire, have, as colonies only, acquired fome degrees of celebrity, fhew, in the traces of aqueducts which conveyed falubrious waters even to fuch cities as feemed to have the leaft need of them*, what Roman magnificence muft have performed in this kind for the embellifhment of the capital of the empire, and the conveniency of its inhabitants.

The firft aqueduct was contrived and built by the cenfor Appius. His example led the public luxury to this ufeful objet ; and, by immenfe works, ftreams and even rivers were brought into Rome. Agrippa, what with improvements of the former works, and additions, within the year of his edilefhip, provided Rome with feven hundred pieces of level waters, a hundred and five of fpringing waters, built a hundred and thirty refervoirs, and, that nothing might be

* For inftance Lyons.

wanting

wanting to the magnificence of thefe works, interfperfed them with four hundred marble pillars and three hundred marble and bronze ftatues. *Si quis diligentius æstimaverit*, cried Pliny at the fight of thefe wonders, *aquarum abundantiam in publico, balneis, piscinis, domibus, euripis, hortis, furburbanis villis, fpatioque advenientium extructos arcus, montes perfoffos, convalles æquatas, fatebitur nihil magis mirandum fuisse in orbe terrarum.* In the learned Fabretti's Differtations, *de 'Aquis & Aquæductibus*, are to be found all the particulars that can be defired, relating to this ftupendous article.

It is in this refpect that modern Rome bears the greateft likenefs to ancient Rome; and for this advantage it is chiefly obliged to Sixtus V. and Paul V. who have rivaled the fplendor and magnificence of the fovereigns of the univerfe. Such are the works of thofe two great princes, that Rome is now the only city which may be faid to be duly fupplied and ornamented with water. That brought by Paul V. to the top of the ancient Janiculum, by an aqueduct of twelve leagues in length, makes one of the moft pleafant fights in this kind which can be beheld.

Out of three mouths opening from a large body of architecture, iffues a river, which turns feveral mills, and after watering part of Rome fupplies the two fountains in St. Peter's Circus. This fuperb *fontanone*, Raphael's famous transfiguration, and Bramantes' antique chapel built on the

* Plin. L. xxxvi.

fpot

spot where St. Peter is said to have been crucified, often drew me towards the Janiculum.

Several other aqueducts bring water to Rome; and so profusely is it distributed among gardens, palaces and public places, that it would seem mere waste in the squares, did not the embellishment resulting from it, and the lively appearance which it diffuses, deserve to come into account. Concerning this I have heard, that at the time of conquering the kingdom of Naples, Don Carlos, now king of Spain, having visited Rome *incognito,* Benedict XIV. would be his Cicero, and shew him in person the chief curiosities. On coming to St. Peter's, the prince admired the height, the plenty, and the fine effect, of the waters issuing from the two fountains which adorn that area. After a considerable time spent in viewing the wonders of St. Peter's, Don Carlos was surprised that the two fountains were still playing; on which the pope told him, that these waters played incessantly, " in the night time for " the moon, and in the day for the people of " Rome."

The Parisians will have it, that, had Lewis the XIVth's magnificence been directed towards this object, there would have been nothing at Rome which Paris need to envy.

Besides, the fountains of Rome are perhaps less to be admired for the plenty of water, than for the taste, the magnificence, and variety of their forms, which have, as it were, exhausted the skill and invention of the most celebrated architects: those in a great measure are owing to Innocent X. Alexander VII. and Urban VIII. That of Trevi

is the work of Clement XII. and his fucceffor:
the richnefs of the architecture in its ground-work,
and the fingularity of the different groupes formed
by the projecting parts, give it the appearance of
a theatrical decoration.

To the Roman antiques, with which I was
moft taken, I think I may add one of a very remarkable kind indeed, and difcovered but a
little before my arrival.

The abbot Mazeas had accompanied the bifhop
of Laon when going to Rome as ambaffador from
France. Though the account given by Spartian
of the magnificence with which the emperor
Adrian had collected for his houfe at Tivoli, the
moft remarkable products of the feveral provinces
of the empire, be but fuperficial, this learned
Frenchman undertook from it to fearch the ground
on which the ruins of that houfe lie fcattered.
Among fome plants quite foreign to the foil of Rome,
and which have perpetuated themfelves on this
ground, he perceived a fhrub emitting a kind of gum,
made ufe of by the labouring peafants for per-
fuming their fnuff. The firft fhrubs of this fpecies
which he examined were weak and knotty; but
advancing towards an eminence intercepting the
north wind, he perceived others very vigorous, and
to be nothing lefs than that valuable fhrub from
which the Arabians gather the balfam of Mecca,
and by the emperor Adrian imported and cultivated in his gardens at Tivoli. The abbot Mazeas,
it is to be prefumed, will communicate to fome of
the academies, of which he is a member, the particulars of his obfervations, and the difcoveries
arifing from them.

MODERN

GOVERNMENT.—The papacy is the moſt abſolute of all the governments in Europe. Its conſtitution, the conſolidation of the prieſthood and prerogative, the eſtabliſhed notion of infallibility, ſet the pope above all ſuperiority, or even equality: and his theocratical authority over the ſubjects, is the ſame as that of the moſt deſpotic general of an order, over the religious ſurbordinate to his obedience. The authority of the European monarchs, beſides being limited by fundamental laws, by the ordinances of their predeceſſors, by their coronation oath, is balanced by intermediate powers, ſuch as the ſtates general, the firſt bodies of the ſtates, &c. The grand ſignor himſelf depends as much on the Janiſaries as the Roman emperors depended on their army; and the muphti, though appointed by him, and removable at pleaſure, is ſo far the more formidable, as, if he tries maſtery with his ſovereign, he is always ſure of carrying his point.

There is not any one law, made either by their predeceſſors or themſelves, from which the popes cannot derogate: they have only, for form's ſake, to declare the law from which they intend to derogate: the want of this form would not hinder the immediate effect of a new law; it would ſerve only to open a future pretext or means of pleading againſt it. Hence thoſe accumulations of derogatories in all bulls, of which they make a part. Of all the pope's ſubjects the jeſuits are they who have moſt ſhackled his authority. The dogmatic and the encyclical bulls, ſuch as thoſe

of

of jubilees, are of no effect with regard to them, unlefs the derogation from their privileges be nominally and explicitly declared.

The political and civil government of Rome is diftributed among congregations, always fitting, and not very unlike the fovereign courts, or rather the councils or commiffions for executing the feveral branches of the prerogative in European ftates: but what keeps up this diftribution at Rome is, that the fenility of the popes difabling them from a clofe application to bufinefs, they rather think on fecuring to themfelves a long enjoyment of their dignity, than of wearing themfelves out by the exercife of the authority annexed to it. Sixtus V has fhewn what may be done by a pope who will put himfelf at the head of his affairs. He did every thing by himfelf, agreeable to the principles of defpotifm, which he brought from the convent; and abrogating the moft effential parts of the adminiftration fettled by his predeceffors, he eftablifhed others, to which his fucceffors have fhewn fuch a regard, that to this day Rome is ftill governed by the maxims of Sixtus V.

He was fo firmly perfuaded, or at leaft he was for having others be fo, of his infallibility, of the fubordinacy of all temporal powers to the power of the keys, and of the prerogatives of the *tiara* over all crowns, that in a fulminatory bull he profcribed the work where Bellarmine the jefuit allows the popes only an indirect right over fovereigns. I have feen, in cardinal Paffionei's library, the only remaining copy of that bull printed *ex typographia apoftolica*, under the infpection

fpection of Sixtus V. Philip II. who connived at
fuch antimonarchical affertions from the popes, and
even from the divines of his own dominions, as
might ferve his defigns againft France, complained
againft this arbitrary bull; and on the repeated
and vigorous remonftrances of that prince, Sixtus V. himfelf and his fucceffors thought fit to call
in all the copies of it.

Farther, in order to a right conception of what
can be done by a pope who is both refolved and
able to govern by himfelf, only compare what
Sixtus V. in the five years of his pontificate,
undertook and executed for the embellifhment
of Rome, and for fixing in it the feat of literature
and arts, to what Auguftus, in a reign of forty
years, and with all the riches of the univerfe at
his command, undertook and executed in the fame
way : the balance of fuch a comparifon will be
in favour of the Cordelier pope.

The Pope's Court.—I never could perceive in
the pope's court, nor in any of its appurtenances,
that ftate and faftuoufnefs with which fo many travellers have been difgufted. A great deal more may
be obferved in the court of the leaft ecclefiaftical
elector. In chapels, confiftories, and all the
occafions on which the pope at the head of the
facred college appears in all his grandeur, never
did I fee but one bifhop, or one abbot, at the
head of his chapter. Thefe ceremonies indeed
are opened by the cardinals fucceffively paying
their adoration to the pope on their knees, and
without fo much as their cap on : it muft likewife
be owned, that when, on the confecration of the
cardinal of York as archbifhop of Corinth, Clement

ment XIII. dined in public, which is very rarely
known, the cardinals were ferved only from the
pope's table, he eating by himfelf; and every
time the pope drank they ftood up, and all the
other dignitaries fell on their knees; but this
ceremonial favours more of the convent than of
grandeur and majefty, and is as little impofing as
the two large feathered fans or fly-flaps which are
a ftated part of the papal pomp.

There was anciently another fort of ceremony,
when fovereigns held the popes ftirrup, and led
their palfrey by the reins. Thefe homages were
the more fingular, as paid to the pope at times
when, not being mafters of Rome, it was purely
their dignity which commanded fuch refpect; and
they have receded from all thofe external claims
of fuperiority, as their temporal power increafed.
I meet with a very remarkable note in the cir-
cumftantial account of every thing that paffed
between Paul II. and the emperor Frederic III.
when that prince came to Rome in 1468. Fabiano
Bencio, fecretary of the chamber, and author of
that account, after relating how Paul II. behaved
towards the emperor, in every refpect, not as a
lord towards his vaffal, but as one fovereign towards another, adds, *Magna fuit humanitas quam
pontifex Cæfari ubique præbuit, et eò major eft habita,
quo pontificalis autoritas nullâ ex parte prifcis temporibus nunc eft inferior; poteftas autem atque vires
longè funt fuperiores. Ecclefia enim Romana, bene-
volente imperio et divitiis, pontificum diligentia
aucta, eò ufque proceffit, ut maximis quibufque
regnis fit comparanda: contrà autem Romani imperii
poteftas*

*poteſtas atque vires adeò ſunt minuitæ atque attri-
tæ, ut, præter nomen imperii, pœnè nihil reman-
ſerit.* He then recurs to former inſtances of the
treatment of ſeveral emperors at Rome; as Conſtantine, whom pope Vitalianus went to meet ſix
miles out of the city; pope Conſtantine, who
being ſent for to Conſtantinople by Juſtinian II.
ſet out immediately; pope Adrian, who received
Charlemagne, before he was emperor, at the foot of
the ſteps of St. Peter's church; pope Adrian IV.
who went as far as Sutri to receive Frederic I. at
his coming to Rome for the imperial crown.
Tunc magna erat, adds the relator, *Romani imperii
poteſtas, magnæ imperatorum vires in Italiâ et extrà
ſatis diffuſæ; tanta autem erat pontificis potentia,
quanta à principibus permittebatur: nunc verò,
cùm rerum mutatio ſit, parvulum quodque humani-
tatis officium pro maximo reputandum!* Theſe ancient examples, by which Paul II. regulated his
behaviour towards Frederic III. ſeem to exclude
all pretence to that ſuperiority with which popes
in the intermediate times have treated ſovereigns,
and little to warrant the forgetfulneſs of dignity
with which on theſe occaſions ſovereigns ſeem
chargeable.

The POPE's TROOPS.---The troops which do
duty at the pontifical palace, eſcorte the pope when
he appears in public, and guard Rome, are divided into different bodies of foot and horſe:
a regiment of foot of twelve hundred men, with
red uniforms trimmed with blue; a troop of hunt-
ers, conſiſting of two hundred men in an uniform
with red trimmings, and who have their hautboys,
baſſoons, and french-horns; a troop of a hundred
light-

light-horfe, in red uniforms faced with blue and a
gold edging; a troop of a hundred cuiraffiers,
with blue uniforms, gold button-holes, and lace
of the fame, and who march with kettle-drums
and trumpets; laftly, two hundred Swifs foot with
cuiraffes, their uniforms even to breeches and
ftockings ftriped with blue, yellow, and red, and
inftead of ruffs, wearing bands; a garb which
makes them look fomething like parifh-beadles.
The other land and fea forces, cantoned in the
ecclefiaftical ftate, I omit.

The places of all the foldiers whofe duty lies in
Rome, are real canonicates : they are new clothed
every year; their pay is a paulo *per diem*, with four
and twenty ounces of bread, falt, oil, &c. The infantry is a medley of deferters from all nations. The
cavalry in a great meafure have been domeftics to
cardinals and noblemen, who procured them this
retreat as a reward for their good behaviour. The
light-horfe have ten Roman crowns per month,
befides the keeping of their horfe; and the cuiraffiers, fifteen fous *per diem*. The captains are all
colonels by *brevet*; their pay is a hundred Roman
crowns *per* month, and that of the fubalterns pro-
portionate, befides an allowance of bread, meat,
&c. from the pope's palace, &c. There are
feveral knights of Malta in this fervice, which to
men of fpirit is the lefs agreeable, being fubject
to the command of prelates; and, what to many is
worfe, the whole corps are cafhiered at every new
pontificate.

TRANSTEVERANS.—Rome has likewife its militia, divided, according to the quarters of the
city, under captains and other officers, who are citizens.

zens. On the ceremony of the *Poſſeſſo* I ſaw the militia of Tranſtevere return into their quarter over the
Sixtus bridge. Never troops were leſs like thoſe
who by their vigour and courage raiſed Rome to
the empire of the univerſe ; yet are theſe Tranſteverans the very flower of the Roman militia, which
dares not compare itſelf to them. Theſe huſband-
men and wine-dreſſers (for ſuch the majority are)
look on themſelves as the progeny of the Trojans ;
whilſt the inhabitants of the other quarters of
Rome, in their account, are only a rabble brought
together by mere chance. At the time of the laſt
conqueſt of the kingdom of Naples, when the
Spaniards paſſed by Rome, the Waloon guards
quartered in this part, committing ſome diſorder,
the towns-people roſe, took arms and oppoſed
their gueſts. This tumult ſpread an alarm which
reached Benedict XIV. Two of the heads, being
condemned to die for non-appearance, went over
to the Auſtrian camp, and offered to bring the
general two regiments of their people. The offer
was readily accepted ; but the peace ſoon following, rendered it unneceſſary. The two de-
linquents returned home, and have continued
without moleſtation. To keep their courage
inured, the Tranſteverans, from time to time,
challenge other quarters to ſtone-fights ; and
generally the victory is on their ſide. As they
have a particular language or jargon, ſo in their
manners and cuſtoms, and even their very ſhape
and appearance, they differ from the other part
of the people.

CHIEF OFFICES.—The ſupreme authority, both
ſpiritual and temporal, is lodged in the pope and
his

his council, which confifts of nephews (of whom
it is very feldom that there is any fcarcity) and
the cardinal fecretary of ftate. Here the principal
affairs are fettled, and even the decifion of thofe
which are to go through the congregations is prepared, thefe affemblies being fo modelled, that
in every thing they conform to the infpiration from
the council above.

By the abrogation of nepotifm, it has ceafed in
apparenza, but not in *foftanza*. Benedict XIV. of
all the late popes, is the only one who, literally
conforming to that law, did not liften to *flefh and
blood*. Though he was not difpleafed with any of
his family, fo little did he concern himfelf about
them, that, receiving an exprefs that his niece was
delivered of a fon, he faid with a laugh, *Io credeva
che la razza de' cogl . . . . . . foffe finita (q).* The
furplus of what the apoftolic chamber annually
yielded for his civil lift, he applied to the benefit
of Santo Spirito.

SECRETARY of STATE.—Cardinal Archinto,
after being fecretary of ftate to that pope as fucceffor to cardinal Valenti, had been continued in his
high poft by Clement XIII. He died very fuddenly,
juft as the Portuguefe affair began to break out:
we faw his funeral, and heard the lamentations with
which it was honoured, with the conjectures and
predictions concerning it. His obfequies as chancellor formed a fpectacle little or nothing inferior
to the funeral even of a pope.

The pofts of camerlingo, chancellor and vicar,
are for life. The firft takes cognizance of all the

(q) " I thought that good-for-nothing breed had been at
" an end."

parts

parts of the finances. Before the second come all affairs requiring the great seal: the income of this post is said to be not less than three hundred thousand livres *per annum.* To the third belongs whatever concerns the ecclesiastical police, the fraternities, the hospital, &c. I have heard that the very public prostitutes were a branch of his department, and that they go before him, and, as it were, make a profession of that calling, declaring the resolution they had taken *far lavorar il terreno.* They are immediately called aside, and that condition is set before them in all its infamy and horror: if they persist, so as to make their appearance a second time before the vicar, they are registered and sent again to the *barigel,* who provides them with a lodging in the streets set apart for that profession. Cardinal Guadagni was still vicar when we were at Rome. This good prelate carried his charity to such a pitch, that a priest representing his distress to him, to make known all its extremity declared to him that he was without breeches: on which the cardinal took off his, and gave them to the priest, as the only relief at that time in his power.

Secretary of the Briefs.—The briefs secretary's office, for which Clement XII. has built on Monte Cavallo, a palace of a more grand appearance than that of the pope himself, has for its head a cardinal, or sometimes only a prelate. This important place was filled by cardinal Passionei, who was put into it by pope Clement XII. and Benedict XIV. confirmed him in it, with the addition of librarian to the Vatican. At the conclaves of 1740 and 1758, cardinal

Paffionei had treated cardinal Rezzonico, (r) who was immediately before him in the facred college, very freely, and fometimes imperioufly and even roughly. The latter being made pope in 1758, without the concurrence of the fquadron of which cardinal Paffionei was the head, and who had repeatedly protefted that he never would come into that election; at the adoration the cardinal, after performing it, delivered to the pope the bulls for his employment, faying, " Moft holy father, " I deliver up to your holinefs the favours with " which your two predeceffors honoured me from " mere kindnefs: your holinefs, who is under no " obligation to me, may confer them on fome- " body more worthy." The pope took the bulls, and after looking on them a while anfwered, " Cardinal Paffionei, perhaps I am more obliged " to you than you think; but, were I under no " obligation to you, the church is under many: " accept then from her hand the confirmation " of my predeceffors favours, if you have any " fcruple of accepting it from mine;" and he added, fmiling, " continue to give me your " advice, with that freedom and candour which " I have often felt."

The fpiritual court has two offices at Rome, that of the inquifition, erected by Paul V. and that of the penitentiary. The firft, of which the pope is always prefident, is like rivers, at their fource of little importance, but increafing in their progrefs. Foreigners of all reli-

(r) That was his way, more or lefs, in the facred college, with all his brethren: all Rome knows how he behaved towards cardinal Tencin in a full confiftory.

gions,

gions, by reason of their bringing a great deal
of money, live freely at Rome without being
molested about their belief, or requiring any
conformity with the religion of the country.
These foreigners make no difficulty of shewing
what they are; and all the commonalty,
whose interest herein is the same as that of the
state, say of them, and that with a laugh,
*Questa gente non crede in Dio: gran' malora per
loro**. It is only the domestics who are tampered
with, and that not by spiritual threatenings, but
offering them pensions, or to make them *sbirri*,
&c. I used to see at the German inn a Swiss
who had been converted in this manner. He
had a pension of ten Roman crowns per month,
and thus was continually smoking and tippling:
he would fain have made such a convert of
a young Saxon, whom my fellow traveller had
taken into his service at Venice. This young
Saxon went, in company with other servants, to
kiss the pope's feet, who being taken with
his countenance asked him what country and
religion he was of: " Of Saxony," answered he
with German frankness, " and of a religion which
" is not yours." " Well, friend," replied the
pope in an affectionate manner, at the same time
giving him a chaplet, " take this from my hand,
" as an earnest of your future reconciliation with
" the church of Rome."

However, should a foreigner be so indiscrete as
to offer at dogmatising, the inquisition would lay
its hand on him, but not till repeated warnings to

* " Those people do not believe in God; so much the
" worse for them."

forbear,

forbear, or to leave Rome. A young Frenchman, whom a friend of mine met with at Bologna, in 1740, told him that he had been in durance for above a week in the prifon of the holy office for an amour with a girl kept by a prieft, who was for making him marry her.

It muft be obferved, that it is now above a century fince the inquifition of Rome has paffed a capital fentence. Every thing there is tranfacted in private by fpiritual and pecuniary penalties: none undergo a public punifhment but blafphemers, and thefe picked out from among the refufe of the city. Their tongue is faftened between pincers made of two pieces of reed joined and tied at the two ends: in this figure they are led to the door of their parifh-church, and there ftand during the time of high mafs.

MASTER of the SACRED PALACE.—The cenfor of books printed at Rome, and in the ecclefiaftical ftate, forms the department of the mafter of the facred palace. This poft is annexed to the Dominican order. The perfon who filled it while we were at Rome was father Orfi, eminent for his birth, talents, and works, among which it is fufficient to name his Ecclefiaftical Hiftory. In his appearance, and in every thing about him, there was a fimplicity, modefty and candour, which would have furprifed even a novice (f). At his houfe I was fpectator of a fcene which for its fingularity deferves relating.

At the time of the *poffeffo* the Jews in Rome are fubject to a very mortifying ceremony, but ftrictly kept up. Near Titus's triumphal arch, the rabbi and elders of the *Ghetto* ftand in a place fitted up at

(f) He died a cardinal, in 1761.

their expence. As the pope is on his folemn
proceffion to St. John de Lateran, they ftep forth,
and on their knees offer to him the Pentateuch
in a bafon full of gold and filver coins. The pope,
making a ftop, touches the bafon with a wand,
and performs the like ceremony on the head or
fhoulders of the chief rabbi, in token that he
accepts of the Jews homage, and allows them to
remain in Rome during his pontificate. The Jews,
that their homage to Clement XIII. might be the
more taken notice of, had purchafed fome original
fonnets, and printed them in a large letter and
paper, like proclamations, and hung part of their
ftation with thefe teftimonies of their allegiance.
The author of thefe fonnets, in expectation of farther gain, digefted them into a collection, to be
fold on his account. The rabbi, who had paid
for them, eftimating their merit by the poet's expectations, feifed the edition, as having originally
purchafed the pieces of which it confifted. The
matter being brought before the mafter of the
facred palace, he fummoned the parties; and I
had the pleafure of hearing them difpute their
claims, with all the vehemency of elocution and
gefture to which the hope of gain could roufe a
rabbi and an Italian poet, to whom the point in
difpute was no fmall matter. Both parties being
heard, P. Orfi adjudged the edition, paying the
expence of it, to the rabbi, who exulted at the
decifion, whilft the poet hung his head. When
they were withdrawn, I took the liberty to efpoufe
the poet's caufe, as connected with that of religion: " Why," fays P. Orfi fmiling, " I have
" given it on the fide of religion. All the money

" that

" that the poet had got from the rabbi he has laid
" out in printing this collection, of which he would
" not have fold half a dozen copies: he would
" have been juft like the dog in the fable, lofing
" its prey in running after the reflection of the
" moon. My verdict againft him was in fact for
" him."

On my leaving Rome, father Orfi gave me, to
deliver to a French bifhop, a piece which appeared
to him of fuch a nature and tendency, that he had
caufed the edition to be feifed and brought
away (s).

PENITENTIARY.—The penitentiary is a harbour
againft the profecutions of the inquifition. It takes
cognifance of all poffible crimes, and grants abfolution from them. The penitentiaries, on prefenting a petition, obtain a licence for abfolving,
which is made out to them *gratis* by way of brief,
in which is left a blank for the finner's name. As
to fatisfactory penalties, it is only fome Spaniards
and Portuguefe who fubmit to them. Thefe are the
creatures one meets with on the ftair-cafe leading
to St. Peter's dome, in the vefture of penitents,
and labouring at peftles twelve or fifteen feet
high, for pulverifing marble to make ftucco.

Thefe abfolutory licences were formerly paid
for, and are a part of the *taxa cancellariæ apofto-
licæ*, which has raifed fuch an outcry againft the
church of Rome. I have a copy of this tariff,
printed at Paris by Galiot du Pré in 1533. In
page 178, is the tax for making out the abfolution

(s) *De Delectationibus cælefti et terrenâ.* Auctore Jofepho
Carpani, S. J. 8vo.

pre.

pro eo qui matrem, sororem, aut aliam consanguineam vel affinem carnaliter cognovit; fol. 181, *pro eo qui interfecit patrem, matrem, sororem, uxorem, aut alium consanguineum, scilicet laïcum; quia, si esset clericus, teneretur interfector visitare sedem apostolicam.* These are rated at seven or eight gros; and, according to the tariff of the value of coins at the end of the collection, each gros was equal to four sols Tournois. Now can it with any reason be inferred from these taxations, which were not pleadable in any civil court of justice, that the court of Rome kept a public office for encourageing all sorts of crimes, absolutions being easily to be obtained? This charge would reach the offices of secular princes; pardons, mitigations, commutations of penalties, &c. being there made out, by order of the prince, after certain knowledge of the cause.

CONGREGATIONS.—The other spiritual or ecclesiastical affairs are divided among various congregations, composed of cardinals and counsellors. These congregations are not unlike the several offices in the European courts: they have their settled meetings; and, in most, the stress of business lies on the secretary, who is always of the pope's immediate nomination. To keep to this comparison, cardinals are at Rome as the counsellors of state in France; and the prelates may be compared to the masters of requests, and counsellors of a supreme court.

The greater part of these prelates belong to the chancery, the datary, and the apostolic chamber. Legations, nunciatures, and places in the Rota, are generally bestowed on them; and several of

E 4

these

thefe places are *cardinalician,* that is, never
quitted but on promotion to the cardinalſhip.
Such are thoſe of governor of Rome, treaſurer
and firſt auditor of the chamber, and dean of the
Rota. A pope of the ſixteenth century had added
this reverſion to the poſts of clerks of the apoſtolic
chamber; and he had fixed on them a ſuitable fine,
that is, four hundred and fifty thouſand livres,
French money, which the incumbents left on
their promotion to the purple. Innocent XII.
judging this to favour of ſimony, ſuppreſſed it,
to the no ſmall vexation of the relations of ſome
of his ſucceſſors, who, however, have found out
other paths leading to the ſame end.

The ſecular tribunals for the affairs of juſtice
and the police are Monte Citorio, the Rota, the
ſenate, the government, and the Conſulta. The
judges of moſt of theſe tribunals are eccleſiaſtics.

Monte Citorio, ſo ſplendidly built by Innocent XII. for all the ſubaltern tribunals to meet in,
is at Rome the ſame as the *Parc civil du Châtelet* at
Paris: all affairs are there tranſacted in writing, and
laid before the judges by way of information: they
are afterwards decided in writing. I have ſometimes been preſent at theſe kind of hearings, where
one or two judges, in long robes, ſit in elbow-
chairs at a table on which is a crucifix. The
lawyer, in his ſhort cloak and band, ſits on one
ſide of the table with his papers ſpread before him.
Having opened the cauſe in a colloquial manner,
he enters on his arguments and thoſe of his ad-
verſary, ſettting forth the former in their full
force, and combating the latter. If, in the
narrative of the fact, the judge perceives any
ambiguity

ambiguity or obfcurity, he calls on the lawyer to clear it up : he likewife canvaffes the arguments, propofes difficulties, makes objections ; in a word, thefe *informations* have more the appearance of a confultation of lawyers, than of a pleading before a judge. At one fitting, I heard a counfellor thus ftate and difcufs five or fix cafes with a facility, clearnefs and precifion, becoming the moft auguft courts of Europe. Appeals from the Monte-Citorio decrees are brought before a particular auditor of the pope's nomination, and from his verdict an appeal lies to the Rota.

The Rota.—This laft tribunal, like the famous Grecian council of the *Amphyctiones*, is compofed of auditors of all Roman-catholic nations. It takes cognifance by appeal of all civil caufes within the ecclefiaftical ftate, and, in firft inftance, of fuits brought before it by foreigners. I never could know what fort of caufes come before it from France : the Gallic liberties feem fcarce reconcileable with the competency of fuch a court. It confifts of twelve auditors, of whom the pope is prefident. The writings and proceffes here know no end ; the duties foreign from judicature, which are incumbent on the auditors ; their neceffary attendance at court ; the long and frequent vacations of this tribunal ; the *fede vacantes* during which the ordinary courts of juftice are fhut up, being all fo many avocations which divert the auditors from their chief functions. Farther, the caufes which come before them, whether in firft inftance or by appeal, are not finally terminated till one of the parties has three uniform verdicts in his behalf ; and thefe

verdicts

verdicts are the more liable to exception, the judges being obliged to infert in them the motive and point of law on which they gave fuch decifion. Befides, all the objects of demands, both principal and incidental, are canvaffed feparately. The recourfe or rehearing is opened before the fame tribunal, which is divided into four chambers or offices. How fuch a form of proceeding, multiplying the writings, and confequently the cofts, muft prolong the final decifion, is eafily conceived ; and this is no longer final than as the party, who has been caft by three uniform verdicts, is pleafed to fit down for thirty or forty years without applying for a fecond hearing before the pope himfelf, which is eafily granted, for reafons to be fet forth in the fequel, and which Muratori *(t)* certainly was not aware of, when he went fo far as to arraign the forms of the Rota.

The auditors, though counfellors of the fupreme court in Rome, are not allowed thofe diftinctions in great ceremonies, for inftance at pontifical chapels, which feem due to their weighty pofts. At one of thefe ceremonies, I have feen an auditor who was a prieft, fub-dean of the Rota, with many ample benefices, and who made a figure in Rome equal to the firft perfons of the court, fuch a one have I feen ftoop to the duty of an acolythe, and humbly carry a candleftick ; fo true is it that extremities are in contact.

SENATOR BILK.—The fenator, who is a fecular judge, and always a foreigner, was a Ger-

(t) See chap. 9. of his treatife *De i difetti della Giurifprudenza*, p. 85. See alfo what Bouchet fays on the fame head in his *Sérées*, p. 331.

man

man * gentleman, whose converfion to the catholic religion was rewarded with this poft, which, befides being for life, gives the rank of a prince, and an apartment in the Capitol. He tries petty caufes and quarrels fummarily, and without appeal. He has for affeffors, four confervators, who are changed every three months. Both thefe confervators, and the fenator himfelf, are appointed by the fovereign, who does not leave to the Roman people fo much as that fmall remainder of liberty, which towns in monarchies freely enjoy, the election of their own magiftrates. In this tribunal is at prefent concentred the *majefty of the fenate and people of Rome,* whofe title it accordingly bears.

GOVERNOR.—The high police is in the department of the governor of Rome, who, with a lieutenant and fome afseffors, likewife judges without appeal. He has every Wednefday an audience of the pope, to which he goes in no fmall ftate; particularly, before his coach walk twelve halberdiers, whofe clothing is like that of the *gentlemen of the fleeve,* who make a part of the king of France's guard. The apoftolic chamber allows him a thoufand *fbirri* under a *barigel* or provoft-martial, five hundred foot watchmen, and three hundred fpies who daily report to him what is doing in Rome. By thefe arrangements the police has long fince been on a footing at Rome, to which Paris was a ftranger before this prefent century: it has an eye to every thing without fhowing itfelf, or caufing itfelf to be felt. The *fbirri,* its minifters, are not in any great efteem: they however keep the populace in

* He was a Swede. *Tranfl.*

awe,

awe, and that fuffices, people of credit having
very feldom any thing to do with the police.
They likewife are a check on the monks, being
their natural overfeers, either to keep them at a
diftance from nunneries, or infamous places, or
to hinder their nocturnal excurfions: but, for a
little money dropped now and then to the *barigel*,
a monk may divert himfelf at his pleafure, and
the police fhall connive at it.

At the theatres, the governor's box, though he
be a prelate, is like that of the fovereign in other
parts. The French embaffadrefs having abruptly
left one of the houfes on account of fome difficulty
concerning the box, and the governor haggling
about the matter, the embaffador fet up the arms
of France over the very box of the governor, went
and feated himfelf among the company there,
ftaying out the whole play, without a word from
the governor.

By a cuftom founded on the manners of the
Romans, the citizens, and even the cardinals
themfelves, inftead of having flambeaus or creffets
carried before them in the winter evenings, only
make ufe of dark-lanterns. On the coming up
of fuch a lantern, any one, whether alone or with
others, who would not be known, has a right to
call out to him who carries the lantern, *Volta la
lanterna*, *i. e.* " Turn the lantern;" and on his
non-compliance rufhes on him with a fword or
poniard: but this is feldom the cafe, the obfer-
vance of that cuftom being a general concern.

The police of health and plenty is divided between an office and two prelates, one of whom is prefect of grain, and the other of the provifions. Report

is made to the health-office of every creature
dying at Rome, men, women, and beasts down to
the very dogs and cats. The office, in considera-
ration of a settled fee, has the bodies removed,
and takes care of their being put under ground.
The most fleshy parts of dead horses, whose
distemper was not contagious, are left to *fachini*,
or porters, who distribute them about as a dinner
for cats; a creature of which the people of Rome
are very fond, but for whom the frugality of
their tables does not provide a subsistence. This
distribution is really something entertaining:
the *fachino*, attended by two mastiffs, has a
large knife in his hand, and on one of his
shoulders a stick, at the ends of which hang the
surloins of horses, which he keeps in balance
by alternately turning the stick from one shoulder
to the other: the cats, on hearing the distributors,
instantly shew themselves at the windows, in the
gutters, and at the doors, according as their dinner is near, or at some distance. I have seen five
or six very fine sleek cats, regularly drawn up at
the doors of several houses, waiting for, and successively receiving their allowance, without any
quarrel, disorder, or confusion: those of the following houses come out into the street; and the more
bold come about the purveyor's legs, and those
of his dogs, who seem to be no wise displeased with
these caresses. One of these purveyors, whom I
once followed all along the street leading from
la Piazza d'Espagna to St. Angelo's bridge, tickled
with my seeming so pleased with his occupation,
did all he could to improve my entertainment both
on his part and the cats: at every piece, before
throwing

throwing it, he held it up a while, faying to them; *Piglia, monfou,* " Take, monfieur," fuppofing me a Frenchman.   This diftribution is performed daily, and at a fettled rate.

The CONSULTA.—The Confulta takes cognifance of the complaints of the people againft the governors, and of appeals from their fentences.   All cities, thofe excepted which have legates, fend their malefactors to Rome, where they are tried. In both criminal and civil proceffes a rehearing may be obtained, and after that a recourfe to the pope ; by which means punifhments fall only on fuch forlorn wretches as are deftitute of all manner of protection, and executions are as rare as crimes are frequent : befides, the greateft malefactors often efcape by means of the afylums, whofe ancient privileges ftill fubfift in all their force.   The corporal punifhments are the *corda,* or ftrappado, fcourging, the gallies, the gibbet, and knocking down.   The laft is inflicted in this manner : the executioner ftrikes the patient on one of his temples with a club, fo that he drops down fenfelefs : then he cuts his throat, and quarters his body, which remains for fome time on the place of execution.   This punifhment may be lefs painful to the criminal than the wheel, but is more fhocking to the fpectators. Under the prefent pontificate there will be no capital punifhments, Clement XIII. having made a vow or folemn promife to the contrary.   The torture is performed only by extending the arms and legs of the party accufed, fo that his body being fufpended, the back bone refts only on a picquet.   Be the proofs ever fo clear and ftrong, the perfon accufed muft himfelf acknowledge his crime, before fentence can be paffed on him.

FINANCES.—The apoftolic chamber is to the pope as land-ftewards to gentlemen of eftates, and as attornies to religious houfes. It manages the revenues of the demefnes, and of the temporal lordfhip of the Roman church, under a form of adminiftration, of which the pope is abfolute mafter. Thefe revenues confift in the produce of the non-alienated demefnes, of the cuftoms, of duties, gabels and taxes on provifions. The real and perfonal impofitions, which are not known in the ecclefiaftical ftate, are made up by a thoufand petty taxes, which, without affecting the freedom of men and lands, yield very confiderable fums. Pins, for inftance, are farmed out as at Naples; and the farmers, to increafe the confumption of their commodity, take care that they fhall be none of the beft. It muft however be owned, that Rome is not peftered, as Venice and Genoa, with that endlefs multiplicity of impofts on the confumptions of inns, and confequently on foreigners. The Romans, equally with them, pay the duties on carriages and baggage, which is collected at the gates of Rome. A very odd circumftance in this duty is, that even the dead, fo far from being exempted, make the moft confiderable article of it. The farmers of the duty required no lefs than a thoufand Roman crowns for admitting into Rome the corpfe of one of the princes Borghefe, who died at Frefcati; but this family fmuggled it into the city under a load of hay. The fame ftratagem was put in practice for conveying away the body of the duchefs de St. Aignan,

O B S E R V A T I O N S

Aignan, though the duke her hufband was at the
fame time embaffador from France at the court of
Rome.

Tobacco has likewife been farmed till the pontificate of Benedict XIV. About the year 1756,
armed bodies of fmugglers ufed to bring tobacco
and other prohibited goods into the very heart of
the ecclefiaftical ftate. The farmers making repeated complaints, the apoftolic chamber determined to difperfe the fmugglers; and for this
expedition it commiffioned the prelate, who at
at that time was prefect of Urbino. This general
got together a little army of *fbirri*, under the
country and city *barigels*; and putting himfelf
at the head of it, he marched directly for a fmall
town, near the frontiers of Tufcany, which was
their chief rendezvous; but all the inhabitants
had fled at his approach, leaving only an old
decrepit creature of fourfcore, and another at the
point of death. This town the prelate made
choice of for his head quarters, walled up the
gates, and fecured himfelf from any outrages of
the fmugglers, who remained mafters of the
country. After taking thefe meafures, he had
the old man and the dying perfon both tucked up.
In a word, the bufinefs was drilled on fo long,
that this hanging, which proved the upfhot of all
that mighty expedition, coft the apoftolic chamber
two hundred thoufand livres: this difpleafed Benedict XIV, to fuch a degree, that he fuppreffed
the farm, and put tobacco on its former commercial footing.

Since this fuppreffion the dealers have contrived
a mixture of bullocks liver dried and pulverifed,

faw-duſt and pepper, which they fell for ſnuff, and for not leſs than the farmers uſed to fell it; and no other could I meet with throughout all Romania, the inhabitants now growing uſed to it.

Grain is the apoſtolic chamber's moſt conſiderable article, and apparently the moſt beneficial to the ſtate, but in reality the moſt hurtful. Formerly this ſtate ſupplied the city and territories of Genoa, and ſome parts of Tuſcany, with grain; and at the ſame time, great numbers of cattle conſumed at Venice came from theſe parts: whereas, ſince the apoſtolic chamber, in virtue of an excluſive privilege, has aſſumed to itſelf the purchaſe and ſale of grain; ſince the landholders and farmers can diſpoſe of their grain to the chamber alone; ſince it is only from the chamber's granaries that bakers can ſupply themſelves; the demands of the Genoeſe have ceaſed, the country people have given over graſiery, and both cultivation and population have been continually declining; in ſhort, that excluſion is moſt truly a perpetual calamity. The grain purchaſed by the chamber being cut and inned at the time of the greateſt heats, it is ſaid, that in the beginning of the rains, the water with which they become impregnated makes ſuch an addition to their volume, as to ſecure to the ſtore-keepers a profit which well makes them amends for wages: but the advantage of meaſure certainly ariſes much more from the different manner of meaſuring, upon receiving and ſelling out the grain of the ſtorehouſes, than from the rain.

The

The DATARY.—The datary, where all collations for benefices are made out, is the moſt certain ſource of the papal revenue, and poſſibly would be the moſt conſiderable, were not a very great part of its produce ſwallowed up, under the appellation of *drink-money*, by a multitude of poſts and employments appertaining to the datary.

Rome has very different thoughts from France concerning the effects of the *concordat* by which Francis I. gave to Leo X. the *annates*, or firſt-fruits, of conſiſtorial benefices in exchange for the right of nomination to thoſe benefices. Not that the Romans ſee it in the ſame light, as the Sorbonne, the parliaments and univerſities of France: ſo far from it, they affirm the pope to have been greatly hurt by that contract; that, of two rights which he was poſſeſſed of, one has been weakened by the loſs of the other; and that the ſituation of things, even in the condition to which they had been brought by the Pragmatic, was leſs diſadvantageous to him.   Indeed, the pope owed no favour to incumbents elected by canons and monks ; and now he cannot refuſe thoſe which the king cauſes to be aſked of him for the ſubjects he names, and whom he gratifies without touching his own pocket, by procuring them abatements in the rates of their bulls.   The cardinals, in order to put a ſtop to theſe favours, as diminiſhing their drink-money, had projected, under the protectorſhip of the laſt cardinal D'Eſte, to prevail with the cardinal-protectors of the ſeveral

crowns

crowns to give up the powers, which as fuch they are invefted with in the rates of bulls; and they had fucceeded : but cardinal D'Efte would not come into that meafure ; he afferted the powers of his place as a prerogative of the crown of France, and carried his point. France, however, never met with better returns for thofe favours than under the pontificate of Benedict XIV. who could refufe nothing to the count De Stainville.

Spain has no lefs reafon to be pleafed with the fame pontificate. During fix months in the year, the pope had, *pleno jure*, the nomination to all benefices in that kingdom, even with cure of fouls, by taking a year and a half's income for each benefice exceeding fifty ducats, and that paid abfolutely without delay or deduction on any account whatever. It is even faid, that the relations of the popes, under fictitious names, received penfions on thofe benefices. In order totally to extirpate fuch abufes, and rid the confcience of his fucceffors of nominations extorted by patrons, by intrigue and importunity, to the prejudice of merit, Benedict XIV. put Spain, in this refpect, nearly on the fame footing with France : but this innovation is, among the Romans, one of the chief complaints againft that pope, who indeed has thereby deprived Rome of great numbers of Spaniards, who reforting thither, either to obtain, or conteft with thofe who had obtained, benefices, or to maintain themfelves in what they had obtained, ufed to fpend, in this capital of the old world, part of the riches of the new. By means of fome arrange-

ments

ments of the like nature, the king of Sardinia is likewife become his own mafter.

BANK-NOTES.—The far greater part of the wealth of the Romans lies in notes of the Spi-rito-Santo bank, and the feveral mounts of piety, whofe names to their papers are what the name of the Eaft-India company was to the bills of Law's fcheme in France. Though the banks and the mounts allow only four *per cent.* intereft, though no more than two and a half or three be actually received, yet fome events, real or forged, are, by the management of an artful jobbery, known to raife their notes to twelve. Innocent XI. laid hold of a time when they were at the very higheft, for offering to reimburfe fuch proprietors who were not difpofed to keep them, by paying to the bank thirty *per cent.* yet without increafe of their capital. Almoft all the proprietors chofe rather to give away, as fo much loft, the thirty *per cent.* than to accept of being reimburfed; for which the pope had before-hand made fure of money at Genoa, at the rate of only two *per cent.*

Other people have fince found means to lodge in the bank and mounts all the Roman coin which they ufed to fend away to Genoa, where all the payments were made in Roman crowns and zequins, whilft Rome had fcarce a fuf-ficiency for daily circulation; and ftill does this lie heavy on it, as the greateft blow it ever received of that kind. Of all the fpecie coined till the pontificate of Benedict XIV. nothing is to be feen but Teftones and Paölis, which have been thought below notice, not from any regard

to

to the public, but becaufe they are fo worn away as to be confiderably below their original value.

The people however are ftill perfuaded, that the bank and the mounts are never without cafh equal to the value of their refpective notes. As for the difficulty of being reimburfed, that paffes for a point of œconomy and prudential management; and he who, on carrying to the bank a note of two hundred crowns, gets ten in cafh, and for the remainder a frefh note of a hundred and ninety crowns payable in eighteen months, thinks himfelf well off.

The funds of the bank and the mounts arife from the immenfe riches of the Spirito-Santo hofpital, which are appropriated to them; from fome branches of the revenues of the apoftolic chamber, which at feveral times the popes have alienated in favour of the mounts, (as in France the king alienates fome funds to the town-houfe of Paris, for making good the annuities payable on his account by that company;) laftly, from the large fums of money daily lodged in thofe places without requiring any intereft.

By means of thefe funds the bank and mounts carry on, under the fhow of charity, a very lucrative trade, lending on pledges without intereft for the term of eighteen months, and to the amount of a hundred and fifty livres French money (about feven pounds Englifh): but, at the expiration of the eighteen months, the pledge, if not redeemed, is fold, unlefs the party keeps up the loan by paying intereft for the eighteen months at three *per cent.* The receptacles of all thefe

effects

effects are like a common wardrobe of the whole Roman people; or rather

Hoc miseræ plebi stabat commune sepulcrum*.

In these places there is a perpetual auction, where nothing is delivered but for ready money. This trade, mean and sordid as it appears, is very confiderable, both in the capitals, and the certainty and proportion of the profit. It affords the people a resource, for which otherwise they muft apply to the Jews : *(u)* and in this point of view it is, that the council of Trent has authorised, and even encouraged it. Plato would not have allowed it in his republic ; but *non in Platonis republicâ agebatur, fed de Romani populi fæce†*.

I have reckoned these objects among the revenues of the popes, for as they are absolute masters of the funds and their produce, they may dip into them *ad libitum*.

Posts.—The various employments in the apostolic chamber, the chancery, the datary, the secretary's office, &c. have been erected into posts. The number of these, the original tax or fine of which is from one thousand to sixty thousand Roman crowns, is said to exceed ten thousand.

---

* Horat. Sat. vii. l. 1.

(u) What the Jews can do in a city, where the people have from the state itself all the refources which in other places are to be had only of that body, is not easily conceived; and indeed they are poor, even to mifery and loathsomenefs : twice a week is the piazza Navona strewed with their filthy rags spread out for sale; and this is the subftance of their whole trade.

† Cic. de Catone.

One

One perfon may hold a plurality, putting in deputies for thofe which are incompatible. To the incumbents who execute them themfelves, they bring in feven or eight *per cent.* fo that at Rome it is the beft way of laying out money. Befides their being fo many fteps leading to the purple, the value of them all, as of the law-employments in France, is ever higher than, and often even double to, what it was at the time of the original fine. Hence the eagernefs for purchafing new-created pofts; an eagernefs which the popes take care not to balk : hence likewife the prodigious number of idlers whom the ftate has on its hands, paying them as if they worked.

Thefe pofts, as in France, though with fome difference, are a part of the fovereign's efcheats. They are loft by death, but may be difpofed of till the age of feventy years, provided that, at the time of refignation, the party has no incurable malady on him, as confumption, afthma, &c. and that the refigner furvives the fale forty days. It is computed, that by thefe meafures there is not a poft which does not revert to the fovereign three or four times every century. The government hath often been advifed to repurchafe them on the footing of the firft fine, as Innocent XII. did thofe of the clerks of the apoftolic chamber; but the popes, ever grafping at prefent emoluments, cannot be brought to plough up a meadow, which every year produces fo plentifully.

To the revenues of the popes muft likewife be added the produce of the falt-pits of Cervia, a very confiderable article; and that of the lottery, which is drawn eight times a year. This lottery is on the fame plan as thofe of Genoa and the military fchool in France; and the people of Rome give into it with all the precipitation of hope, incited by prefent neceffities and the fpirit of calculation: in fhort, the lottery is to this people the locuft which confumes what the caterpillar had left.

By thefe revenues it was, that Sixtus V. befides the ordinary expences of court and government, and even doubling thefe expences by undertakings worthy of ancient Rome, found means to accumulate, during only the three firft years of his pontificate, the three millions of gold which he laid up in the caftle of St. Angelo, certifying this depofit by three bulls inferted in the *Bullarium magnum*. This depofit is faid to have remained hitherto untouched.

GOVERNMENT-SPRINGS.—This curfory glance on the government of Rome fufficiently lays open its fprings, the weaknefs and fubtilty of which are fcarce perceived by thofe, who, having found the machine wound up, have nothing to do but to fet it in motion.

Love and fear are the two great hinges of all government; and its fcope is, or fhould be, to direct the actions of men for the public good. That of Rome is of fo particular a nature, that it does not concern itfelf about any fuch fcope, nor has it thofe fupports. Protected againft foreign enterprifes by a refpect for religion, and without fufficient forces to command refpect at home, it derives its fafety from this, that it is the intereft of the feveral parties which compofe it, not to defire, but even to dread its diffolu-

tion;

tion ; and that the want of dutiful and affectionate sentiments in the subjects is made up by the most substantial securities for their fidelity.

Such securities the sovereign has obtained, by getting into his hands all the wealth of his subjects, and all the objects of their dearest hopes. By these means it is that the nobility and commonalty of Rome, and all the ecclesiastical state, are connected with the papal government.

By the bank, the mounts of piety, and the posts, the pope is master of their wealth, as in those receptacles are included all the moveable riches of Rome and its dependencies. Of the immoveables and lands he is master by the monopoly of their produce to the apostolic chamber ; by the accounts which are always kept dependent between the landholders and farmers and the apostolic chamber, which takes care never to be before-hand with them; lastly, by the difficulties raised to retard the clearance of accounts : and, if to these embarrassments and fetters be added the endless length of law-suits, scarcely any can be imagined more forcible and intricate.

A Roman has a son in a post leading to higher employments, which may throw open the road of fortune to all his family : at first he had a smaller, of which he received the price in bank-bills, which remain in his port-folio. All this Roman's debts, both active and passive, lie in these papers. Another part of his substance lies in the bank or the mounts, having been placed there by himself, his father, or one of his ancestors. He has a suit for an estate, as plaintiff; in another, for a succession, he is defendant : one is but just entered on, and

of

of the other he may pretty well guefs the iffue from two correfponding verdicts already given. Now can fuch a one, without fhuddering, think on a revolution which may overthrow that conftitution to which he finds himfelf tied in fo many refpects? Will the ivy ever wifh for the fall of the tree, round which it twines as its fupport?

PEOPLE of ROME.—Thefe ties, great and fmall, are common to the prince, and to the citizen of any fubftance. As to the lower clafs, it is connected with Rome and the government by the conftant low price of bread, the holidays, and church-folemnities; by the places of *fbirri* and of fpy, or by the hopes of being one; by the eafinefs of procuring patrons; by the multiplicity of reliefs for the poor; by the endowments through which they hope to procure fettlements for themfelves and their children; in a word, by all the refources which floth can defire, and which are not to be met with under any other government. Thefe were the very fame allurements by which the populace of ancient Rome was kept together: *Retinete*, faid Cicero to them, in oppofition to colonifing fchemes, *retinete iftam poffeffionem gratiæ, libertatis, fuffragiorum, urbis, fori, feftorum, cæterorumque omnium commodorum**. As to the other refources which I have juft now fpecified, the fame Cicero in another place makes a due eftimate of them: *Frumentariam legem*, fays he in his fpeech for Seftius, *C. Gracchus ferebat : jucunda res plebi Romanæ; victus enim fuppeditabatur largè fine labore. Repugnabant boni quod ab induftriâ plebem ad defidiam avocari putabant*. To the picture of the

* Cic, *contra* Rullum.

lazy

lazy and precarious life of the Roman people Ta-
citus adds thefe difgraceful lineaments: *Languef-
cit induftria, intenditur focordia cùm nullus ex
fe metus aut fpes ; et fecuri omnes aliena fubfidia
expectant, fibi ignavi, aliis graves (x)*. So that
the people of modern Rome may fay, " We
" are beggars, but it runs in our blood."

The condition of all the citizens of Rome
is as fingular as the conftitution under which
they live; and it is in this particular that modern Rome is moft like the ancient city. In
its moft happy times, that is, to the year 650
from its foundation, according to Cicero, there
were fcarcely two thoufand houfe-keepers in
it, *qui rem haberent**. And it is much to be
queftioned, whether as many could be found
among the hundred and fifty thoufand fouls,
or thereabouts, which modern Rome is reckoned
to contain.

The great officers of ftate, and eight or ten ancient families, but eclipfed by four or five whom
the triple crown has enriched and promoted,
thefe, together with foreigners, fupply the public
luxury: but in this luxury alms bear a very
confiderable part. We have feen the richeft
Roman prince not fpending above twenty-four
fous a day for his table, and the furniture of
his houfe fuitable to fuch parfimony, yet dif-
tributing millions in alms of various kinds.

(x) I had thought of ftriking out the Latin with which
the original text is interlarded, and of replacing it with
French tranflations ; but I was diffuaded from it in favour of men of letters, to whom no tranflation would
be an equivalent.

* Off. L. ii. c. 21.

This

This fuperabundancy of charities, which to floth are as honey to hornets, anfwers the *congiaria* of the emperors, and is productive of the like effect.

The middle ftate, every where elfe formed by the citizens and trades-people, is unknown at Rome. There is no medium between opulence and poverty. " The rich," fays Mr. Sandys*, " are the " richeft of men ; and the poor, the moft in- " digent creatures in the world; an excefs never " known in a well-governed ftate." Extremities exactly touch each other; every member of the ftate either gives or receives alms. No fmall part of the wages of the numerous retinue of the cardinals and nobles confifts in alms, under the foftening appellations of *buone mancie, good feftivals, Far-Agofto, welcomes, good journies.* The eldeft of every family, under the refpectable title of *Decano*, is in this refpect the folicitor, the receiver, and the cafh-keeper, to his fellow fervants: in fhort, among the Romans themfelves, it is a faying, " that there is not a " burgefs of Rome but would fell the very fun " for three Paölis."

The perfons of eafy circumftances are not to be fought for among the lower dignitaries of the church ; nor among the fet of lawyers called *Curiales*; nor among thofe marquiffes and counts who, with the title of *Maeftri di camera & Scudieri*, are as profoundly verfed in ceremonials as the Germans are in the civil law; nor, in fine, among the placemen belonging to the different offices of the court: all thefe live more on hope than on

* Account of the State of Religion, c. 7.

fub-

subſtance. The demiſe of a pope and the va-
cancy occaſioned thereby, together with the ſuſ-
penſion of all kinds of buſineſs, reduce them
to objects of alms. The only claſs, which a
decent competency and the privilege of indepen-
dency put on a footing with all the other ranks,
are the conſiſtorial counſellors. In this claſs
Benedict XIV. had ſpent the fineſt twenty years
of his life, and there acquired that ſprightli-
neſs, wit and urbanity, which ſtuck to him on his
exaltation, and ſo happily counterbalanced the
many diſagreeable circumſtances of the pontificate. I have heard, that when a young lawyer, he took a trip on a party of pleaſure to
Genoa with ſome of his brethren of the gown,
who were for returning by ſea: " Do as you
" pleaſe," ſaid Lambertini, " you who have no-
" thing to riſque; but as I ſhall come to be
" pope, I muſt take care how I truſt Cæſar
" and his fortune to winds and waves."

In fine, the deſcription given by Mauro of the
precarious life of the Roman people includes
every claſs, both of court and city.

In Roma miſeria e ſperanza*.

" Rome is made up of wretchedneſs and hope."

A deſcription chalked out on that which Juvenal has left us of Rome in his time:

Hic vivimus ambitiosâ paupertate omnes.

A fondneſs for ornament and parade is the
hobby-horſe of the Roman people : to this all
other inclinations give way : it regulates and directs

* Capit della Fava.

the

the expences of the rich and the great : what
it faves in good cheer, or comfortable living,
it lavifhes on entertainments, equipages, liveries, and external fhow. And equally ambitious are the people amidft all their penury :
fhambles, the butchers and their ftalls, are all
fet off with linen as white as fnow : the frui-
terers fhops are difpofed in curious defigns, as
if for a fight : the fhoe-maker, the very cob-
ler, decorates his ftall with fnips of gilded leather. When fome public feftival is at hand,
a whole family fhall, for a day or two in
a week, abate of their ufual food, even of
bread, that they may coach it at that time in
the public places ; and thofe families, for whom
fuch an expedient would not anfwer, take other
meafures. The mother, dreffed like a *duegna*,
attends on her *zitella* (daughter) in all her finery :
the father follows in a livery, and his hair in
two twifted queues. Should fome *Appius* caft
a look or defire on this *Virginia*, the *Virginius*
at her heels would not offer to renew the tragedy which fuppreffed the authority of the *De-
cemviri*. This paffion for glitter and parade
(and it rages not lefs on parents than daughters) is an open door to intrigues. It is found
with the loweft poverty : all thefe *zitelle*, fo
very fpruce and fhowy at the public places,
have fcarce a gown to their backs at home :
one fhift is their whole ftock, which their good
houfewifery will not allow them to lie in, and which
every Saturday, after going through a flop-wafh,
is difplayed at the window till perfectly dry.
From this itch of feeing and been feen, the
people

people of Rome are more given to ftaring about than any other in the univerfe : the fame multitudes of fpectators always croud to the fame feftivals and the fame ceremonies.

It is very feldom that there is any thing new in them ; but when this happens, all eyes are greedily fixed on the novelty. Without any fuch defign, without fo much as a thought of it, I made myfelf a fhow at Rome by a taffaty umbrello which I ufed to carry about in my walks. The trades-people came out of their fhops, the better to fee a fight which was altogether new to them : they were quite amazed, that a man on foot fhould take on himfelf the honour of an umbrello, which princes them-felves only ufe on the greateft ceremonies : the very colour excited their wonder, all the ce-remony-umbrellos being red, and mine was green.

The Pope.—From the people let us proceed to the fovereign ; that is, to him who, though the chief of the ftate in dignity, and often in age, is for the moft part the laft in knowing what is tranfacted in it. His quality, as firft of the bifhops, overwhelms that of firft of fovereigns, under a ceremonial which makes his life as weari-fome and doleful as that of a young queen of Spain. He is ever alone *per la dignita*, immer-fed in temporal affairs, if difpofed for bufinefs ; encumbered with congregations, moft of which are held at his palace, and with ecclefiaftical folemnities ; furrounded by a court, the greater part of whom do not care how foon he breathes his laft, or rather daily wifh it ; in fhort,

all his relaxations and diverfions amount to no
more than fome excurfions in the city under pretence of devotional ftations, and to a public
audience or two in a week to foreigners in general,
converfing with thofe whom he happens to like beft.
    All popes have not been flaves to this trou-
blefome ceremonial.   Leo X. and Sixtus V. found
means to fhake it off.   Innocent XI. himfelf,
though by the Romans ranked among the faints,
during the far greater part of his pontificate
fmuggled himfelf from the ecclefiaftical folemnities.   A cold or defluxion often ftood him in
good ftead on the moft indifpenfable occafions.
Ever invifible, he governed his dominions as
God governs the world.   His melancholy caft
and the aufterity of his temper, infecting all
about him, fpread a gloom in which Rome was
involved during his pontificate.
    Benedict XIV. had excluded this ceremonial
from a little apartment which he caufed to be
built in the gardens of Monte-Cavallo : thither
he generally retired after dinner to drink his
coffee, and, with fome of his moft intimate
familiars and felect foreigners, would facrifice to
pleafantry and laughter as if he had not been the
pope.   His excurfions into Rome were generally
on foot, with a large cane in his hand ; and, fo
far from confining himfelf to the fand which is
ftrewed every day in thofe ftreets through which
the pope paffes, he would even ftrike into little
bye-ftreets, where never pope was feen : he has
more than once ftopped at the door of a public
houfe where people were making merry, and
would fay *con gufto* to abbé Bouget, his ufual
                                        attendant

attendant in thefe walks; "I warrant ye, mon-
"fignor Bouget, there's rare wine there." Thefe
freedoms, which Benedict XIV. allowed himfelf,
the people of Rome could by no means digeft:
they, and even his very guards, ufed to fay of him,
*E un birbante quefto papa**. And I myfelf have
often heard them fay, relating to the daily ram-
bles of Clement XIII. at the beginning of his pontificate, *Sará un birbante quefto papa come l'altro†*.

It was with much greater reafon that Rome
complained of Benedict the XIVth's manifeft
averfion to bufinefs, which, though no perfon
was more capable, he totally left to cardinal
Valenti. Any thing might be obtained from him,
taking him by this averfion; and this was the
French embaffador's way, to whom, ftarting up
from his feat, when he found himfelf urged too
home, he would fometimes fay, "Well then, tell
"your king, for whom I have fuch an affection,
"and who requires fo much of me, to come and
"take my place." The affaffination of January 5,
1757, is perhaps the only thing he ever laid to heart.
He has more than once been known to break
off audiences on important affairs, when folicited
to enter into a difcuffion of them, crying out in
a pettifh angry manner, *Mi faranno morire*, "They
"will be the death of me." Such a flave did he
continue to that love of life, that he could not
prevail upon himfelf to fign the bull, urged by
cardinal Saldagna, for the fuppreffion of the
jefuits in Portugal, till his laft illnefs, and then

* "This fame pope is a black-guard."
† "This pope will be fuch another black-guard as the
former."

not till all his phyficians had pofitively affured
him that there was no hope of his recovery.
Some time after that fignature, he put his hand
to another bull, relating to the beatification of a
jefuit, and delivered it with thefe words; *Cum dilex-
iffet fuos, ufque in finem dilexit illos.* Though he did
not love thofe fathers in his heart, they have obtained from him as many favours, and even facrifices, as from any of his predeceffors; and concerning this he would fometimes fay, *Grandemente
confido nelle preghiere di quefti buoni padri per viver
lontano*. There were very few occafions which
did not produce fome genteel raillery, atticifm,
or fmart faying, from him. During the laft conclave, an Englifh gentleman made a collection of
them, with which it is to be hoped he will favour
the public; and what Cato faid of Cicero would
be no unfuitable motto, *Habemus profecto facetum
confulem.*

That hilarity, which in him difperfed all the
gloom of the papacy, is generally derived from the
tranquillity congenial to a fine foul : it is as nearly
allied to candour and probity, as it is remote from
falfity and meannefs. Befides the qualities productive of chearfulnefs, Benedict XIV. was long
eminent for an unparalleled difinterestednefs, and
a truly chriftian difregard of all the advantages,
which his ftation put in his hands for the promotion of his family. The Romans cannot but rank
him among the beft popes, if not among the
greateft; that is, when they fhall begin to forgive
his having held the pontificate eighteen years; for

* " I depend greatly on the prayers of thofe good fathers,
" that I fhall have a long life."

every

every Roman building hopes of mending his
ſtation on a change of the pontificate, nothing
rankles him more than a pope's longevity. In
eſtimating the merit of thoſe popes who have
reigned with the greateſt luſtre, they diſtinguiſh
the man from the prince and the prelate : for inſtance, Pius V. ſay they, was only a good pre-
prelate ; Sixtus V. a cruel man, a great prince,
and bad prelate ; Paul V. an ambitious and rapacious man, an enterpriſing but weak prince, a
middling prelate. There are but three popes
whom they will allow to have been great princes,
good prelates, and worthy men ; Clement VIII.
Clement IX. and Innocent XI. auſtere as his
pontificate ſeemed to their fore-fathers. They now
begin to rank Clement XI. with them ; and Benedict XIV. I make no doubt, will come in for his
turn : he has the very ſame right to their eſteem
as Clement IX. whoſe chief merit is, to have done
as little for the Roſpiglioſi, as Benedict XIV. for
the Lambertini.

Did the popes, to inſure the immortality of
their name, conſult the example of their predeceſſors, the inutility of the moſt ambitious efforts
for fixing grandeur and opulence in their families
would put them on diſintereſtedneſs, as the moſt
certain way, though the leaſt frequented.

When we were at Rome, the laſt prince of the
houſe of Pamphili was ſtill living : he had no children, and his death was to be followed by the long-
expected opening of Innocent the Xth's will,
wherein he had arbitrarily diſpoſed of the immenſe
wealth which he had accumulated for his family.
On our return we were informed that prince Pam-

phili

phili was dead, and that, on opening this famous will, Innocent had intailed the whole between the Dorias and the Colonnas.

The latter had already got into their hands the vaſt inheritance of the Barberini family, after all the expedients of Urban VIII. for eterniſing his name. This holy father had carried them ſo far as to appoint, by a bull *ad hoc*, that, in caſe of the failure of the male branches of his name, his eſtates, of which he made a perpetual intail, ſhould, excluſively even of lawful daughters, go to male baſtards, even though the iſſue of monks or nuns. The intail however has not gone beyond the ſecond degree, his nephew leaving only two children, one of whom was cardinal Barberini, who died dean of the ſacred college in 1739 ; and the other a daughter, married into the Colonna family. The cardinal-dean had a baſtard, who bore the name of Maffeo ; but here that unreaſonable appointment, by which he was to ſucceed in the intail, to the excluſion of the lawful daughters, was ſet aſide ; and he had only a penſion allowed him, the eſtate going to the Colonna family in right of the cardinal's ſiſter. The prince her huſband has condeſcended to bear the name of Barberini, and by a *mezzo termine* has taken that of Paleſtrina as a principality belonging to the intail, but which hereafter muſt ſit down with the bare honour of being allied to the houſe of Colonna.

I have heard, that cardinal Salviati, founder of the orphan hoſpital, and one of the richeſt prelates of the ſixteenth century, had a clauſe in his will, which, though very ſingular, was yet better grounded than that of pope Urban.

In

In the want of iffue male to inherit the large
provifion he had made for his family, an orphan of his hofpital was to be chofen by lot
for the intail : a difpofition which puts one in
mind of that of Crates, whofe children being
minors, he ordered that their fucceffion, which was
to remain fequeftrated till they came of age,
fhould be delivered up to them if they proved
to be of mean parts ; otherwife, to be diftributed among the weakeft of their fellow citizens.

These ambitious fettlements, which are very
common at Rome and in all the ecclefiaftical
ftate, meet with great encouragement. The eldeft,
and all the children of the beft families, if they
have either talents or ambition, betake themfelves to the church, as the only way leading to regard, riches, and the moft fubftantial honours,
leaving the bufinefs of perpetuating their name to
thofe of their brothers who are unfit for any
thing better ; or who, voluntarily facrificing themfelves, are in their families like drones among
bees, or as our fex was among the Amazons.

Had the popes confidered the celibacy of the
clergy in a political light, had they reflected
what a check it is to the peopling of their
ftates ; they would, as princes, have done as
much to profcribe fuch an unnatural and pernicious regulation, as, in quality of popes, they
have done to ftrengthen it, and give it an irre-
vocable ftability.

Intails are no lefs ruinous to cultivation, than
celibacy to population. An ufufructuary deals
with the lands which come to him by this

tenure, as a beneficiary with church-lands, or a truftee with an eftate in chancery; *Oves bis mulget in horâ ; et fuccus pecori et lac fubducitur agnis.* He takes care not to be at any extraordinary expences for keeping the lands in heart: he never concerns himfelf about augmentations or improvements, to which property alone can incite. It is indeed fomething amazing, that, in countries which feem intent on agriculture, fo ftriking an example fhould be overlooked, and that intails are not limited only to thofe houfes, which by their important fervices have deferved that the ftate fhould intereft itfelf in the prefervation of them. Why are eftates, got at any rate, to be perpetuated among the defcendants of individuals, often fuch as were battened at the public expence? The leaving of thefe poffeffions open to fale will be an incitement to the induftry of new families ; and, fhould thefe ruin themfelves by improving their purchafes, ftill would this imprudence be a general good.

In fome countries this has been taken into confideration, by limiting intails to three degrees. It would have been better if, excluding from intails real eftates, which are the chief object of them, they had been limited to deeds of gift, and other fuch effects, of which the mifmanagement, and even the diffipation, do not affect the ftate.

I have faid above, that among the later popes Clement VIII. is one whofe memory is moft beloved among the Romans. The portrait of this pontiff, drawn from the life by a cotemporary, has fome fingular features of refemblance

between him and Clement XIII. now reigning:
" The prefent pope," fays Mr. Sandys*, " is ac-
" counted a fenfible, good-natured man ; not over
" cunning, but very clofe and tenacious ; eafy
" with his friends, and very devout in his reli-
" gion, of which he feems thoroughly perfuaded.
" He is often feen to weep ; which fome will have
" to be from an habitual tendernefs of heart, while
" others attribute it to piety and devout contri-
" tion. At his maffes, proceffions, &c. his eyes
" are always bathed with tears ; fo that, as the
" laft pope was a *Democritus ridens*, this is a fe-
" cond *Heraclitus plorans*."

Every body knows that Clement XIII. was,
like his predeceffor, exalted to the pontifical
chair quite unexpectedly both to the public and
himfelf ; but it is not fo well known, that after France had fet afide cardinal Cavalchini, the
French cardinals had it in their power to place
the triple crown on the head of cardinal Porto-Car-
rero. This cardinal, the laft of his family and
of his name, having, by dividing his fucceffion and relinquifhing his fubfiftence, broken all
the national ties which linked him to Spain,
profeffedly made Rome his country. Under
an exterior not very promifing, he added
to Spanifh phlegm a large portion of Italian fubtilty. Embarking in the world only as knight
of Malta, he might of himfelf and by his own
merit have rifen to great fortune, even without
inheriting his patrimonial eftate. *Obfequium ami-
cos, veritas odium parit,* was the fundamental
rule of every part of his behaviour ; fo that

* Account of the State of Religion.

G 4 Benedict

Benedict XIV. ufed to call him fometimes *lo*
Spagnoletto, (i. e. the Spaniel) fometimes *Laus per-*
ennis. In the conclave of 1758, as chief of the
Spanifh faction, to which the political union of
the two crowns had joined the French and Au-
ftrian factions, he was the foul of the three, and
had at his difpofal thirty-five votes, which would
have been ftrengthened by cardinal Paffionei's
fquadron. The unexpected exclufion of cardinal
Cavalchini was a thunder-clap to the French
cardinals themfelves, who, being quite novices
to the intrigues of the conclave, had been drawn
in to join in his election : but the game being,
by this exclufion, to be played over again, they
might have offered the *tiara* to cardinal Porto-
Carrero; whereas they only afked him how
they muft proceed. " This is the inftant for the
" Holy Ghoft," anfwered the Spaniard, *terram*
intuens modeftè. The meaning of this language
efcaping even the fagacity of the cardinal De
Luynes, fome more fteady and refolute meafures immediately decided the election for Clement XIII.

As they were carrying him from the conclave to
St. Peter's altar, a common man, clinging to a pillar
of the grand ftair-cafe leading from the great hall,
called out with an enthufiaftic vehemence, *Della*
parte di Dio, fantiffimo padre, l'emendazion di quefta
città piena di fceleratezza e d'abominazioni*; and
repeated it feveral times without any menace, or
fo much as a reproof.

FOREIGNERS.—Till the pontificate of Alexander VII. Rome had been the centre of the nego-

* " For God's fake, moft holy father, reform this city,
" fo full of wickednefs and abominations."

ciations and political motions of all Europe: a
perpetual congrefs might be faid to be held there
of embaffadors reputed the very beft heads of their
feveral courts; and they who were in the embaffadors fuite, vied, as it were, with each other in
doing honour to their nation by the decorum of
their behaviour. Accordingly, there is nothing
which the celebrated marquis de Bedemar, in the
inftructions he drew up for his fucceffor in the
embaffy at Venice, recommends fo ftrongly as a
very fcrupulous choice of the perfons who are to
compofe his retinue.

Though Rome be no longer fuch a crouded theatre, yet is there always a great concourfe of foreigners of all nations drawn hither by curiofity, devotion, and the conclaves. Thefe foreigners are
above difguife: the Englifhman behaves as at London, the Spaniard as at Madrid, the German as
at Vienna, and the Frenchman as at Paris: but
the manners of thefe nations are not equally fuitable to thofe of Rome; and from thefe manners it
is that the Romans form their judgment of the
different nations. The conclaves bring to Rome
a number of young noblemen, of whom the
greater part, having no other motives for this
journey than thofe of intereft and fortune, look
on it with the fame eye as Ovid confidered his
exile from Rome: they contemn the people, the
language, and every thing which they might and
fhould make a matter of entertainment; and fometimes they fhew this contempt in a manner the
more difobliging to the Italians, as very few nations
are fo delighted with being efteemed by foreigners.
Thefe young fparks judging of the Romans from
the

the 'ferioufnefs which they put on in public, it brings to their remembrance the governors and mafters from whom they have been lately delivered; and to this ferioufnefs they oppofe frolic, volatility and giddinefs. Being at length obliged to keep at home, and not finding there entertainments to compenfate for thofe of public converfe, they give themfelves up to laffitude and difguft, which increafing by communication, fends them away from Rome, quite out of humour with the Romans, who are not much better pleafed with them *(y)*.

This, and this alone, is the real fource of the unjuft prejudice of the Romans againft the French; a prejudice of as long ftanding as Rome itfelf, and from which Cicero faid of the anceftors of the latter, *Si homines ipfos fpectare convenit, non modò cum fummis civitatis noftræ viris, fed cum infimo cive Romano quifquam ampliffimus Galliæ comparandus eft**.

France, in its negociations at Rome, makes ufe of munificence to footh, or loftinefs to fupprefs, this prejudice. The cardinals of Efte, who under Francis I. and Henry II. † reprefented France at Rome, made ufe of the former way for dazzling the eyes of the Romans, to which they were in fome meafure ftimulated by the example of the embaffadors of Charles V. who even in

---

(y) " What a thoughtlefs people are we !" faid Montaigne : " to make known our vices and follies to the world " by reputation, is not enough ; but we muft needs go to " foreign nations to make fights of ourfelves." *Effays*, L. ii. c. 27.—In another place he extols ' the wifdom of Plato's laws, prohibiting travelling under the age of forty or fifty.

* Pro Fonteio.

† See their lives in Brantome.

- magnificence

magnificence (z) would outdo his rival. The cardinal of Lorrain carried it even farther than the cardinal of Efte ; but this oftentation was part of the fcheme which that ambitious prieft had formed for the grandeur of his family. Of late no foreign minifter at Rome has fhone with a luftre equal to the cardinal de Rohan : he outdid himfelf in his negociation for promoting the abbé Du Bois to the purple, backing it with toys and trinkets to the amount of forty or fifty thoufand livres. In his clofet he had tables covered with them, and dealt them about indifcriminately. A Roman was fure of a prefent ; and on his leaving Rome, he expreffed a concern that he had not been able to give away all his ftore. A continuance of fuch liberalities would in time remove all pre-judices, and reconcile the Romans to the French intereft, did France think fuch a purchafe worth its while. Rome is ftill what it was when Jurgurtha, at his departure, looking back on it, cried, *Urbem venalem, fi emptorem invenerit !*

Loftinefs is ftill a more certain way of operating on the Romans. That of Lewis XIV. in his dif-putes with the holy fee, has impreffed on them fuch refpect and veneration for the memory of that prince, as in their idea place him on a level with the Antonines, the Conftantines, and the Charle-magnes. Of that glorious prince Henry IV.

(z) " It behoves you, Sire," faid the bifhop of Tarbe to Francis I. in his difpatches of the 27th of March, 1530, " to " bear in mind, that this is a place of great importance to " you : and your fervice requires, by all means, to fend hither " a man of fpirit, and who is able to fpend high ; for, " among other follies of the Italians, take my word for it, " nothing goes farther with them."

they

they have no knowledge but from that difgraceful abfolution to which he fubmitted for cogent reafons of ftate, which they know nothing of, and from the memorial of that abafement *(a)* which his minifters weakly allowed to be fet up in one of the moft frequented places of Rome *(b)*, with this infcription, which remained till the laft pontificate *(c.)*

D. O. M.

CLEMENTE VIII. PONT. MAXIMO,

AD MEMORIAM

ABSOLUTIONIS HENRICI IV.

FRANC. ET NAVARR. REGIS CHRISTIANISMI.

Q. F. R. D. XV. KAL. OCTOB. MDXCV.

What was intended by the four initials in the laft line, I know not.

One of the late embaffadors from France made a very happy experiment of what may be effected

(a) This was chiefly cardinal Du Perron's doings, who afterwards fhewed what he thought on the fubjects of the two powers, when he oppofed the article moved by the *Tiers Etat.*

(b) In the piazza de Santa Maria Majore.

(c) Purfuant to that condefcenfion, of which the famous Aretin wrote to Francis I. in this manner: *Ecco il religiofo coftume de i voftri predeceffori che vi facendo confentire à le richiefte de i Pontifici, non vi lafcia fcorgere in che modo le lor lingue di mela, moffe da i cori d'affentio, fono fimili à le paffione delle femine le quali hanno in un occhio pianto di duolo, e nel altro lagrima di infidia.* "You follow the implicit devotion of your pre-" deceffors, who complied with all the demands of the popes;" and this hinders you from perceiving that, if they carry" honey on their tongues, their hearts are full of wormwood," and that, like women, their grief is only to deceive." Vol. ii. p. 12.

among the Romans by a freedom accompanied
with dignity, a steady and resolute conduct, and
sometimes even a little loftiness in very critical
cases : by such a carriage he brought them to all
that could have been obtained by artifice, liberality, and intrigue, and thus gained, to his court
and the French name, a consideration of happy
influence for all the objects of his ministry. I
have heard, that at a time when he had some difpute with the papal court, there came suddenly on
his hands a prince of his nation, with a numerous
attendance of young adventurers, who had accompanied him from a desire of seeing Rome.
The embassador being by his station governor of
these sparks, so far from recommending reserve
and circumspection to them, encouraged them
to live gaily, and not tie themselves down to the
dull rules of the Italians; and, as for the conse-
quences, he would take them on himself. The
frolics of so many young gentlemen left to themselves made that noise which he had foreseen,
and spread an alarm that at once put an end to
the dispute.

This minister was one of those *brave and gallant
gentlemen of the blade*, whom, from a multitude
of well-chosen instances, Brantome proves to be
preferable to gowns-men, even for the embassy
of Rome, *where the honour of the prince often
suffers for want of the embassador's making a bold
and spirited reply**. Exclusive of the cases mentioned by Brantome, the most common objects
of negociation must very often be extremely per-
plexing to a prelate. "You, who are a bishop,"

* Life of Francis I.

it is urged to him, " you who may soon expect
" to be a cardinal, put yourself in our stead, or
" rather make it your own case : see, consider,
" yourself, what we can do concerning your
" proposal ; weigh it in the balance of the sanc-
" tuary, &c." What firmness is to be expected
from a minister, in whom the combined characters
of priest and embassador are continually thwarting
each other ?

There are few countries where a true judgment
is formed of new comers so speedily as at Rome :
*Gens emunctæ naris, natura cui verba non potuit
dare*, says a famous jesuit* of the modern Romans.   Their concern to study one another, produces a habit which forms them to this sagacity :
this is the pole-star by which they steer their
behaviour towards those with whom they are to
have any intercourse, or dealings.   They cannot
be long imposed on, either by a dull or pro-
mising mien : to them this is no more than the
persona tragica, the mask to the fox.   A show of
frankness, an airy carriage, puts them out of their
bias, and puzzles them the more, as being less
a-kin to that gravity in which they muffle themselves, that others may not see into them.

GRAVITY of the ROMANS.—This gravity never
leaves them in public, not even in the parties
of pleasure which seem contrived to shake it
off.   At a formal dinner with a prelate I happened to let fall a joke somewhat roguish : this
turned the eyes of the Italians towards the prelate,
who smiled, yet with an air of uneasiness : this
smile was the signal which set the whole company

* Vavassor de ludicra dictione.

a laugh-

a laughing as if they never would have given over ;
and it was not fo much at the joke, and my ignorance of their cuftoms, that they laughed, as
to fee one another laughing in the houfe where
they were.

In private, however, they make themfelves
amends for the conftraint they obferve in public.
Nothing can be more chearful than their clubs,
where a knot of trufty friends freely give themfelves up to that tranquil gaiety, which is fuited to
the natural ferioufnefs of their character, and in
which confifted the *urbanitas* of the ancient Romans.
There one may laugh even at perfons who are part
of the company ; there the *fpropofiti* of a foreigner
efteemed fo far as to be admitted into thofe meetings, and who is never reproved in public for dia-
lectical miftakes, are made matters of merriment;
there they laugh more, and more heartily, than in
any other place on earth ; laftly, there a thoufand
tales are circulated, of which the Romans have an
inexhauftible fund ; and fuch excellent relaters are
they, that their manner always gives an air of
novelty to their ftory. Let the following ferve as
a fpecimen of them.

In the combat between St. Michael and the devil,
the archangel, perceiving that his fpear was rather
an incumbrance than of any fervice to him, fhot
up again to heaven, and fnatching a thunder-
bolt hurled it at Lucifer, fo that his body flev
about in fhivers: his legs fell in France ; and
hence the petulancy of the French, their paffion
for rambling, and the difficulty of fettling them:
Lucifer's head was carried as far as Spain ; and to
this is owing the pride, the ftiffnefs, and over-
bearing

bearing carriage of the Spaniards: the hand with
which the fiend ufed to pilfer, Naples got; and
that with which he fqueefed, was Genoa's portion:
his ftomach was picked up in Germany: laftly, the
leaft honourable parts of his body alighted in Rome,
e per quefto, add they, *tutti noi Romani fiamo
cogl*......*

The Italians have retained thofe words which
other languages have cafhiered, as politenefs and
good manners came to prevail among them.
The objects expreffed by thefe words are an
ample field for the convival mufes. In a word,
Italy fwarms both with obfcene *(d)* and devout fonnets. Their infancy is accuftomed to nudities, as
were the Greeks and Romans, and as the favages
ftill are. Their ears are as little moved with the
expreffion, as their eyes with the reprefentation, of
objects, the indecency of which has been leffened
by habit. It was from a deep-rooted cuftom, that
after Benedict IV. was exalted to the pontificate,
one of the moft obfcene words in the Italian language equally efcaped him, both in his anger and
his mirth; that is to fay, it was almoft always on
his tongue. This word, and its counter-part, are
the moft common oaths, or rather interjections,
among the Romans. *Per Dio* (by God) is feldom
or never heard, on account of the penalties pro-

* "And this has made all us Romans fuch wenchers as
"we are."

(d) I have brought from Naples a collection called *La Cic-
ceide*, the third edition. This collection contains four hundred
and twenty fonnets or madrigals, proving four hundred and
twenty different ways, that one Don Cicceio is *in terminis a
cogl*..... This kind of wit is the foul of the *Murtoleide* of
Marino, &c.

ñounced againſt blaſphemers ; whereas *per Dio Bacco* is in every body's mouth.

The merriment of private clubs never ſhows it-ſelf in public but during the carnival : no where is that entertainment carried ſo high as at Rome; it is a perfect tranſcript of the ancient *Saturnalia*, in all its frolics. I have heard of a thouſand ſcenes, the agreeable levity and feſtivity of which gave me ſome concern, that I was not at Rome in ſo jocund an interval : yet the ſight perhaps would have fallen ſhort of my ideas ; *minuiſſet præſentiá famam.*

RELIGIOUS.—I have ſaid, that among the inha-bitants of Rome nothing is ſeen of the mediate claſs between opulence and indigence ; of that body of citizens among whom, in other ſtates, is found the *aurea mediocritas.* Inſtead of that creditable claſs, one ſees an innumerable crowd of regulars of all orders and all colours ; a ſet of mortals, to whom the air of Rome is as heat to flies, multiplying them, and making them more buſtling, more obſtinate, and more troubleſome ; and of whom it may more properly be ſaid than of the ruſtics, *Fortunatos ſua ſi bona nôrint !*

And indeed they might quietly enjoy the fruits of the labours of their founders and primitive fa-thers : they are free from the trouble of acquiring, and that of enjoying, which not ſeldom is the greater of the two : every circumſtance concurs to ſecure them in a peaceable life, which they might divide between ſtudy and the duties of their function ; but, as if engagements and vows only irritated the paſſions, they ſeem to have no ſenſe of the advantages of the monaſtic life, wholely fixing their eyes on some disagreeable circumstances of it. Scarce is there, in all Rome, a religious, without a system of promotion, or without personal views and concerns quite foreign from any views and concerns of his order : every one peremptorily follows the clue which he fancies will lead him to regard, opulence and dignity : the success of some stimulates the hopes and efforts of others ; whilst few are they whom the examples of so many who fail by the way, deter from engaging in the competition. In a word, the monks are at Rome like the abbé de Moliere's little vortexes in the physical world.

The Coriphæus of these intrigues was, during our stay at Rome, the procurator-general of an order, to the supremacy of which he aspired in his way to the highest preferments. The suppleness of his body seconded that of his mind. I used to meet him in all the drawing-rooms : he was frequently whispering with the leading men ; and he had wormed himself into all affairs and secrets. It is said, that he very nearly missed being made a cardinal by Benedict XIV. In a word, he had lately ruined one of his brethren, a rising man, at whom he had taken umbrage. A private conversation, which he once drew me into, was of great use to me in knowing the man. He began with mighty compliments on my being so much in favour with a cardinal, to whom he never could be allowed access : " You alone," said he, " when with his emi-
" nence, have constantly seen *cœlos apertos* ; which
" gives me the highest idea of your talents for in-
" sinuation. There is no place where you can turn
" this talent to greater advantage, both to your
                                        " friends

" friends and yourfelf, than Rome; and thus you
" may reap both pleafure and profit from your tra-
" vels." I anfwered him, that no Carthufian
minded profit lefs than myfelf; that, however, I
fo far relied on the cardinal's goodnefs, as to expect fuccefs in any proper folicitation, either for
myfelf, (fhould I, contrary to expectation, come
to ftand in need of it) or for others, whom I fhould
think deferving of his countenance. " That's the
" very thing I meant," replied the monk; " and
" a friend whom you don't think of ftands in need
" of your interceffion." On my defire to know who
this friend was, he named a gentleman of Lower
Britany, whom, he yet allowed, I did not know,
but whofe friendfhip would be the fruit of the
good offices which it lay in my power to do him;
and fuch a friendfhip as fhould be cemented by an
acknowledgement which he intirely left to my dif-
cretion. Being aware of his drift, I told him that
with me the abfent were always in the wrong; and
that the motives which he intimated, might determine me in favour of perfons who were on the fpot.
This declaration puzzled him; and after fome
paufe, he defired our interview might be ad-
journed till the day after the next: this I readily
agreed to, it being the very day fixed for my departure.

About the fame time, died at Rome a Celef-
tine, who had diftinguifhed himfelf in the profound
fciences. Ten thoufand Roman crowns were difcovered in his apartment: his friends faid that he
intended them for founding a library; but all the
monks gave out, that he was for dying a bifhop at
leaft.

What

What every regular does to attain diftinétion for himfelf, and rife above his fellows, every jefuit does for his order. Intereft, regard, profits, the various gains, acquifitions, and fruits of merit and induftry, are all referred to the common ftock for augmenting the intereft, the opulence, and grandeur of the fociety; a grandeur which receives increafe both from the clofe union of its members, and the difcord which a felfifh fpirit has produced in the other orders. Amidft the fruitlefs clamours of thofe bodies, the fociety makes its way, like a clofe battalion, with united ftrength, defpifing the diforderly attacks of light troops : on one fide *plena omnia confiliorum videmus*; on the other, *plena verborum omnia**.

The oftentatious fhow which the jefuits make of their opulence, perhaps may not exactly fquare with found policy. All Rome knows, that in the courfe of that year, when with regal fumptuoufnefs they built the palace which the abbé de Canillac fince lived in, they expended on that palace, and purchafes made at Rome or in the environs, four hundred thoufand Roman crowns, without borrowing a fingle bajoco : yet they continue begging; and, agreeably to the primitive inftitution, *Giefu*'s houfe fubfifts, fay they, only by thefe gatherings, which bring in fums anfwerable to their fuperb expenditures. When we were at Rome, there died a rich Florentine prelate, who ufed to give them about fifty louis per month as alms; and this good work he crowned by making them his fole legatees. All his effects which were at Rome went according to the will ; but, as for

---

* Cic. de Orat. L. i.

the

the immoveables which lay in Tuscany, the imperial ministry at Florence thought fit to secure them
for the testator's family.

The only corps from which the jesuits have to
fear, (and yet they seem to make no account of it) is
the congregation of the *(e) Scuole Pie*. This congregation, which was formed in the last century,
on the model of the brethren de St. Yon in France,
has already its *literati* and its esteemed writers ; it
is likewise possessed of great wealth, and its interest is daily on the increase. The administra-
tion of this body, being no less political than
that of the jesuits, catches hold of every thing
the latter overlook, insinuates itself into all the
voids left by them, takes advantage of all their
mistakes, and possibly may prove the stone which
shall overthrow this Colossus, and set itself up
in its stead.

The other orders are above their wants, and
well settled in town and country : *fruuntur paratis*
under the privileges which the popes have heaped
on them. The Franciscans I think call the collection of theirs *Mare magnum* ; and this sea has
broken down all the boundaries which the ancient

(e) Lascelles, who saw this institution in its infancy,
speaks of it in this manner, Tom. i. p. 3. 304. " They
" are a company of good religious, going bare-legged and
" with sandals : they teach poor children the first rudi-
" ments to fit them for the college of the jesuits, *gratis*;
" and, besides teaching them, attend them when they go
" into town, that they may not bring back or practise any
" of the corruptions of the age."
The fathers initiated in this humble profession have no
higher views : they affect neither erudition, wealth, or
splendor ; a great reproach to the would-be wits so common among us.

H 3   ecclesiastical

ecclefiaftical laws had fet up. How rapidly thefe privileges have fpread, appears only from comparing the prefent ftate of the Francifcans with the bull of Sixtus IV. who, being a Francifcan, granted to his brethren, as a very fpecial favour, to fing high mafs in their convents among themfelves, but with the doors fhut, and an hour before public fervice.

A reducement of moft of the new orders to their primitive ftate would prove the total diffolution of them; whereas reformation has ftrengthened that of the Benedictines, dividing it into congregations of a conftitution ftill better calculated for temporal than for fpiritual views. This order is fecured from revolutions by its right of elderfhip, by the nature of its poffeffions, by the manner of the adminiftration of them, by its having long fince fet bounds to its acquifitions; laftly, by the weight which it derives from the great number of creditable perfons, who in Italy embrace it, in hopes of getting abbies, (the far greater part of which are ftill regular) and afterwards of rifing to the pofts which thofe abbies ufually lead to.

Yet is it one of the pope's and his minifters chief bufineffes, to elude and fhift off the projectors coming daily with fchemes for the foundation of new orders, or the reformation of the more ancient. Cardinal Valenti, fecretary of ftate to Benedict XIV. was befet by two monks who were for reforming their difcipline under his aufpices; and the manner how he got rid of their importunities was this: having, after much folicitation, admitted them into his clofet, he told
them

them that the Holy Ghoft, whom he had confulted about their pious intentions, had infpired
him to add to it, that its authors fhould fet an
example of the difintereftednefs and humility on
which the reformation was to be grounded, by
renouncing all dignities and fupcriority. The
reformers extolled the infpiration, and the cardinal heard no more of them and their project.

RELIGION.—Such of the Romans as are virtuous,
are not fo by halves ; and modern Rome ftill
includes, in the practice of virtue, that fublimity of which ancient Rome fet a pattern firft
to the Pagans, and then to the Chriftians. Models of this kind are fcarce ; but in what city,
or what country, are they very common ? They
are the more to be wondered at in Rome, as
public inftruction in that city is very little edifying, and the common exercifes of religion are fo
many external obfervances, which feem to be addreffed only to the fenfes.

Italy and Rome indeed are full of congregations, fraternities, and foundations, of a religious
nature. From the frequency of jubilees there is
no want of miffions and preaching. The principal object of fuch inftitutions as thofe of the
Jefuits, Philippins, &c. is the inftruction of the
people. Laftly, canonifations daily hold forth
new patterns of a fanctity almoft cotemporary.

CONGREGATIONS.—But congregations, divert-
ing the people from the parifh-churches, draw
them out of the canonical path laid down by
the church through the miniftry of paftors.
The conventicles fet up one againft another by

H 4   the

the new religious orders, hold their meetings privately; fo that the inftructions delivered there want that publicity, which both the welfare of the ftate, and the gofpel, require in the functions of its minifters. The directors of fuch affemblies may be fuppofed lefs intent on inculcating the facred truths, than infufing into their followers a blind and exclufive zeal for the prejudices, the concerns, and profperity, of the order under whofe banner they have lifted.

FRATERNITIES.—The fraternities promife no better fruit. A certain number of feculars form a fociety, where, on Sundays and the feftivals, they perform in common the canonical office. Every fraternity is diftinguifhed by the colour of the domino in which the brethren muffle themfelves. The greateft noblemen join in one or other of thefe focieties, which were never thought of till about four hundred years ago. Death itfelf makes no feparation, the brethren always taking care to be buried in the chapels where they meet. The prior of the fraternity is commanding officer; the very priefts, who enter into it, being fubject to his orders. In the choir he acts the prieft's part; and whilft the other officers attend to their feveral pofts, fome walking about, as vergers, with ftaves of the colour of the fraternities, others as acolytes, &c. the prior gravely chants out the laft leffons, the laft anthems, the Pater-nofters, &c. Moft of thefe gentry know not a word of Latin: from one Sunday to another they are ftudying their parts; but on the more folemn days, as in Paffion week, when under a neceffity of performing
extempore,

extempore, they often fall into ftrange impro-
prieties, as edifying to their ignorant brethren,
as they are comical to Latinifts. I have heard
that this verfe of the *Tenebræ*, *Vos fugam capietis, ego autem vadam immolari pro vobis*, was
pronounced by a very grave prior in this manner, *Vos* furcam *capietis, ego autem vadam* in malora *pro vobis*.

The feftivals of thefe fraternities are fo many
contefts of magnificence : the leaft gay of thefe
fhows is that exhibited in the octave of All
Souls by the *Fraternity of Death*, which is one
of the richeft. In a very fpacious vault under
their chapel, one firft comes to a kind of a hall
hung with red paper, and having pilafters and
niches, the bafes and chapiters of which are made
of real death's heads, with lights fo difpofed
within them, and bits of paper laid over the
eyes and the jaws, as to fhed a dim and red-
difh glimmer, the only illumination in this lugubrious place. In the niches are large deficcated
fkeletons, among which I was fhewn that of the
beautiful Paula, whom her red treffes ftill covered
down to her middle. This fame **Paula** was a
modern Roman beauty, who difappointed an attempt on her chaftity by imitating the example
of the ancient Lucretia : the fatal ftab is indicated by a breach in the fkin over her breaft. Farther on, in another vault, refembling a large burial-
place lighted with torches, are laid feven or eight
dead bodies, as natural reprefentations of the
progreffive degrees of putrefaction. In this manfion of death, in the midft of a fpectacle, the
fadnefs of which is increafed by the ftrong *fætor* of
the

the bodies, amidſt the loud thumps with which a crowd of well-meaning ſouls were bruiſing their breaſts, I obſerved ſigns were made to the *zitelle*, or girls, to keep them in heart; whilſt on ſeveral of that ſex, who were left to themſelves, the horror of this exhibition had its intire effect, being carried away in a ſtrong *deliquium*, without the leaſt ſign of ſenſe or knowledge.

On this octave all Rome flocks to St. Gregory, that is, to the monaſtery on mount Celius, on the very ſite of the houſe in which this pope was born, and near the place which the Romans called *Clivus Scauri*. St. Gregory relates, in his Dialogues, that, having cauſed thirty maſſes to be ſaid for the ſoul of one of his monks, this ſoul appeared to him, in an effulgence of glory, to inform him that, by means of thoſe interceſſions, God had releaſed him out of purgatory. Such is the origin of this act of devotion, to which I followed the crowd. It is become a point of honour to have one's name entered for thirty maſſes, which are paid for before-hand. The firſt viſit is made to the great church, which was intirely rebuilt by the learned cardi-nal Quirini, with very ſplendid embelliſhments. From thence we reſorted to a private chapel, noted for having the table where St. Gregory every day uſed to entertain twelve poor perſons : there were once thirteen, though only twelve had been ad-mitted ; the thirteenth was Jeſus Chriſt himſelf. Next is ſeen the chapel of St. Sylvia, St. Gregory's mother. On the two walls of this chapel Guido and Dominichini painted, in competition, the martyrdom of St. Andrew, two pieces which all connoiſſeurs cannot ſufficiently admire. I was

told,

told, that when they were finifhed and laid open, a woman coming into the chapel, and her eyes alighting on St. Andrew falling on his knees at the fight of his crofs, fhe expreffed her aftonifh-ment at the excellence of the piece with a kind of enthufiafm ; and that afterwards, turning towards the St. Andrew whom his perfecutors are ftretching out on the inftrument of his torture, fhe burft into a flood of tears. The ftatues of St. Gregory and his mother, at the farther end of thefe two chapels, are either by Michael Angelo, or copies from him. On going out of St. Gregory's the crowd turn off into narrow and crooked ftreets, extending among gardens, fmall churches, and ruins, all over the inhabited furface of mount Celius, which is no fmall piece of ground. During this ramble the pilgrims fay prayers, and repeat the chaplet for the dead.

I accidentally fell in with a more entertaining feftival, given, I do not know not on what account, by the fraternity of the Holy Ghoft. The morning-office was juft over. After taking a view of the chapel, which was decorated in high tafte, I went into the adjoining apartments, which I found ftrewed with flowers and odoriferous herbs, and the walls covered with boughs and feftoons. On entering a large hall, I was ftruck with the fight of the whole fraternity fitting round a very elegant ambigu : one of them was pleafed to come to me with a very polite invitation to par-take of their entertainment. The wine was excel-lent, and fpread among the brethren a chearfulnefs, which however did not carry them beyond the ftricteft decency.

St.

St. Anthony brings together a concourse of another kind. On his festival, all the horses of Rome, dressed out in the finest trappings, make their appearance before his church, where, for a fee, according to the circumstances or devotion of the owners, they are sprinkled with holy water. The pope's stable itself is not exempt from this aspersion. Some will say, that, the better to keep it up, the monks of St. Anthony and the coachmen and grooms of great houses, whose example supports it, go halves*. To its rise I am an utter stranger. It seems, however, something extraordinary, that the coachmen and grooms should not have given the preference to St. James, who has a little church in the neighbourhood of St. Peter's, called *Scossa Cavalla* ; the origin of which is mentioned in all the descriptions of Rome.

SERMONS.—I once spent a whole day in following the exercises of a mission occasioned by a jubilee of Clement XIII. The morning was taken up with a conference, two sermons, and a solemn mass : the afternoon's exercises were two sermons, and a grand exposition of the host. The conference turned on some punctilios, by which casuists estimate sins. Of the two preachers, who alternately stood on a large *estrade*, covered with a black carpet, one was a buffoon, who stuffed his discourse with a thousand tales, right or wrong ; yet so excellent a pantomime, that his gestures and grimaces gave a considerable relief to his stories, among which, to

* *Vid.* Script. Antiquit. Rom. *De Conso et Consualibus.*

my

my great furprife, was that of father Philip's geefe, even as it ftands in Boccace. Indeed I was fo fhocked at it, as to mention it with fome difpleafure to a cardinal, who crying out, " What " a novice you are in the world !" fhewed me, in St. Antonine's fermons, that very tale with all its embellifhments. The manner and matter of the other preacher were of a piece, the former quite lifelefs, the latter ftiff, and laid out in jejune divifions and fub-divifions ; the whole very mean. One of his fermons was on God's mercy towards a finner ; mercy before converfion, and mercy after converfion. The firft part was built on all creatures, animate and inanimate, confpiring againft the finner, whom they would deftroy did not God put a curb on their endeavours ; and the fecond expatiated on the favours conferred by God, by the virgin, and by the little Jefus, on all the devout women of the later ages. The fermon concluded with an act of contrition, and a proteftation of the whole congregation never to fin any more; which they expreffed by uttering the word *Mai* with all their force, and at the fame time weeping and fobbing, and beating their breafts. I have heard, that at the conclufion of one of thefe acts, the preacher made proclamation, that it had been revealed to him, that one of the congregation refufed to be converted, and therefore he was going to find him out, and drag him to the altar ; that he actually did come down from the *eftrade*, and buftled along through all the rows, and then returned to his

roftrum,

roftrum, where he declared to the congregation, that this hardened wretch had at length re-lented, and was firmly determined to give him-felf up to God.

The pulpit being one of the paths leading to fortune, the Lent and Advent ftations are much coveted by all who conceit themfelves poffeffed of oratorial talents: thefe ftations like-wife excite a fpirit of rivalry between all the religious orders, and often manifeft the preva-lence of intrigue over merit.

Benedict XIV. had procured one of the prin-cipal pulpits at Rome for a regular of his coun-try, who, unhappily for both, did not top his part. A converfation at the pope's palace falling on the preachers, the profoundnefs of one was ex-tolled, the devotion of another, the delivery of this perfon, the compofition of that; not a word of the Bolognefe, till a by-ftander, think-ing to ingratiate himfelf with the pope, con-centred all thofe elogiums in his favourite: the pope, who was not to be impofed on, angrily interrupted the flatterer, *Siete come la piattola che gira, e rigira, e fempre torna al cogl.* . . . .

The orders, moft in repute for erudition and underftanding, keep to the common way of inftruction. Of this I gave an inftance in the Dominicans at Venice. I was once prefent at a conference which the Jefuits hold every Sa-turday. The fubject of this conference was the neceffity of giving one's heart to the bleffed virgin; and it was proved both by the misfor-tunes which have happened to thoufands of

people

people for neglecting this duty, and by the advantages it procures to those who carefully observe it. The second part turned on the story of a young princess: she had made a solemn offering of her soul and body to the virgin Mary: by the death of her two brothers she unexpectedly became heiress to her father's dominions, who, without minding her peremptory refusals, and her declared aversion from marriage, promised her hand to the heir of a neighbouring state : all the youth and charms of the future bridegroom could make no impression on the devout princess : in a word, the night preceding this forced marriage she spent in prayer, and called on the holy virgin to display her power in supporting the solemn engagement which she had contracted with her: her prayers were heard ; one of her eyes sunk in ; a loathsome leprosy spread over her body, and the most beautiful princess in the universe instantaneously became a frightful object. This story, with all its appurtenances, on which the preacher's imagination luxuriantly expatiated, took up the greater part of the conference, and let me into the reason why a French Jesuit, whom I had met at the church-door, was so very urgent with me not to go in.

The sermons made by the novices of all orders, at the corners of streets, to the meanest of the people, are futile declamations on purgatory, hell, &c. All the truth lies in stories, the ridicule of which is the less glaring from the custom of hearing them. The people know nothing of religion but by these tales, which

to

to them are fo many articles of faith: accordingly, when, at the fight of the Egyptian idols
placed in one of the rooms of the Capitol,
a prelate cried out, " Good God! is it poffible
" that a whole people fhould fo long have
" worfhiped fuch objects?" he received for anfwer, " It is not the people, but the priefts,
" who are to be wondered at."

This ignorance, in which Rome, and almoft
all Italy is kept, has neceffarily an influence on
their manners. The unprincipled, ignorant commonalty, are without any other impreffive docu-
ments than the punifhments of criminals; and thefe
are very rare. The torments of the other life,
fo often thundered in their ears, might be a curb
to a people lefs acute, lefs hacknied in diffimu-
lation, and lefs concerned to doubt of fuch a
ftate.

In the fame principle I thought I perceived
the caufe of the indifference of this fame people for the intereft and perfons of its fovereigns;
an indifference which at Rome is not a matter
of wonder: but one is furprifed to meet with
it likewife in a neighbouring ftate, whofe fovereign is of no more concern to the people of
that ftate than the Grand Turk.

The form of inftruction, the forfaking of the
parifh-churches, the contempt of the fecular clergy,
are perhaps the refults of a fyftematic plan for
eftablifhing ignorance, which, efpecially at Rome,
is the very foundation of the regular clergy's intereft, and the ftrongeft fupport of the fovereign's
greatnefs.

This ignorance, confidered in a political view,

is

is not without its reafons, which I fhall fpecify from
Muratori*: " Since the fettlement of the Lombards
" in Italy, the church has, for a long fucceffion of
" ages, enjoyed a repofe and tranquillity which
" might be envied. Vices of all kinds indeed tri-
" umphed bare-faced, but the people believed what-
" ever the church taught them : and if this be any
" advantage, ignorance, the mother of fuperftition
" and a thoufand evils, produced it: not that it is to
" be defired, that the people, and efpecially the
" clergy, fhould have only a nominal acquaintance
" with the principles of its belief ; yet where the
" people and the clergy do not affect any great
" compafs of learning, and relying on tradition,
" keep to what they learnt in their childhood, no
" herefies are to be apprehended, provided however
" that occafions be wanting. Thefe are always
" more dangerous for the ignorant than the know-
" ing : it is through learning, and its attendant
" pride, that all herefies have fprung up in the
" church : not that religion has any thing to fear
" from learning and knowledge ; they are its
" fureft fences, yet eafily thrown down, if not
" refting on fubmiffion and humility. In a word,
" throughout that long feries of barbarous ages, the
" public belief owed its ftability and prefervation
" to the ignorance and incapacity of the people and
" clergy to engage in thofe queftions and difputes,
" which, by difturbing the quiet of the church,
" have often made Europe a fcene of bloodfhed."

It was merely from the fame principle, that an
Italian regular, being afked whether he believed
the tranfmigration of the *Santa cafa*, made anfwer,

* Differt. 31.

" In believing every thing, the only inconveniency
" is to be reckoned fimpletons and noodles;
" whereas feeming to doubt of any one point is
" very dangerous, as he who doubts of one point
" may incur a fufpicion of doubting of all, the
" motives of belief and doubt being nearly the
" fame in all. Therefore we chufe to be reckoned
" noodles in believing all, rather than expofe our-
" felves to trouble, by frivolous doubts concerning
" any article whatever." An admirable expedient,
truly, for believing nothing by believing every
thing; and as convenient as that, in virtue of
which, a great number of devotees, ftill modeftly
ranking themfelves with faints, indulge themfelves in every gratification, and all with a clear
confcience, from the maxim *Sancta fanctis.*

The purgatory, the rofary, the ftations to which
the people throng on Sundays and holidays, the
finging of litanies every evening before the Madonnas at the corner of the ftreets, the lighting a wax
taper on Saturday evening before an image of the
Virgin, which no houfe is without, together with
the *angelus's* at noon and in the evening, make
the fum and fubftance of the moft ufual religious
obfervances at Rome. Concerning the laft, I remember that a young *mezzano,* or procurer, was
propofing to me an amour; for at Rome this
creditable employment is ingroffed by the men.
In the midft of his overture, the *angelus* ftrikes,
and my gentleman immediately doffs his hat, and,
ftill keeping clofe to me, fays the prayer very
devoutly. When over, he afked me my anfwer;
which was, that during the *angelus* I had been
favoured with the gift of continency.

I muft

I muſt not diſmiſs the article of inſtruction, without obſerving, that for ſome years paſt the parochial prieſts, to recover their eſteem, take very great pains in catechiſing the children, and, to animate them by emulation, have ſettled prizes, rewards, and honours. Of theſe the chief is the title of *Emperor della dottrina chriſtiana*, which is conferred, but after the ſtricteſt examinations, on the boy who is moſt expert in every part of the catechiſm. This inveſtiture is performed with the ſplendor which accompanies all Roman ceremonies. The emperor, attended by a court and a retinue all in *gala*, and the ranks regulated according to the proficiency of the children, has an audience of the pope, and afterwards is admitted to the cardinals, the perſon ſtyled King of England, the embaſſadors, and all the great perſonages at Rome. If theſe exerciſes do not terminate in memory only, great advantages may be expected from them, both in knowledge and morality; a change which will equally appear both in the people and the clergy. It may be forwarded by the choſen books in all languages, which ſome cardinals of late cauſe to be tranſlated into Italian, and printed at their own expence, to be diſtributed among the people. I heard one of theſe cardinals anſwer one of his brethren, who was praiſing his great liberality in this article; " Why, what can " we do leſs? we neither adminiſter the ſacra- " ments, nor preach; ſo that this is the only way " we have to ſerve the church, and not be uſeleſs " drones in it."

CANONISATIONS.—Canoniſations make no farther impreſſion on the Romans than what a certain legate expreſſed in theſe words; *Iſti novi*

fan{ti faciunt dubitare de antiquis: and as to the
ceremonial part, all they mind about it is, that
it fills Rome with company, and caufes a good
deal of money to be fpent. To the laity the
new faints are perfons of another world, whofe
virtues are fcarce applicable to common life:
they are founders, regulars, brothers, fifters, of
orders which have money enough to anfwer the
expences of having the great gates of heaven
opened to them: the hopes of attaining to thefe
honours is what prompts thofe who, from a religious caft, or want of abilities, decline worldly
honours, to enter into thofe orders, and fupports
them in the trying courfe of their perfeverance.
I have been told, that fince the popes have
referved to themfelves an exclufive right of be-
ftowing thefe honours, St. Roch is the only
fecular, who has obtained a public worfhip; and
this worfhip is but a bare toleration. The
time may perhaps at length come, when fome
pope, by the canonifation of fome European laic,
known by his countrymen to have difcharged,
in gradu heroico, the duties of a fon, a hufband,
a father, and a member of fociety, fhall fet
before the men of the world a pattern of virtues within their fphere.

The rooms, in which lived the faints cano-
nifed during the two laft centuries, have been
converted into oratories, which are open to the
devotion of believers, and the curiofity of foreigners, who vifit them on account of the excellent collection of paintings in them.

The chamber of St. Staniflaus Cofka, in the
novitiate of the Jefuits, is remarkable for its
paintings,

paintings, fome autographical letters of St. Ignatius framed and glafed, but chiefly for the image of that faint lying on the bed in which he died: it is as big as life, and for workmanfhip accounted the mafter-piece of the famous Le Gros, who wrought the young Jefuit's vefture from a block of black marble, with the head, hands, and feet, in exquifite white marble.

The Philippins of the *Chiefa nuova* have fhewn the fame regard to the chamber where their founder died. There they fhew his bed, his mattreffes, his crucifix, and fome of the furniture which belonged to him. There are few houfes in Rome of a more fuperb architecture, or containing more valuable productions of the fine arts: yet thefe very good fathers, it feems, amidft all this fplendor, have retained *that piety, and truly apoftolic fimplicity*, which father Mabillon had admired in them. Thofe qualities I likewife admired in P. Bianchini, nephew to the prelate of that name, who has been immortalifed by M. Fontenelle; and thefe virtues derived no fmall luftre from his fhare of that vaft knowledge for which his uncle was fo eminent.

FUNCTIONS.—All civil and religious ceremonies, attended with pomp and fplendor, at Rome are diftinguifhed by the appellation of *Functions*, and are no mean *fuccedaneum* to the fhows for which the Roman people had fuch a rage.

Of all thefe *functions* the moft brilliant is that of the *Poffeffo*, or the pope's cavalcade when he goes to take poffeffion of the church of

St. John Lateran, accounted the firſt church in Rome, and the mother church of all chriſten-dom. I ſaw Clement the XIIIth's *Poſſeſſo*, which was full three miles in length, reaching from the Vatican through the whole extent of Rome. This is the only ceremony in which the pope appears in all his ſpiritual and temporal gran-deur. He is preceded and followed by above two thouſand horſemen divided into ſquadrons, the variety of which makes a very entertaining ſhow. The moſt brilliant of. theſe ſquadrons is that of the cuiraſſiers; whoſe officers, being completely armed in the old manner, give an idea of the gorgeouſneſs of ancient military ſpectacles : the richneſs of the armour, all of the moſt curious damaſk work; the embroi-dered half-mantle, or *paludamentum*, hanging from the right ſhoulder; the ſaſh, in ſome round the waiſt, in others over the ſhoulder; the *ai-grette* and plumage ſhadowing the helmet, form a garb with which all the modern gewgaws will not bear any compariſon. The cuiraſs and head-piece of the Swiſs guards put one in mind of the Ligue's infantry in the frontiſpiece of *La Satyre Ménipée.* The Roman barons are on horſeback in black, and cloaked; with ſhort hair, frizzled and full of powder; pumps and white ſtockings, and their hat under the arm : every one is preceded by four pages cloaked likewiſe, in long hair and embroidery : about the bridle and ſtirrups walk grooms; and his train conſiſts of twenty footmen in glaring li-veries. The cardinals, the upper and lower dig-

nitaries,

nitaries, and all the pope's houfehold, in ceremonial habits, made a part in this cavalcade;
and even father Orfi himfelf, though turned
of eighty, as mafter of the facred palace. The
leaft fhowy, and at the fame time the leaft
convenient accoutrements, are thofe of the cardinals : their hats, which are quite flat, are faftened to their head only by ftrings tied under
the chin : their long mantles cover the horfe's
whole body, like a caparifon; and the two
corners of the cloaks being made faft between
his two ears, the rider has no means of clearing himfelf in cafe of any accident, which indeed is little to be apprehended, feveral footmen going on each fide of the horfe, and
watching its fteps. All the fineft horfes in
Spain and Sicily are produced on this occafion; and their beauty, and graceful ftatelinefs
of motion, are no fmall addition to the fpectacle.
A Venetian, who was juft come from Conftantinople, where he had feen the new fultan go in
proceffion to St. Sophia's mofque, affured me,
that, fetting afide the beards and turbans, it
was exactly like the pope's.

They who led the cavalcade having moved
forward, I faw Clement XIII. get on horfeback,
at the foot of the Vatican great ftair-cafe, by
means of fteps which reached to the ftirrup.
Being a Venetian, he had a right to take
every advantage, though in the interval from
his election to the *Poffeffo* he had not been wanting to practife in Monte-Cavallo gardens. The
pad which he rode was a very beautiful white
mule, a little dappled, and led by grooms.

I 4   The

The pope in his left hand had a fwitch, which he ufed now and then to make his mule quicken its pace; and with his right, he was continualiy blefling the people. Being feated in the faddle, his fetting off was proclaimed by a general difcharge from the caftle of St. Angelo, on the top of which was difplayed the church's banner. At this fignal all the people, with whom the neighbouring ftreets were crowded, fell on their knees, calling out, *Santo Padre, benedizion.* The pope was fo affected with this fuperb commencement, that I faw the tears run down his cheeks : afterwards, mingling with the crowd which lined the ftreets, I heard, among the invocations of *Santo Padre, benedizion,* fome, who with a hollow voice muttered, *e groffe pagnotte,* (" and large loaves.") Some were reckoning their age by the *Poffeffos* which they had feen : I heard others obferving that Benedict XIV. made his proceffion in an open chair, with a chaplet in his hand. What would thefe good folks have faid of a pope, who, to difplay all his prerogatives, had made his appearance as a prince, and armed *cap-à-pié?* However, in the proceffion were particular perfons, one carrying a helmet, others gauntlets, which, I was told, were thofe of the pope.

The cavalcade from the Vatican to St. John Lateran took up near two hours. On their arrival, the greater part, and all the people, difperfing over the large fquare before that church, the pope, the cardinals, and fome prelates, after taking poffeffion, went up to a gallery over the great door. There the pope on his
throne

throne repeated fome prayers relating to the ceremony : they were very appofite, and pathetically
pronounced ; and the people obferving a profound
filence, every word could be diftinctly heard all
over the fquare. On the conclufion of them the
tiara was put on the pope's head, and his firft
folemn benediction was anfwered with an univerfal fhout of the people, and a difcharge of all the
artillery in Rome. This ceremony is fo ftriking,
fo auguft, fo truly glorious, that a Genevan,
who was prefent, owned to me, that at the inftant
of the benediction he felt himfelf a catholic.

Another ceremony, which makes Rome all
alive, is the prefentation of the pad ; in which I
could not help obferving, that the creature, which
is taken out of the pope's ftables, and has been the
fame for feven or eight years, is ufed to kneel down
before the pope on its fore legs, which it does
very gracefully. On its croup is a large filver
flower, with its ftalk and leaves, and in its calix
the cedule or acknowledgment of homage, which
is annually prefented to the pope in the name of
the king of Naples, as his liege-man. This *function* is accompanied with a fire-work, played off
three evenings fucceffively, in the Farnefe fquare.
The decoration of every evening is different, the
laft is the moft brilliant, and they all vary from
the decorations of the preceding years. That of
1758, defigned by the architect Pofi, reprefented
a large Chinefe coffee-houfe, diftributed, on each
of the two grand fronts of the decoration, into
nine rooms differently furnifhed. In the middle
of the decoration ftood a Chinefe octagon tower,
of nine ftories diftinguifhed by rough cornices,

at

at the angles of which hung little bells. The fire was diftributed and ferved with all the dexterity and exaƈtnefs for which the Italian engineers are fo eminent.

The eighth of September, being the nativity of the virgin, was celebrated by a *funƈtion* which is repeated only every tenth or twelfth year. The Minerva Dominicans carried in proceffion the Madonna of the Rofary. This Madonna, who is as big as life, and dreffed in the neweft fafhion and richeft ftuffs, frizzled, powdered, perfumed, and all over ribbons, laces and jewels, is feated on a lofty throne, in the midft of a machine fuperbly ornamented, and being very heavy is carried by thirty men, among whom the burthen is equally diftributed by means of thofe interlaced levers, in the management of which the porters at the feaports are fo very dexterous. The Madonna, with all the Dominicans of Rome before her, and the general at their head, was followed by two hundred girls, from fourteen to feventeen years of age; walking two by two in an uniform of white ferge, and veiled; every one with a wax-taper; and one body had garlands on their heads. After morning fervice they had received the portions diftributed annually by the fraternity of the Rofary, which is very rich. Thefe portions are about two hundred and fifty French livres for thofe who are difpofed to marry, and twice the value for thofe who will embrace the convent. The latter headed the proceffion, and were honoured with the diftinƈtion of the garlands. The veils of all rather fhade than cover their faces. I did not fee one that might be faid to be pretty, and very few of a tolerable fhape. The portions
they

they receive in bills, which are paid by the cafhier of the fraternity on their marrying, or taking the veil.

Ten or twelve fraternities give fuch portions; and there is no regulation againft a girl's offering herfelf to each of thefe fraternities, and receiving the portion. They who have intereft may offer themfelves two or three times at the fame fraternity; and the aggregate fum of thefe portions makes a ftock, which with induftry and œconomy will fet up a frugal pair.

Rome is full of thofe foundations, for which religion lays opulence under contribution; fuch as the confervatories, fome of which are for orphans, fome for children brought thither by their parents, and not feldom taken from them when their poverty endangers their morals; fuch as the houfes of reformation for difobedient children, or who are taking bad courfes; houfes for young women tired of a loofe life, and others for wives under the misfortune of having bad hufbands. I never could hear of any fuch afylums for hufbands in the like woeful cafe. The devotees in general concern themfelves more about women than men: befides, from the Italian manners, the happinefs of a hufband depends on himfelf.

As to thefe foundations, might they not be improved to the benefit of the ftate? In the confervatories, and houfes of reformation, children are brought up only for a town life: embroidery, knitting, needle-work, finging, and mufic, is all the children are taught, according to their difpofitions; and the trades, to which fome houfes put them out, attach them ftill more ftrongly to a

town

town life. If in thofe houfes, which might be
fcattered among the environs of Rome, part of
thefe young folks were trained up to rural occupations ; if the charities of which they are the
objects, were employed to fettle them in the
country, to provide them with a little cottage
and neceffaries, and fix them there by the property of fome fmall fpot to clear and improve ;
were the apoftolic chamber, were the great
landholders, in imitation of the methods which
have peopled our northern countries, to farm
out fuch parts of their eftates as now lie wafte
for want of hands; fuch management would
preferve thefe young people, now left to themfelves, from perifhing in licentioufnefs, floth, and
difappointed expectations ; the Campania of
Rome would fill apace, without thinning the
town, and every year be productive of a new
fwarm of one or two hundred families ; in a
word, as colonies were the ftrongeft fupport of
the grandeur of ancient Rome, fo would they
relieve modern Rome from that difmal folitude
and fcandalous indolence in which it now lan-
guifhes. But thefe are vain fpeculations ; the
manifeft preference given by fraternities to religious vows, too plainly evinces how very far
thefe pious focieties are from any œconomical
views : it may likewife be a part of the government's fyftem, that the population of the
ecclefiaftical ftate fhall remain as it is. *Vacua
fe jactet in aula.*

THEATRES.—Among the fhows at Rome we
are not to forget theatres for operas and plays.
Thefe theatres, which are open only in winter,

are under the cognifance of the governor of Rome. The communions, which differ from that of Rome, make a great outcry againft the pope for this toleration, and exult in contrafting Geneva and Rome. But the leifure of the people and nobles at Rome, overthrows this comparifon : Modern Rome, nay Chriftian Rome, has retained all the inclinations of Pagan Rome; and the Royal-Pontiff, to whom it is now fubject, cannot but tolerate what the Conftantines, the Theodofius's, &c. were not able to extirpate. At Rome, and all over the ecclefiaftical ftate, agreeably to the cuftom among the ancient Romans, women are not allowed to tread the ftage, whilft, all over Italy, the parts of men are generally acted by women.

Let us farther examine whether it be reconcileable with civil and religious policy, that the theatres of Rome fhould be filled with eunuchs. The operation, by which thefe men are fo debafed, the Roman laws, which the popes have adopted, prohibited under the greateft penalties ; but the want of fuch for the theatres, for facred and prophane mufic, &c. filences the law ; fo that of thefe wretches it may be faid, *Genus hominum quod in civitate noftrâ (Româ) et vetabitur femper, et femper retinebitur.* One would be amazed at the number, could an account be taken only of thofe within the ecclefiaftical ftate (e). For my part, I never could
join

(e) *Horum tædio*, faid Ammian Marcellinus, *veterem laudare juvat Domitianum, qui licet patri fratrique diffimilis, memoriam nominis fui inexpiabili deteftatione perfudit, tamen receptiffima inclaruit lege, quâ minaciter interdixerat, ne intra terminos*

join in the pleafure which the Italians take in
thefe effeminate voices : they proceed from bodies fo little a-kin to them, and thofe bodies
are formed of parts fo ill put together, their
motions on the ftage are fo clumfy and aukward, that I fhould ever prefer an ordinary
voice in a natural body to the fineft *mufico*.
Their notes never conveyed to my heart that
fenfation, which a female or a boy's finging
excites : this difference perhaps is founded in
nature, which taught the Greeks to call a fine
voice *the flower of beauty*.

This ftate is a path to fortune in Italy, where
they are fo capricious as even to pay thofe unnatural parents who thus facrifice their children ;
as to reward infamous pimps who carry on
this horrible trade almoft openly ; and, in a
word, to fhower opulence and regard on thofe
whofe organs retain nothing of their original
ftate.   But to twelve of thefe prodigies what
numbers of wretches linger in diftrefs, under the
torturing fenfe of their former and prefent condition !

One of thefe monfters, on his return from
Madrid, where his voice had gained him a
moft exorbitant fortune, was giving Benedict
XIV. a particular account of the profits, employments, and honours, which had been heaped

*terminos jurifdictionis Romanæ, quifquam puerum caftraret :
quod ni contigiffet, quis eorum ferret examina, quorum pau-
citas difficile toleratur.* Liv. xviii. p. 141, Ed. Rob. Steph.
See a vehement invective againft the violation of human
nature, in the fifteenth of thofe Satyrs, the authors of
which have concealed themfelves under the name of Q.
Sectanus.

on him: " So," faid the pope, when he had
made an end, " you have found there what
" you had left here."

Having given fuch a detail of the prefent
ftate of Rome, it will doubtlefs be defired,
that I had touched on the morals of this great
city; that I had fketched out a *fcandalous chronicle* of the princes of priefts ; in a word,
that I had fhewn how far modern Chriftian
Rome is like ancient, or Juvenal's Rome. On
this head I may be permitted to fay, that my
ftay was not long enough in a country, where
pleafure is carried on with no lefs myftery,
contrivance, and circumfpection, than bufinefs;
where that publicity is carefully avoided, which
in other parts is its chief relifh ; where the fortune of moft people depends at leaft on the
apparent regularity of their behaviour. I have
indeed heard of notorious libertinifm in fome
people who think themfelves above cenfure;
of connexions formed by intereft, and fupported by ready money ; of intrigues of aban-
doned women ; I have collected fome merry
fayings of Benedict XIV. on thofe connexions
and intrigues ; that, for inftance, occafioned by
a lady's fumbling a long time in unhitching
an extraordinary watch which had been given
her, to fhew it him (f) : but nothing of what
I obferved can warrant the unjuft prejudices
which prevail in fome countries againft that
purity of manners, and regularity of behaviour.

(f) *Lafciate, lafciate: deve fempre il voto effere dirempetto
al fanto :* " Let be, let be; the offering fhould always be
" over-againft the faint."

which

which does honour to the far greater part of the facred college and the upper prelature. All thefe illuftrious perfonages, with little exceptions, feem to have taken for their rule of conduct a letter of the greateft politician of Italy, the very celebrated Lawrence de Medicis, to his fon John, who was afterwards Leo X. The value of this letter, on account of the perfons by whom and to whom it was written, its fubject and manner, induced me to infert it here, the collection to which it belongs being very fcarce.

* *MESSÉR Giovanni, voi fiete molto obligato à M. Domenedio, & tutti noi per rifpetto veftro, perche oltre à molti beneficii & honori, che ha ricevuti la cafa noftra da lui, ha fatto, che nella perfona voftra veggiamo la maggior dignità che fuffe mai in cafa. Et ancora che la cofa fia per fe grande, le circonftantie la fanno affai maggiore, maffime per l'età voftra, & condition noftra.*

Però il primo mio ricordo è, che vi sforziate effer grato à M. Domenedio, ricordandovi ad ogn'hora, che non i voftri meriti, prudentia, ò follecitudine,

ma

---

* "Son John, you, and all of us on your account, are "greatly obliged to God Almighty, as, befides many other "kindneffes and honours which our family has received from "him, it is by his means that we behold in your perfon the "greateft dignity that ever our houfe enjoyed ; and though "the thing be great in itfelf, the circumftances make it "much greater, efpecially at your age and in our condition.

"The firft thing I have to put you in mind of is, that you "endeavour to prove yourfelf grateful to God Almighty, con- "tinually remembering that it is not any merit, prudence,

"or

*ma mirabilmente eſſo Iddio vi ha fatto Cardinale;
& da lui lo riconoſciate, comprobando queſta conditione con la vita V. ſanta, eſſemplare, & honeſta.
A che ſiete tanto più obligato, per haver voi già
dato qualche opinione nella adoleſcentia voſtra da
poterne ſperare tali frutti. Saria coſa molto vitu-
peroſa, & fuor del debito voſtro, & aſpettatione
mia, quando nel tempo, che gli altri ſogliono acquiſtar
più ragione, & miglior forma di vita, voi domen-
ticaſte il voſtro buono inſtitùto. Biſogna adunque,
che vi sforziate alleggerire il peſo della dignità, che
portate, vivendo coſtumatamente, & perſeverando
ne gli ſtudii convenienti alla profeſſion voſtra.
L'anno paſſato, io preſi grandiſſima conſolatione,
intendendo, che ſenza che alcuno ve lo ricordaſſe,
da voi medeſimo vi confeſſaſte più volte, & com-
municaſte. Nè credo che ci ſia miglior via à
conſervarſi nella gratia di Dio, che lo habituarſi*

in

" or intereſt of yours, but that ſame God, who made you
" cardinal : and of this ſhew your acknowledgement in doing
" credit to his choice by the exemplary decency and holineſs
" of your life : and to this you are the more obliged, having
" already raiſed an opinion that ſuch fruits might be expected
" from your youth. It would be extremely culpable, and
" contrary both to your duty and my expectation, ſhould
" you, at a time when others improve in reaſon and the
" practice of virtue, run counter to your good beginning.
" It is therefore neceſſary for you to endeavour to lighten the
" weight of the dignity you are inveſted with, by a decent
" tenour of life, and adhering to the ſtudies ſuitable to your
" profeſſion. I was exceedingly rejoiced laſt year to hear
" that, without any advice of others, but purely of yourſelf,
" you confeſſed, and received the ſacrament, oftener than you
" had been uſed : and I do not conceive there is a better
" way for preſerving ourſelves in the grace of God than to per-

K " ſevere

*in simili modi, & perseverarvi. Questo mi pare il
più utile, & conveniente ricordo, che per lo primo
vi posso dare.*

*Conosco, che andando voi à Roma, che è sentina
de tutti i mali, entrate in maggior difficoltà di
fare quanto vi dico di soprà, perche non solamente
gli essempi muovono, ma non vi mancheranno par-
ticolari incitatori & corruttori: per che come
voi potete intendere, la promotione vostra al Car-
dinalato, per l'età vostra, & per l'altre conditioni
sopradette, arreca seco grande invidia; & quelli,
che non hanno potuto impedire la perfettion di questa
vostra dignità, s'ingegneranno sottilmente diminuirla,
con denigrare l'opinione della vita vostra, & farvi sdrucciolare in questa stessa fossa, dove essi sono
caduti, confidandosi molto, che debba lor riuscire
per l'età vostra. Voi dovete tanto più opporvi à
queste difficultà, quanto nel collegio hora si vede
manco*

" severe in the frequent use of such means. This seems to
" me the most suitable and beneficial counsel that I can at first
" recommend to you.

" I know, that as you are going to Rome, that sink of all
" corruption, it will be the more difficult to conform to what
" have said above, as, besides the contagion of bad examples,
" you will not want bad counsellors and seducers ; for, as
" you may well think, your promotion to the cardinalate
" will, both on account of your age and the circumstances
" above mentioned, bring much envy on you ; and they who
" have not been able to hinder your acquisition of this dignity
" will leave no stone unturned to bring a slur on it, by degra-
" ding the opinion entertained of your life, and causing you
" to slip into the same ditch into which they themselves are
" fallen : and this, they promise themselves, they shall
" bring about by reason of your age. Against these difficulties
" you must make head with the greater vigour, as little virtue
" is now to be found in the college ; though I remember to
" hav

manco virtù, & io mi ricordo pur'havere veduto in quel collegio buon numero d'huomini dotti, & buoni, & di santa vita : però è meglio seguir questi essempi, perche facendolo sarete tanto più conosciuto, & stimato, quanto l'altrui conditioni vi distingueranno da gli altri. E' necessario, che fuggiate, come Scilla & Cariddi, il nome della hippocrisia, & il nome di mala fama, & che usiate mediocrità, sforzandovi in fatto fuggire tutte le cose, che offendono in dimostratione, & in conversatione, non mostrando austerità ò troppa severità, che sono cose, lequali col tempo intenderete, & farete meglio a mia opinione, che io non le posso esprimere. Voi intenderete di quanta importanza, & essempio sia la persona d'un Cardinale, & che tutto il mondo starebbe bene, se i Cardinali fossino, come dovrebbono essere, percioche farebbono sempre un buon Papa, onde nasce quasi il riposo di tutti i Christiani. Sforzatevi dunque d'esser tale voi, che quando gli altri

" have seen in it a good number of learned and virtuous men,
" men of holy lives. But it is better to follow these examples;
" and by so doing you will become the more known, and
" the more esteemed, as the condition of others will distin-
" guish you from them. It will behove you to avoid, as the
" worst of evils, the character of hypocrisy and libertinism;
" and observe a medium and temper, diligently shunning
" every thing which may give offence in action and in conver-
" sation; not affecting too much rigour or austerity: but these
" are things which you will see into in time, and, I promise
" myself, will perform better than I can set them forth. You
" will understand what weight the example of a cardinal
" carries with it; and that it would go well with all the world,
" were cardinals what they ought to be, as then they would
" always make a good pope, on which the quiet of Christen-
" dom so much depends. Endeavour therefore to be such,

*altri fuſſino coſi fatti, ſe ne poteſſe aſpettare queſtó
bene univerſale.*

*Et perche non è maggior fatica, che converſar bene
con diverſi huomini ; in queſta parte vi poſſo mal dar
ricordo, ſe non che v'ingegniate, che la converſation
voſtra con gli Cardinali, & altri huomini di conditione, ſia caritativa, & ſenza offenſione : dico, mi-
ſurando ragionevolmente, & non ſecondo l'altrui
paſſione : perche molti volendo quello che non ſi dee,
fanno della ragione ingiuria. Giuſtificate adunque
la coſcientia voſtra in queſto, che la converſation
voſtra con ciaſcuno, ſia ſenza offenſione. Et queſta
mi pare la regola generale, molto à propoſito voſtro,
perche, quando la paſſione pur fà qualche inimico,
come ſi partono queſti tali ſenza ragione del l'amicitia,
coſi qualche volta tornano facilmente.*

*Credo per queſta prima andata voſtra à Roma, ſia
bene adoperare più gli orecchi, che la lingua. Hoggi-
mai*

" that, if others were like you, this univerſal good might be
" expected from them.

" And, as nothing requires greater watchfulneſs than to
" converſe becomingly with different perſons, I am not able
" to give you any farther advice in this, but only that your
" converſation with the cardinals and other perſons of rank
" be courteous and affectionate, and void of all offence,
" ſtill acting on reaſon, and not by others paſſions ; as many,
" requiring that which ought not to be, do violence to rea-
" ſon, and turn right into wrong. Therefore conſult your con-
" ſcience, that it may approve of your care ſo to order your
" behaviour with every one, as to give no offence. And
" this ſeems to me the general rule, very ſuitable to your
" purpoſe ; for where paſſion excites an enmity, as ſuch
" break from friendſhip unreaſonably, ſo ſome time or other
" they eaſily cloſe with a reconciliation.

" This being your firſt time of going to Rome, I am incli-
" ned to think that your ears ſhould be more buſy than your
" tongue.

*mai io vi ho dato del tutto à M. Domenedio & à
santa Chiesa, onde è necessario, che diventiate un
buono Ecclesiastico, & facciate ben capace ciascuno,
che amate l'honore, e lo stato di Santa Chiesa, &
della Sede Apostolica, innanzi à tutte le cose del
mondo, posponendo à questo ogn'altro rispetto. Nè
vi mancherà modo, con questo riservo, d'aiutar la
città & la casa : perche questa città fa l'unione della
Chiesa, & voi dovete in ciò esser buona catena, & la
casa ne va con la città. Et benche non si possono vedere gli accidenti, che verranno, così in general credo,
che non ci habbiano à mancare modi di salvare (come
dica) la capra, & i cavoli, tenendo fermo il presup-
posto, che anteponiamo la Chiesa ad ogn'altra cosa.*

*Voi siete il più Giovane Cardinale non solo di tutto
il Sacro Collegio, ma che fosse mai fatto infino à qui,
& però è necessario, che dove havete à concorrere con*
gli

" tongue. I have now given you wholely and solely to God
" Almighty and holy church ; which makes it incumbent on
" you to become a good ecclesiastic, and thoroughly to convince
" every one that you have at heart the honour and prosperity
" of the holy church, and of the apostolic see, preferably to
" every thing in the world, postponing all other concern and
" regard to that: and with this reserve, you will not be the
" less able to benefit the city and your family : for in this city
" consists the union of the church ; and, here, it is your
" duty to be the auspicious link for connecting our family
" with the city ; and, though what accidents may happen
" cannot be foreseen, yet in general I believe, that means
" will offer themselves of saving, as the proverb runs, *both*
" *the goat and the cabbages* ; yet inviolably adhering to the
" above maxim of preferring the church to every other re-
" lation.

" You are the youngest cardinal, not only of all the sacred
" college, but that has hitherto been advanced to that dig-
" nity ; so that, when an assembly is to be held, it will become

K 3 " you

gli altri, fiate il più follecito, il più humile, fenza farvi afpettare ò in Cappella, ò in Concifterio, ò in Deputatione. Voi conofcerete prefto li più, & li meno accoftumati. Co i meno, fi fuol fuggir la con-verfatione molto intrinfica, non folamente per lo fatto in fe, ma per l'opinione, & à largo converfar con ciafcheduno.

Nelle pompe voftre loderei più prefto ftar di quà dal moderato, che di là; & più prefto vorrei bella ftalla, & famiglia ordinata, & polita, che ricca, & pompofa. Ingegnatevi di vivere accoftumatamente, riducendo à poco à poco le cofe al termine che per effer hora la famiglia, e il pardon nuovo, non fi puo.

Gioie, & feta in poche cofe ftanno bene à pari voftri, più prefto qualche gentilezza di cofe antiche, & belli libri, & più prefto famiglia accoftumata, & dotta, che grande. Convitar più fpeffo, che andare à conviti, & non però fuperfluamente. Ufate per la perfona voftra cibi groffi, & fate affai effercitio, perche in
                                                                 cotefti

" you to be the moft diligent and moft humble, and not be
" waited for either in the chapel, confiftory, or *deputation*.
" You will foon know who are the beft-mannered and the moft
" ill-mannered. Any intimate commerce is to be avoided with
" the latter, not only for the thing itfelf, but as affecting your
" character: in indifferent matters converfe openly with all.

" As to figure, I could rather recommend being within
" moderation than beyond it, and fhould prefer a regular
" and neat way of living to fhow and magnificence; thus
" gradually reducing things to what cannot fo well be done
" now, with a fettled family and a new mafter.

" Jewels and filks little fuit your ftation; but it would
" be right to have an elegant library and collection of
" antiques, and a family more remarkable for their learn-
" ing and good breeding, than for their number. Give en-
" tertainments oftener than go to them, but without excefs.
" Let your food be plain, and ufe a good deal of exercife; for
                                                              " in

peſi ſi viene preſto in qualche infermità, chi non ci ha cura. Lo ſtato del Cardinale è non manco ſicuro, che grande, onde naſce, che gli huomini ſi fanno negligenti, parendo loro haver conſeguito aſſai, & poterlo mantenere con poca fatica, & queſto nuoce ſpeſſo, & alla conditione, & alla vita, allaquale è neceſſario che habbiate grande avvertenza, & più preſto pendiate nel fidarvi poco, che troppo.

Una regola ſopra l'altre vi conforto ad uſare con tutta la ſollecitudine voſtra ; & queſta è, di levarvi ogni mattina di buon' hora, perche oltre al conferir molto alla ſanità, ſi penſa, & eſpediſce tutte le facende del giorno, & al grado, che avete : havendo à dir l'officio, ſtudiare, dare audientia, &c. ve'l troverete molto utile.

Un' altra coſa ancora è ſommamente neceſſaria ad un par voſtro, cioè penſar ſempre, & maſſime in queſti principii, la ſera dinanzi, tutto quello che havete à
fare

" in theſe countries, without ſuch care, diſorders are ſoon con-
" tracted. The dignity of cardinal, being no leſs ſecure than
" it is illuſtrious, is apt to make men remiſs : they think they
" have made a great acquiſition, and that it is to be ſupported
" with little or no fatigue ; which is often very detrimental
" both to the rank and the morals, both which require ſtrict
" watchfulneſs ; and I would adviſe you to be rather diffident
" than over confident.

" One thing I would eſpecially recommend to you, to be
" very diligent in, and that is early riſing ; for, beſides the
" healthineſs of this cuſtom, you compoſedly deliberate on and
" go through the buſineſs of the day, and thoſe of your par-
" ticular ſtation, as praying, ſtudying, giving audience, &c.
" ſo that you will find a great advantage of it.

" Another thing likewiſe extremely neceſſary to one in your
" ſtation, eſpecially as you have newly entered on the dignity,
" is, on the evening to think on all that you have to do the
K 4　　　" next

*fare il giorno seguente, accioche non vi venga cosa
alcuna immeditata. Quanto al parlar vostro in Con-
cistorio, credo farà più costumatezza, & più lauda-
bil modo, in tutte le occorrenze che vi si proporranno,
riferirsi alla Santità di Nostro Signore, pensando, che
per esser voi Giovane & di poca esperienza, sia più
officio vostro rimettervi alla Santità sua, & al sapien-
tissimo giudicio di quella. Ragionevolmente voi sarete
richiesto di parlare, & intercedere appresso a Nostro
Signore per molte specialità. Ingegnatevi in questi
principii di richiederlo manco che potete, & dar-
gliene poca molestia : che di sua natura il Papa è più
grato à chi manco gli spezza gli orecchi. Questa parte
mi pare da osservare per non lo infastidire ; & così
l'andargli inanzi con cose piacevoli, ò pur quando
accadesse, richiederlo con humiltà & modestia, doverà
sodisfargli più, & esser più secondo la natura sua.
State sano. Di Firenze.*

LORENZO DE' MEDICI.

" next day, that nothing may come on you unpremeditated.
" As to your speaking in the consistory, it will be more polite,
" and more commendable, in all occurrences which may come
" on the carpet, to refer yourself to his holiness. Your
" youth and little experience must incline you to think it be-
" comes you to lay your private opinion at his holiness's feet,
" and leave all affairs to his wise judgement. In all pro-
" bability, you will frequently be desired to intercede with
" his holiness for some particular favour : but, it being still
" young days with you, be very sparing of such intercessions,
" and give him as little trouble as possible ; for the pope him-
" self is naturally more affable and kind to those who trouble
" him the least with requests. This is the part I would have
" you act, in order to avoid disgusting him ; and let your con-
" versation turn on things agreeable to him ; or when any
" thing of that nature happens, to ask it with humility and
" modesty will please him better, and more coincide with his
" temper. Farewell.
" Florence.   LORENZO DE MEDICI.

F I N E   A R T S.

Music.—That melancholy, which generally prevails in the constitution and temper of the Italians, is the chief source of their fondness as well for the arts as for poetry and music. It is this melancholy which has filled Italy with epic poems good and bad, but all instances of a perseverance in the poets, of which every nation is not capable. This perseverance has been of infinite service to genius towards the production of those master-pieces, in all the entertaining arts, for which Italy is famous : *Alterius sic altera poscit opem res.* I saw at Rome an abbé of one of the first families in Bologna, who applying himself closely for ten years together to the spinnet, (two of which he had spent at Naples without minding any one thing else) had brought that instrument to such a perfection, as to make it perform equally to the best harpsicord. Music, besides being an entertainment to the Italians, is a passion, is a want ; a want, relative to their constitution, which, the louder the music, the more deliciously it affects.

On the promotion of cardinal Priuli, the prince of Viana gave a grand entertainment, for which the finest music at Rome had been procured. I happened to sit next to a prelate, to whom I was a stranger, and who asked me how I liked the music. I answered, that, from the pleasure the connoisseurs expressed at it, I could not but think it excellent ; but, for my part, I only heard a noise. " I like your frankness," said the prelate with a smile : " but have patience ; five or six months " hence, you will feel harmony in what now seems

" only

" only noife. You are, in this refpeƈt, like one,
" who after living under ground fhould be fud-
" denly brought into open light: his eyes would
" be too much dazzled to perceive any thing, and
" it would be only by degrees that he could come
" to diftinguifh objeƈts." But, replied I, what if
your *virtuofos* aim more at noife than harmony?
" That's the very criterion," returned he, " by
" which you will know the bad performers: it is
" by that the celebrated Tartini judges of them.
" The Neapolitan *virtuofi*, that is, the beft fiddles in
" Italy, queftion their own abilities till tried before
" him. You muft needs think, that in order to
" obtain a favourable verdiƈt they exert every art
" of fkill, ftrength and fupplenefs: their fingers
" fly, their ftick crackles; and when they have
" done, Tartini coldly fays to the greater part,
" *That's notable, that's fmart, that's very ftrong*;
" *but*, adds he putting his finger to his heart, *it was*
" *not felt there.*"

ARCHITECTURE.—To fpeak of Rome without
faying a word about St. Peter's, would be like leaving that city without having feen the pope. This
bafilic even furpaffes its celebrity; it is among the
works of art, as the fea in the fcene of nature, the
only objeƈt adequate to the idea which man is capable of forming to himfelf of grandeur, majefty, and
immenfity. It was finely faid by father Mabillon,
Tam divinæ fabricæ majeftatem rudi calamo violare
non audemus: nonnulla funt quæ nullo melius modo
quàm filentio & ftupore laudantur. After viewing
it, he who employs his eyes only about buildings,
might imitate thofe devout Muffulmen, who on
leaving Mecca put out their eyes, becaufe, after
having

having feen that facred place, they cannot expect
to behold fuch another auguft fpectacle.

The immenfe revenue belonging to this cathedral
fuffices both for the continual repairs which fuch
a ftructure requires, and the decorations daily
added to it. The repairs within the church caufe
no diforder or impediment : they are done with
flying fcaffoldings. I have feen fome of thefe fcaffoldings fixed to the great cornice of the nave,
and to us below they feemed like cobwebs.

The defign formed by Clement XI. for putting
into mofaic all the mafter-pieces of painting, which
will thus be immortalifed, muft require a prodigious
expence, both in the workmanfhip, and the various
cryftaline paftes which are the bafe of this work.
When I was at Rome, I faw this work carrying on
in copies of Guido's *St. Michael*, Carravaggio's
Chrift in the fepulcre, and Raphael's *Transfiguration*. For the convenience of the copyifts, the
original of the latter, which was painted on a
very compact affemblage of walnut-tree boards,
ftood on a fcaffold raifed behind the altar of St.
Peter Montorio, where it had been placed on
Raphael's death, and where it has remained though
done for Francis I. king of France, who had partly
paid for it. I have more than once found this
place quite empty, and been alone with this *ne plus
ultra* of painting. This is a carelefsnefs which
does honour to the Romans : the refpect which the
artifts and the common people bear to mafterly
performances (g) is the fafeft and moft honourable

(g) Yet I have heard that the paintings by the fame Raphael in the Vatican, as his *School of Athens*, his *Sacrament*,
&c. have been very much abufed by young painters putting
oil papers on the heads, for taking them off.

guard

guard that can be placed about them: fuch a guard has been much wanted to the paintings in the Carthufian monaftery at Paris.

The decorations in hand during our ftay at Rome were exceeding coftly: befides new-pointing and repolifhing the grand canopy and St. Peter's chair (*h*), the whole infide of the chapel del Santiffimo was to be embellifhed with all new work. The firft repair was by moft connoiffeurs looked on with an evil eye: they, as I faid before, lamented the taking away of that ineftimable *patina* which the Greeks accounted the flower in works of this kind (*i*), This reftoration was in their eyes a real degradation. In the chapel del Santiffimo they found great fault with the paltry tafte of the mock tapeftry on the walls; but the mofaic on the floor was crowned with univerfal praifes. The principal piece of this mofaic is a group of fheaves, vine-leaves and bunches of grapes: no painting can come nearer to the beauties of nature.

The Romans are not wanting to think very highly of the beauty of their city, and the fplendor of St. Peter. This idea of theirs indeed is confirmed by the concourfe and admiration of all nations, whom curiofity is daily bringing to Rome. Accordingly, when any one feems to wonder at their having no inclination for travelling, they coldly anfwer, *Eh! dove ritroveremo quefta*

(*h*) This canopy, which is exactly of the fame height as that of the front of the Louvre at Paris, is fo proportioned to the ftructure in the centre of which it ftands, that at firft fight it does not feem fo lofty as that of Val de Grace at Paris.

(*i*) See Plutarch's Treatife why the Pythian, &c. *initio*.

bella

bella cupola ? " Where ſhall we meet with ſuch
" a fine cupola ?"

According to Michael Angelo's plan of St.
Peter's, in the Vatican library, the form of it was
to have been that of a Grecian croſs ; that is, of
four naves of equal proportions and length, terminating at an altar as their common centre. The
nave facing the area has ſince been lengthened
with two arcades, and the entrance covered with
a portal which takes up the whole of it, and was
not in Michael Angelo's deſign. In this deſign,
each nave had a projecting portico in the ſtyle of
that of the Pantheon : and this portico would neither have hid, nor broke in on, the external decoration of the whole of the edifice, which Michael
Angelo had no leſs provided for than the interior ;
and it would have appeared with the greater advantage, as St. Peter's was to have been inſulated
on every ſide *(k)*. By ſuch porticos it had ſtood
diſtinguiſhed from all modern edifices, the out-
ſides of which make no manner of appearance but
by a portal, and that void of the neceſſary proportion with the parts, which indeed have little

(k) It was by way of imparting a ſymmetry to all theſe
parts, which are foreign from Michael Angelo's deſign, that
cavalier Bernini raiſed that ſtately periſtyle round St. Peter's
ſquare. A Venetian embaſſador, in his Account of Rome
under the pontificate of Alexander VII. is very ſevere on the
pope for this undertaking, which, ſays he, coſt three millions
in French money. What would this Venetian have ſaid to
the magnificence of Francis I. who appointed the celebrated
Serlio, *per Generale ſopra Fabriche regie, con proviſione di tre-
cento ſcudi per ſoſtegno de i ſuoi biſogni ?* " ſuperintendant of
" the royal works, with an appointment of three hundred
" crowns to ſupply his neceſſities ?"

or none among themselves ; for the architect totally leaves them to the mason. In short, the
beauty of the churches at Rome is like that of
the princess in the Psalms : *Omnis gloria filiæ regis
ab intùs.*

With the palaces it is otherwise ; their outsides
display all the inventions of genius and the delicacy
of art. These palaces line the streets and squares,
which thus owe their greatest ornament to the di-
versity and number of those vast structures. This
external decoration is so far the leading object of
those who build, that several fronts, which have
been long since completed, are yet without the
palaces for which they were made. Such is the
palace of cardinal Sciarra Collona, protector of
France. Behind one of the most grand fronts
in the whole Corso, the master lives, in some
slight apartments hastily run up on the inside of
the front, till the palace intended for him is taken
in hand.

This fondness for grandeur prevails no less in
the inward distribution of the palaces. Every
conveniency gives way to it. Beyond a continued
range of halls, salons, and parlours, some little
corner forms the master's apartment. I visited
a cardinal when sick, who lives in one of the
largest and most splendid palaces in Rome; yet
his whole apartment consisted of a little dark
smoky hole, only eight feet long to a breadth
of six.

The Romans however begin to grow tired of
having houses only for others, and in the new
buildings consider themselves a little. The Corsini
palace, lately built on the same spot where the

famous queen Chriftina lived, between the Tiber
and the Janiculum, though not laid out with all
thofe conveniences which at prefent are the capital
view of French architecture, yet has many more
than all the ancient palaces ; and this, I think,
makes ample amends for any lofs with refpect to
magnificence.

But no where does this tafte fhine with greater
luftre than in thofe country palaces known by
the name of *Vignas.* Here the families of the
popes of the two laft centuries have, as if ftri-
ving to outdo one another, accumulated the
riches of all modern arts, and the very fineft
monuments of the ancients. Here it is efpecially,
that an idea may be formed of what Rome was,
and what it is. The gardens belonging to thefe
palaces, neither in difpofition nor culture, come
up to thofe of our northern countries : but a
turn or two in the Corfo, towards the clofe of the
day, in coaches moving a fnail's-pace, and the
fafhes of which are drawn up at fun-fet, is all the
airing known at Rome, even in the fineft part of
the year. In general, the Romans, like the
Chinefe, know not what to make of our walks
and airings, in which we have no farther view
than that of going and coming back.

Though gardens for mere ornament are neglected, the kitchen-gardens for the legumes and
herbs, on which the greater part of the Romans live, are cultivated with the greateft care.
Indeed, to judge of the culture of thefe vegetables
by their beauty and goodnefs, one would think
that the Roman kitchen-gardeners at leaft had de-
parted from the privilege *di far niente,* " of doing
" nothing :"

" nothing :" but their number is much lefs than
in other parts. The exuberance of the foil, the
plenty and cheapnefs of dung and manure, their
very fcrupulous care in the choice of feeds, *hæc funt
illorum veneficia.** The watering of thofe gardens,
which one would think as toilfome as it is neceffary
under fuch a parching fky, puts them to no manner
of trouble: the mountains within the circuit of
Rome pour into thefe kitchen-gardens both the
furplus and the remainder of the waters of their
public and private fountains; and thefe waters by
fkilful management are made to run into trenches
between the beds, thus plentifully watering them
morning and evening.

PAINTING.—Churches, chapels, palaces, religious houfes, private houfes, all Rome, are fo full
of paintings, that, fo far from fpace being left
for frefco-paintings, there is not fo much as room
for pictures in oil. Were it poffible, that amidft
fuch abundance, and the fatiety refulting from it,
painting ftill produced more mafter-pieces, it
would be given to underftand, *Pulcrum, fed non
his locus:* and thefe mafter-pieces would meet
with no buyers *(l).* Accordingly, what mafters
                                                    it

* Apud Cicer. de C. Furio.

(l) The Italian ftates and princes, I think, might turn
this fullnefs to the advantage both of themfelves and the art.
Were the prohibition of exportation limited to the capital
pieces of the great mafters, the paintings of the fecond clafs
would form a commerce, which, befides bringing money
into their country, would always leave a field open for the performances and emulation of living artifts. Thefe artifts, in
their turn coming to be ancients, would fucceffively enjoy the
value which paintings derive from antiquity, and would
                                                    fupply

it has, are intirely employed by foreigners. I
could not conceal my wonder at the fight of fome
fubjects taken from the *Metamorphofes*, which are
doing in frefco on the ground-floor cielings of a
palace in the Longara. Thefe paintings would
fcarcely pafs in our northern countries : the young
artift who performed them had however all the
hilarity of his calling : befides a general underftanding of mufic, he played a fine fiddle, and
from his fcaffolding gave us five or fix voluntaries
with all the fwiftnefs and fkill of a Neapolitan.
The prince who employed him as a painter, put
me in mind of that French general * who had a
fecretary † to drink for him.

The capital hands in the Roman fchool are
Placido Coftanzi, Sebaftiano Conca, Pompeo
Battoni, and John Paul Panini. I ufed to vifit the
firft, then prince of the academy of St. Luke : he
was employed on a large altar-piece for a nunnery
in Franche Comté : this was the fecond or third
for which he had commiffions from that province.
My vifits and our talk did not in the leaft interrupt
his work, which was very eafy, and in the large
ftyle of the Roman fchool. In the few pieces of
thofe mafters which are remaining at Rome, this
large manner is enhanced by a colouring beyond
that of the ancients.

Thefe laft, and the clofets filled with their

fupply curiofity with valuable pieces, which other pieces
would fucceffively replace. Thus the feveral fchools of Italy
would become a kind of manufactories, which, animated by a
certain fale, would be able to anfwer a continual demand.

* The duke of Vendome.

† Campiftron.

works, I fhall omit, only relating fome facts concerning that deceit which has ever been bufy in multiplying them. I have feen four or five originals of the fame Holy Family of Raphael, of which the only original is in the collection of the Palais-Royal at Paris. One of the fuppofititious originals fills the place of honour in cardinal Albani's gallery, where it is the only one with a curtain before it.

In cardinal Valenti's collection *(m)*, now in the hands of abbé Valenti his nephew, is fhown the little *rock Magdalena*, one of Correggio's mafterpieces ; and this fame Magdalen I fince met with among thofe paintings of the houfe of Farnefe, which were fent away to Naples, and placed in Capo-di-Monte palace. Though that of cardinal Valenti be extremely beautiful, though it has a bloom and luftre wanting in that of Capo di Monte, there is all the reafon in the world to fuppofe, that the real original, done by Correggio for the Farnefe his fovereigns, is that in the poffeffion of the heir of the family.

I happened to be with fome foreigners, when a fmall picture was brought to them for fale as an original Baffan : it had all the characters of that mafter, and the appearance of antiquity requifite for the deceit ; but I accidentally perceived that the canvas on which it had been painted was

(m) In this collection are feveral fmall pieces by Raphael, which, being fent away to Spain, had been confufedly put up in the Corridors, and the darkeft communications in the Efcurial, till, being taken notice of by cardinal Valenti when nuncio in Spain, the queen, who had a great love for him, gave them to him to place them in a light fuitable to their merit.

quite

quite new; a blunder the more palpable, as the impoftor had taken care to mount it on an old frame. I only told him who feemed the moft taken with it, to examine it *folio verfo*.

One of the moft valuable pictures of the Sachetti collection, which Benedict XIV. purchafed, and confecrated to the public in a hall of the Capitol, raifed in me another fort of fufpicion. It reprefents in little the battle of Arbella; and in the whole, and the particulars, there is fuch a near affinity and refemblance with that of Le Brun, among the battles of Alexander painted for Lewis XIV. that, at firft fight, one feems a copy of the other. Such a refemblance whetting my curiofity, I made it my bufinefs to inquire after the age and date of the Roman picture. It feems it had been befpoke of Pietro di Cortona by a king of Spain, who had left both the fubject and the price to himfelf: the king dying while the work was in hand, the painter finifhed it, and made a prefent of it to cardinal Sachetti, his patron, as a token of his gratitude.

Of his motives for fuch gratitude I have the following account. Peter Berretini, having a ftrong inclination for painting, left Cortona, his native place, at the age of ten or eleven, and came to Rome, without any other means of fubfiftence than an acquaintance with a countryman of his, then a fcullion at cardinal Sachetti's. The Cortonian fheltered him in his garret, gave him fhare of his ftraw bed, and for two years fubfifted him with the fcraps which he ufed to purloin, till being promoted, he obtained the garret for his countryman's fole ufe, together with the run of the kitchen. The young

L 2

draughts-

draughts-man, without any other mafter than
genius and inclination, fpent fome years immerfed
in clofely ftudying ancient and modern paintings.
The palace Sachetti, being at the extremity of
Rome towards the Vatican, lay at a great diftance
from the parts beft adapted to the ftudy of
antiquities. To hufband time, Berretini, without
any other provifion than bread, ufed to go and
ftay feveral days in thofe parts, taking up his abode
at night in the work-fhop, that is, in the middle
of the ftreet, or under fome portico. His mefs-
mates (thefe abfences being frequent) were under
no apprehenfion ; however, he having once been
a fortnight without making his appearance, and
his generous countryman having fent about to
inquire after him to no purpofe, he was thought
to be dead, or to have gone back to Cortona ;
and in confequence his garret was difpofed of.
The new inhabitant, finding it full of papers,
fketches and defigns, tied them up together, and
delivered them to the Cortonian, who took it into
his head to prefent them to the cardinal. The cardinal, judging of the author's abilities by his
fketches, ordered the cook to make frefh inquiry,
and, if his countryman came to light, to bring
him to him. At length he was found about St.
Gregory's, in a lonely monaftery, where the monks,
pleafed with his clofe application to work, had
offered him fhelter, and a place at their fecond
table. He was brought back to the palace, where
the cardinal received him in the moft obliging
manner, had him new clothed, put him out to
board, and placed him with Ciarpi, at that time
one of the beft mafters at Rome. Fired with the
                                          liberal

liberal encouragement and public countenance of fuch a patron, Berretini foon arofe to eminence, the glory of which he referred to his Mecænas, who had been fo long a time without knowing it, and now infifted on his living under his roof, and with him, as one of the family, and as a friend. The efteem and favours of Urban VIII. and Alexander VII. who employed Berretini as painter and architect, equally promoted both his reputation and fortune, which he had the moderation to enjoy without quitting his profeffion : part of it he dedicated to the honour of his art, repairing the academy of St. Luke, and rebuilding and endowing St. Martin's church *(n)* belonging to that academy, and for the enlargement of which he gave away his own houfe; laftly, by contriving the vault which runs all under the church, and which by his fkill and munificence is come to be one of the fineft things in modern Rome. In it is his tomb, which he himfelf had prepared *(o)*.

To return to his *battle of Arbella*, its date may be fettled by that of the deceafe of the king of Spain, who had befpoke it. This king is not Philip IV. who died in 1665, as at that time Pietro de Cortona was not lefs than fixty-nine years of age, being born in 1596: he died four years after, turned of feventy ; and this painting fpeaks

(n) Over the great altar of this church is the celebrated *St. Luke* of Raphael, the joining of which has been warped by the humidity of the place, which, befides, is too remote from the eye.

(o) The fineft piece of painting of his at Rome, and one of the moft fublime that perhaps the genius of painting ever planned or executed, is the cieling of the falon in Barberini palace.

a pencil in all its vigour. The king in queftion muft, then, have been Philip III. who died in 1621, when Pietro de Cortona was in the twenty-feventh year of his age; and by that time eminent talents have generally reached their zenith; fo that his *battle of Arbella* muft have been confiderably prior to Le Brun's battles, who was not born till 1619.

The laft painter of high reputation in the Roman fchool is Carlo Maratti. His works, both in public and private buildings, have taken poffeffion of all the voids which were not filled up by the performances of the ancient mafters; and in this refpect he may be looked on as *ultimus Romanorum.* Befides his eminent fkill in the art he profeffed, his talents for poetry and mufic were not lefs admirable; and the difclofure of them was owing to love. In his early youth he was fmitten with a Roman beauty, but of a rank and fortune far above his hopes; yet Carlo had undertaken to raife fuch a fortune by means of his pencil, as fhould warrant his addreffes. Love however anticipated the execution of his fcheme, uniting the lovers by a clandeftine marriage. The family to which the young artift had prefumed thus to fteal an affinity, profecuted him as a feducer, and got the marriage fet afide. This feparation, affecting both honour and love, was a double incitement to Carlo for accomplifhing the project on which he had founded his firft hopes. The productions of his application foon infured his fuccefs, raifing him to the prefidentfhip of the Roman fchool; a ftation, at that time, of very great honour. In this high reputation he applied to his bride's family, requefting the re-union of what
they

they had feparated: his folicitation, being backed by all the greateft perfonages in Rome, was agreed to, and a fecond decree annulled the former: the faithful pair were reftored to each other, and a tender affection, never interrupted till death, com‧penfated for all paft afflictions.

During that long perfecution, Carlo compofed many very pathetic verfes on his fufferings, which he fet to mufic; and, on the happy turn of his affairs, he fang his felicity in ftrains not lefs melo-dious. Several of thefe compofitions are ftill re-membered among the polite Romans. I have heard fome repeated, and do think that none of the moft diftinguifhed poets in this kind, whether an-cient or modern, have produced any thing more impaffioned, more tender, and, at the fame time, more decent. It is obferved, that moft of the great artifts cultivated the agreeable talents. To men-tion only their chief and pattern, there is a very good collection of poems by Michael Angelo, printed at Florence in 1726.

Carlo Maratti at firft limited his pencil to Ma-donnas. Amidft the variety of expreffion, and the airs of the head, they all appeared to be of one family: *Facies non omnibus una, nec diverfa tamen.* The image of his dear fpoufe, as ever pre-fent to his mind, was the architype of his defigns (o). I often ufed to fee an Annunciation of his over the great altar of a chapel near Santo-Spirito hofpi-tal: the virgin in this piece had an air of fpright-linefs, and even of coquettry, which might have

(o) Pliny, cenfuring this kind of prototypes, not uncom-mon among our modern painters, as an infult on religion, fays of one Arellius, a Roman painter, *Flagitio infigni cor-rupit artem, Deas pingens fub dilectarum imagine,* L. lxxxv. c. 10.

been in character for a Magdalen before her converfion : the greater part of this air, however, was
owing to a real pearl necklace on her neck, and a
filver demi-crown, both faftened to the picture.
All the veneration of the Romans for mafter-pieces
of the art has not yet been able to reform this filly
cuftom : their devotion is daily disfiguring and
fpoiling ineftimable pictures, by a thoufand foole-
ries of this kind.

To conclude this article of painting in a manner
agreeable to the connoiffeurs, and ufeful to the
artifts, I fhall infert a letter * written by the famous
Aretin to Michael Angelo on the report, at Venice, that he was going to paint the Laft Judgment in Sixtus the IVth's chapel at the Vatican.
This great piece was finifhed by the time Michael
Angelo received the letter; for which he thanked
Aretin, acknowledging that the ideas which he
fuggefted of that grand fubject were fuperior to
thofe of his own growth. Let artifts and connoiffeurs judge whether there was more truth than politenefs in this declaration of Michael Angelo,
who accompanied it with feveral defigns by his
own hand, for which Aretin returned him thanks
in a letter of the 20th of January, 1538. The
letter in queftion is of the 15th of September, of
the foregoing year. What Aretin fays of painting
in the beginning of this letter, he unqueftionably
wrote as dictated by the celebrated Titian, his
godfather and intimate friend. It may be accounted
a mafterly commentary on the 6th chapter of the
35th book of Pliny.

* Lettere de l' Aretino, vol. i. fol. 153 v. In Parigi,
1609, in-8.

Al

* Al divino MICHEL AGNOLO.

*SI come, venerabile huomo, è vergogna della
fama, e peccato de l'anima il non ramentarſi di Dio,
coſí è biaſimo della vertù e dishonor' del giudiſio d'
ogni un chi hà vertù, e giuditio, di non riverir' voi,
nelle cui mani vive occulta l'idea d'una nuova natura :
onde la difficultà delle linee eſtreme (ſomma ſcienza
nella ſottilità de la Pittura) vi è ſi facile, che con-
chiudete nell'eſtremità de i corpi il fine de l'Arte :
coſa, che l'Arte propria confeſſa eſſer' impoſſibile di
condurre a perfettione ; per cio che l'eſtremo (come
ſapete) dec circondare ſe medeſimo, poi fornire in
maniera, che nel moſtrare cio, che non moſtra, poſſa
promettere delle coſe che promettano le figure della
Capella, a chi meglio ſa giudicarle, che mirarle. Hor'
io che con la lode e con l'infamia, ho ſpedito la maggior'
ſomma de i meriti, e de i demeriti altrui ; per non
convertire in niente il poco ch'io ſono, vi ſaluto. Nè
ardirei*

* To the divine MICHAEL ANGELO.

" As not to be mindful of God, is a ſtain to reputation,
" and a guilt in the ſoul ; ſo, O reſpectable man, is it a ſlur
" to ſkill, and a diſgrace to the judgment of any one who has
" any ſkill and judgment, not to reverence you, in whoſe
" hands lies concealed the idea of a new nature. Hence the
" difficulty of the out-lines (in which painting ſhews its utmoſt
" art and delicacy) to you is ſo eaſy, that in the extremities of
" the bodies you exhibit the utmoſt extent of the art : though
" perfection herein be what the art itſelf owns impracticable ;
" for the extremity (as you know) ought to ſurround itſelf, then
" be finiſhed in ſuch a manner that, expreſſing what it does not
" ſhew, it may give to underſtand what they, who can rather
" judge than admire, may expect to ſee performed in the cha-
" pel. Now I, who either by praiſe or abuſe have employed
" myſelf on the greater part of the merits and demerits of
" others, that I may not reduce to mere nothing my inſigni-
" ficancy, do pay you my reſpects ; nor ſhould I preſume thus

" far,

ardirei di farlo, se il mio nome accettato dalle orecchie di ciascun Principe, non havesse scemato pur' assai de l'indegnità sua. E ben' debbo io osservarvi con tal' riverenza, poi che il mondo ha molti Rè, & un' solo Michel-Agnolo. Gran' miracolo, che la natura, che non può locar si alto una cosa, che voi non la ritroviate con l'industrià, non sappia imprimere nelle opre sue la maestà, che tiene in se stessa l'immensa potentia del vostro stile, e del vostro scarpello : onde, chi vede voi, non si cura di non haver' visto Phidia, Apelle & Vitruvio, i cui spirti fur' l'ombra del vostro spirto. Ma io tengo felicità quella di Parrhasio, e de gli altri dipintori antichi, da poi che il tempo non ha consentito, che il far' loro sia visso fino al dì d'hoggi : cagione che noi, che pur' diamo credito a ciò, che ne trombeggiano le carte, sospendiamo il concedervi quella Palma, che chiamandovi unico Scultore, unico Pittore, & unico Architetto, vi darebbero essi, se fusser' posti nelTribunale degli occhi nostri.

Ma

" far, had not my name, which has reached the ear of every
" prince, greatly diminished its original unworthiness : and
" it becomes me to respect you very highly ; for, if there be
" many monarchs in the world, there is but one Michael An-
" gelo. What a wonder, that Nature cannot place anything
" at such a height but your skill can reach it, nor stamp on
" its works that majesty which resides in your chissel and bu-
" rin ! so that he who sees you is very easy about not having
" seen Phidias, Apelles, and Vitruvius, whose geniuses
" were only the shadow of yours. But I look upon it as a
" happy circumstance for Parrhasius, and the other painters of
" antiquity, that time has not allowed their works to be seen
" in our days ; and therefore, as I give credit to the records
" of the ancients, I must defer giving you that palm which
" they would confer on you, were they to judge with our
" eyes, declaring you the only sculptor, the only painter, and
" the only architect. But, it being so, why not content
" yourself

*Ma se così è, perche non contentarvi della gloria ac-
quistata fino à qui? A me pare, che vi dovesse bas-
tare d'haver' vinti gli altri con l'altre operationi;
ma io sento, che con il fine de l'Universo, che al presente dipignete, pensate di superare il principio del
mondo, che già dipigneste; acciò le vostre pitture
vinte dalle pitture istesse, vi dieno il triompho di voi
medesimo.*

*Hor' chi non ispaventarebbe nel porre il pennello à
così terribil' suggetto: io veggo in mezzo de le turbe
Antichristo con una sembianza sol' pensata da voi.
Veggo lo spavento nella fronte de i viventi: veggo i
cenni che di spegnersi fà il Sole, la Luna, e le stelle:
veggo quasi esalar' lo spirto al fuoco, a l'aria, a la
terra, & a l'acqua: veggo là in disparte la Natura
esterrefatta, sterilmente raccolta nella sua età decre-
pita: veggo il tempo asciutto, e tremante, che per
esser' giunto al suo termine, siede sopra un'tronco secco:*

e

" yourself with the glory you have already acquired?
" Ought you not to rest satisfied in having surpassed others in
" other performances? But I perceive you intend, that the
" End of the World, which you are at present painting, shall
" exceed its Beginning, which you have already painted, so
" that, your performances being outdone by themselves, you
" shew yourself superior to your ownself.

" Farther, who would not dread employing his pencil on
" such a tremendous subject? I see, amidst the multitude,
" Anti-christ with a visage which none but you could have
" imagined: I see the countenances of the living convulsed
" with terror: in the sun, moon, and stars, I see the symp-
" toms of approaching extinction: I see fire, air, and water,
" expire: I see effete Nature apart, her contracted posture
" the emblem of her decrepitude: I see Time, withered and
" trembling, sitting on a dry stump of a tree, as being come
" to its period: and while I perceive every one shuddering

" at

*e mentre sento dalle trombe de gli Angeli scuotere i
cuori di tutti i petti, veggo la vita, & la morte opresse
da spaventosa confusione ; perche quella s'affatica di
relevare i morti, e questa si provede di abattere i
vivi : veggo la speranza, e la disperatione, che gui-
dano le schiere de i buoni, e gli stuoli de i rei : veggo
il theatro delle nuvole colorite da i raggi che escano da
i puri fuochi del Cielo, su i quali frà le sue militie si
è posto a seder' Christo cinto di splendori, e di ter-
rori : veggo rifulgergli la faccia, e scintillando fiamme
di lume giocondo, e terribile, empie i ben' nati di alle-
grezza, & i mal' nati di paura. Intanto veggo i mi-
nistri de l'abisso, i quali con horrido aspetto, con gloria
de i Martiri, e de i Santi, scherniscono Cesare, e gli
Alessandri : che altro è l'haver' vinto se stesso, che il
mondo : veggo la Fama con le sue corone, e con le sue
palme sotto i piedi, gittata-là frà le ruote de i suoi
carri : in ultimo veggo uscir' dalla bocca del figlivol'
di Dio la gran' Sententia : io la veggo in forma di due
strali*

" at the clangor of the angels trumpets, I see Life and Death
" labouring with dreadful opposition : I see the former strain-
" ing every nerve to raise up the dead, and the latter no less
" eager in destroying the living : I see Hope conducting the
" band of the blessed, and Despair at the head of the guilty :
" I see the clouds fulgid with rays issuing from the heavenly
" fires, on which Christ sits environed with glories and terrors
" amidst his blessed hosts : I see his countenance, which,
" emitting corruscations of a benign and terrible light, fills
" the virtuous with joy, and the profligate with terror : in
" the mean time, I also see the ministers of the abyss with
" frightful countenances insulting such as Cæsar and Alexan-
" der, pointing to the glory of martyrs and saints ; to overcome
" one's self being quite a different thing from conquering the
" world : I see Fame with her crowns and palms trodden
" under foot, and she herself lying among the wheels of her
" shattered car : lastly, I see the final sentence issue from the
" divine

ftráli, uno di falute, e l'altro di damnatione; e nel vedergli volar' giufo, fento il furor' fuo urtare nella machina elementale; e con tremendi tuoni disfarla, e rifolverla: veggo i lumi del Paradifo, & le fornaci dello abiffo, che dividono le tenebre cadute fopra il volto de l'aere; talche il penfiero, che mi rapprefenta l'imagine della rovina del noviffimo die, mi dice: fe fi trema, e teme nel contemplar' l'opra bel Buonaruoti, come fi tremarà, e temerà, quando vedremo giudicarci da chi ci dee giudicare?

Ma crede la Signoria V. che il voto, che io ho fatto di non riveder più Roma, non fi habbia a rompere nella volontà di veder' cotale hiftoria? Io voglio più tofto far bugiarda la mia deliberatione, che ingiuriare la voftra virtù: la qual' prego, che habbia caro il defiderio ch'io ho di predicarlo.

Di Venetia, Il xv. bi Settembre 1537.

" divine mouth : I fee it like two arrows, one of falvation,
" the other of damnation; rapidly flying downwards in
" its vindictive wrath, darting on the elemental machine,
" and, with loud claps of thunder, ftriking creation to ruins :
" I fee the lights of paradife, and the furnaces of the abyfs,
" glaring amidft the palpable darknefs which involves the
" ethereal expanfe. So that the thoughts raifed in me by the
" imagery of the deftruction attending the laft day, intimate
" to me, " If thou feareft and trembleft thus whilft only
" beholding Buonaruoti's works, how will thou fhudder and
" fear when thou fhalt fee the Omnipotent Being himfelf fit
" in judgment ?"

" But do you think, fir, that, though I have made a vow
" never to fee Rome again, my ftrong defire of feeing fuch a
" picture will not break that vow ? Yes, fooner than thus
" affront your incomparable fkill, I will give the lye to my
" refolution ; and I beg your kind approbation of my defire
" to celebrate your talents.

" Venice, the 15th of Sepember, 1537."

• The paintings of Sixtus's chapel reminded me of the Salle Royale, which ferves as a diftribution to the chapel, and the apartments adjoining to Bernini's great ftair-cafe. The reafons of that appellation being given to this hall, are at Rome a riddle, folved only by the will or fancy of the pope who built it. But, from the paintings which are fpread all over it, an attentive eye is at no lofs to fee into thofe reafons : thefe paintings reprefent the feveral triumphs of the Roman church over its enemies, of whom crowned heads are made the majority.

SCULPTURE.—Sculpture has now little elfe to do at Rome befides copying antiques for foreigners ; and being flightly performed, no better are they paid. The laft pontificate was a bad time both for fculpture and painting. The real Mecænases of the fine arts are thofe, among the rich and great, who build and embellifh their houfes. The production of mafter-pieces depends not in the leaft on their knowledge and tafte : they are atchieved by the emulation which the great number of undertakings excites among artifts: this emulation had the like effect in Greece, and efpecially at Athens, where every petty citizen employed painters, fculptors, and engravers. In a word, to ufe the comparifon which Socrates applied to himfelf, builders are the *accoucheurs* * of the artifts ideas.

The greateft *accoucheurs* of this kind, which modern Rome has to boaft of, in the fixteenth century were Julius II. Leo X. Sixtus V. and in the laft, Urban VIII. and Alexander VII. All the great artifts of Italy, all the known mafter-pieces, belong to one or other of thefe pontificates.

* Men-midwives,

In

In the two laſt flouriſhed Bernini and Algardi *(q)*. The latter was under the former ; but, if
their talents are to be judged of by their works,
Algardi was ſuperior in many reſpects. His Attila
is perhaps the grandeſt piece that ſculpture ever
produced. Among all the wonders of St. Peter's
there are few or none which come up to it. In
the very eſſays of that artiſan you ſee nothing of
that ambiguity and tameneſs objected to thoſe left
by Bernini at Naples : for inſtance, that coloſſus
of a virgin in the Carthuſian monaſtery. The
latter, when his powers were at their height, never performed any thing more beautiful, or more
energetic, than the two figures of natural bigneſs,
at the altar-piece of Our Lady of the Victories *(r)*
in the *Thermæ Dioclefianæ* : he has taken the very
inſtant when a cherub lets fly an inflamed arrow at
St. Tereſa's heart. At the feet of the angel, who
is repreſented ſtanding, half naked, ſmiling, and
of a celeſtial beauty, lies the Carmelite nun in a
trance, ſtretched at full length upon the ground,
with her breaſt prodigiouſly raiſed, and in a ſort of
palpitation ; her eyes reverſed ; all the nerves and
fibres of her body under a contraction, which
appears in the diſorder of her features, of her
whole perſon, and the ſeveral parts of her drapery :
the impreſſion of the trance is ſhewn even in the
toe of the left foot, being extended out of the altar-piece. If Bernini took the model of this con-

(q) I looked for this maſter's name in *le Dictionnaire des Beaux Arts*, but could only find that of Aldegraef.

(r) This Madonna was brought from Germany, in the beginning of the laſt century, by a bare-footed Carmelite. To
this image, and their prayers to it, the Romans attribute every
advantage gained by the Chriſtians over the Turks, ever ſince
the battle of Lepanto, incluſive.

vulſion

vulfion from nature, his having hit on, and fixed
its rapidity, is the higheft pitch of art : if it be
the work of his ftrong imagination, it is not lefs
wonderful, that he fhould have fo perfectly reprefented the movements of thofe convulfions, the
fight of which was referved for the eighteenth century, or that he fhould fo well have filled up the
fketch drawn by Virgil in his picture of the Sybil :

Non vultus, non color unus,
Nec comptæ manfêre comæ ; fed pectus anhelum
Et rabie fera cordâ tument.

Nothing is more amazing than that fuch a piece
fhould ftand in fuch a place, the pannel of an altar.

In the Piazza Navona, a vault, faid to be the
very *fornix* where St. Agnes was expofed to the bru-
tality of the Pretorian foldiers, is now a little chapel,
the altar of which has no other ornament than an
image of the faint in femi-relievo, almoft as big as
life, and quite naked ; but her long treffes feem
accidentally to cover fome parts of a moft beautiful
body. Algardi has accompanied this critical fituation with an air of decency, pudicity, and fanctity,
perfectly fuitable to the figure, and the place
it ftands in.

The laft fculptor who did the moft bufinefs at
Rome, and has acquired a growing reputation, is
Peter le Gros, a native of France, who died at
Rome, 1719, aged fifty years. His fate was
like that of the famous Pouffin : the fame caufes,
that is, the fame jealoufies, the fame malignant
practices, induced both to leave their country,
and determined them to fettle at Rome, which
was fo wife as to avail itfelf of their country's
ingratitude.

S7.

St. Luke's Academy.—The kind of inactivity into which the fine arts are fallen at Rome, has made no alteration in the condition of St. Luke's academy, in which are cultivated the three daughters of Defign ; Painting, Sculpture, and Architecture. This academy was founded in the fixteenth century by Mutiano, an able mafter of the Roman fchool. In the laft century its reputation was raifed by Pietro de Cortona, and in the prefent it has received a confiderable encouragement in the prizes inftituted by Clement XI. for the pupils of the three arts.

On one fide of the church of St. Martin, which belongs to this academy, are feveral contiguous apartments for its fchools. The principal piece is a vaft hall, the fides of which are covered with the performances of academicians. In a clofet is kept Raphael's head, as taken out of his tomb feveral years after his death. Over this relique, on which the academy places a very great value, is cardinal Bembo's famous diftich :

Hic ille eft Raphaël, timuit quo fofpite vinci
Rerum magna parens, & moriente mori.

I don't know whether M. Rollin, or P. Bouhours, have ever brought this high-flown diftich to the teft : I am inclined to doubt whether it would have turned out to its advantage.

On the 18th of September I partook, jointly with all Rome, of the fpectacle exhibited by the academy, for the nineteenth diftribution of the prizes founded by Clement XI. ; a fpectacle performed with that grandeur and magnificence which the Roman genius ftill retains. The large hall in

Vol. II.   M   the

the Capitol was the scene of the exhibition : it was
hung all over with crimson damask and velvet,
edged with broad gold lace and fringes, and illuminated with lustres and branches: at one end
of it was a semi-circular *estrade*, or small theatre, in
the centre of which stood a chair of state, and over
it the portrait of the reigning pope under a canopy,
than which nothing could be richer ; over it a gallery ; all concurring to the general decoration of
the hall.   Facing the theatre were placed, likewise
in the form of a semi-circle, *fauteuils* for the cardinals ; and on the right and left two galleries,
one for the pretender, who at Rome is styled King
of England ; the other for embassadors and foreign
ministers.   Twenty cardinals, who honoured the
ceremony with their presence, having seated themselves, the *Arcadia*, or the society of the Arcadians,
took their places along the first seat of the theatre.
The academy of St. Luke, which was at the expence of the spectacle, filled the second.   Mon-
signor Carrara mounted the *rostrum* ; and immediately from the gallery was heard a symphony composed for the occasion, and executed
by the best instruments in Rome.   This was succeeded by an Italian oration delivered by M. Carrara, and which lasted about half an hour.   In it
the orator set forth the eminent services which the
fine arts have received from religion, and those
which the fine arts render to religion.   A fresh
symphony proclaimed the distribution of the prizes,
which are silver medals of different models, nine
for three classes in painting, and a like number
for sculpture and architecture.   On an Italian,
and especially a Roman, being called, the hall
rang

rang with fhouts, claps, &c. but a young Frenchman (M. Berton of Befançon) having been called
up for the firft prize of the firft clafs of fculpture,
thefe applaufes fubfided into a deep filence, which
afterwards rofe to a murmur. This filence animated all the foreigners who were at the ceremony,
and they loudly expreffed their pleafure at a Spaniard's obtaining the next prize. Two French
youths, and a young artift from Scotland, were
likewife crowned in different claffes. The diftribution of the prizes was performed by the cardinals,
from whom the conquerors came to receive them,
and who could not but be charmed with the condefcenfion, kindnefs, and commendations with which
their eminences accompanied this ceremony. After another fymphony, and in the midft of frefh ac-
clammations, the Arcadians read, in turns, fonnets, and fome other pieces compofed by them, in
honour of the fine arts and the victors ; for, all
over Italy, a *function*, a country wake, the feftival of a fraternity, a monk or nun's taking the habit, a thefis or any collegiate act, produces fonnets:
fuch a ceremony without a fonnet would be a *par-
tridge without orange.*

The emphafis with which thefe productions are
read, efpecially by their authors, was obferved to
the height in thofe which followed the diftribution
of the prizes. The fonnets amounted to twenty ;
and with them was intermixed a very poetical prediction on the viciffitudes of the Capitol, which
abbé Golt put in the mouth of Saturn ; and an ingenious dialogue by abbé Pezzi, between him and
the Marcus Aurelius in the Capitol, on the gran-

deur

deur of modern Rome. The dialogue ended in the following verſes :

Sè il Tarpeo di virtude é ſi fecondo,
Se i figli tuoi vantan ſi bel ardire,
Sempre, ô Roma, ſarai ſcuola del mondo.

Among the ſonnets I took notice of two, the thought of which ſeemed to me new, appoſite, and well expreſſed. In the former the anonymous author made a reply to theſe verſes of Virgil, *Excudent alii ſpirantia molliùs æra,* &c. and to the prediction contained in them, which not a little depreciates, the object of the feſtival. The author of the ſecond was Dr. Melani, who introduced Poetry complaining to Painting and Sculpture of the preſent diſparity of their fortune. This ſonnet bids fair to paſs the Alps.

Anch' io ſeggo ſublime in Campidoglio,
Pingo e ſcolpiſco anch' io. Se la poſſente
Cetra mi reco in man, fracco l'orgoglio
Del Tempo, e rendo al Di le forme ſpente.

Quel che voi fate, anch' io far poſſo e ſoglio ;
Mà creſce il mio valor. Del gran Clemente
Voi non potete, io ben potrò, ſe voglio,
Co' i carmi effigiar l'auguſta mente.

Noi ſiam ſorelle al par ben nate e oneſte ;
Mà chi ſù i marmi o ſulle tele ſuda,
Oltre l'onor, cibo ne tragge e veſte.

Per me viene ogni età ſempre più cruda,
Che io piena d'aura e d'armonia celeſte
Mi veggo in mezzo à voi povera e nuda.

STUDIES and LITERATURE.—Of all the cities in Europe it is at Rome alone that literature has conftantly met with aids, refources, encouragements, and objects of employment. Accordingly, it is the only one which can reckon an uninterrupted feries of celebrated *literati*. If this fucceffion be not equally fhining through all its periods, yet, even in the moft obfcure, Rome was ftill the depofitary of learning; and it is fhe from whom have always iffued the firft fcintillations, which have been productive of the moft fignal improvements.

Since the laft, in which Nicholas V. and his fucceffors had fo great a fhare, fcientific affiftances and refources have greatly increafed at Rome. Colleges, fchools, feminaries, public and private libraries, every thing concurs to infpire youth with a tafte for fcience and literature, and to facilitate the culture of the intellects.

Befides the Vatican library, which both for the ftores of learning in all kinds contained in it, and the manner of accommodating the public, may be looked on as the capital library in the univerfe, thofe of La Sapienza, the Propaganda, the Auguftinians, the Cazanate at the Minerva, &c. are open every day, morning and evening.

Cardinal Cazanate, the founder of the laft, has fhewed a munificence becoming a fovereign in the funds for its maintenance and its increafe; in the falaries of the librarians and their affiftants; and in founding two lecturefhips, in which eight doctors of different nations, that is, the choice of the whole Dominican order, daily declaim on St. Thomas's doctrine. The firft object which pre-

fents

fents itfelf to the eye on entering into this fpacious hall, and no lefs fplendid than fpacious,
is the ftatue of the founder inviting the lovers
of literature to make ufe of the helps which he
has provided for them. This ftatue is of white
marble, as big as life, and intirely worthy of Le
Gros the artift, who has improved the exact likenefs with an air of grandeur and benevolence,
dignity and affability.

The private libraries are lefs ufeful to the learned
in the quantity and choice of the books, than by
the eafinefs of admiffion, and politenefs of the librarians. Such are the Pamphili, Barberini,
Borghefe, Chigi, Altieri, Albani libraries, &c.

I ought to have reckoned, even among the public libraries, that of the Corfini palace, though
it be fo only *per la cortefia* of the noble proprietors.
It is open every day, and at every hour, under
the direction of meffieurs Bottari and Foggini,
who divide their attendance between that and the
Vatican. The refpectable age of the former ren-
ders him at Rome what Neftor was in the camp of
the Greeks. He is a great divine, of an exemplary piety, verfed in all learning the profound
and elegant, of fine judgment, and with all the
Florentine amenity ; fo that his converfation, his
informations, his advice, are equally efteemed by
the learned, the *literati*, the artifts, natives and
foreigners. The abbé Foggini, fo well known
to the learned world by his fine edition of the
Medicean Virgil, and the collection of the works
on the belief of the church of Rome concerning
Grace, is equally able, and equally ready, to ob-
lige thofe who ftand in need of his affiftance.

The

The head houfes of orders have generally valuable collections of books, and are very eafy of
accefs. I fhall mention only that of the fathers of
the oratory, which has produced the works of the
cardinals Baronius and Bona, thofe of father Ray-
naldi, &c. and in which are preferved all their ma-
terials and manufcripts. The librarian was about
publifhing the letters and different treatifes of cardinal Baronius. Among the latter I perufed one,
written with great folidity and force, infcribed to
Clement VIII. on the neceffity of granting the abfolution, which Henry IV. king of France had
long been foliciting. I was affured, that this treatife was what mainly determined the pope to make
an end of that great affair. I have forgot the
French embaffador's reafon in declining the dedi-
cation, for which the editor defired his permiffion.

About thirty years ago Rome had three cardinals particularly diftinguifhed for their opulence
in books; Davia, Gualterio, Imperiali : the firft
was always reading, and never wrote any thing;
the fecond was always writing, and never read;
and the third neither read nor wrote. His library now belongs to cardinal Spinelli, who, both
for the learned and himfelf, makes that ufe of
it which becomes a nobleman of his learning,
judgment, and communicative affability. This
valuable treafure is under the fuperintendency of
M. Simeoli, his theologian, and one of the firft
divines of the Roman communion.

In that of cardinal Paffionei, fo well known to
all Europe, were collected the beft, the fcarceft,
and the moft remarkable performances in all
kinds, and all languages ancient and modern, the

Jefuit writers excepted. Of thefe the cardinal would often boaft that he had not fo much as one. In forming this ineftimable library he had employed all intervals from bufinefs, his travels, his long ftay in all the parts of Europe, the intereft of his rank, and the connexions arifing from his poft as librarian to the Vatican, and fecretary of the briefs. He was his own librarian, and knew every book as perfectly as if they had not been above a hundred. His doing the honours of it himfelf was the more pleafing to the learned, as no body could better affift and enlarge their views.

One of Benedict the XIVth's chief diverfions was to put cardinal Paffionei *in furia*, by attacking him in what he moft valued himfelf on, his books. His palace and apartment overlooking that of the cardinal, put him in the way of enjoying that entertainment at pleafure.

His eminence had fome original anecdotes of letters written by the celebrated father Paul Sarpi's own hand. He took a delight in frequently quoting fcraps of thefe letters, as exciting a curiofity which he never could be prevailed on to gratify. He even could not be brought to it by folicitations and inftances, which the pope himfelf had made to him in the name of the learned procurator Fofcarini *(s)*. The pope, turning this refiftance to a double advantage, that is, obliging M. Fofcarini and teafing the cardinal, found means to convey out of his library that volume of which he was fo very chary, placing in its room another, the outfide of which was perfectly like it. On this fuccefs, the cardinal

(s) Since Doge of Venice.

being

being one day with him, he turned the converfation on Fra. Paölo and his letters. The cardinal,
as ufual, with great pleafure mentioned fome paffages, and the pope feemed to doubt of the reality:
Paffionei infifted, Benedict denied ; till at laft the
cardinal, wrought up to the heat which was intended, ftarted up, fhot away to his library, and
returned with the volume of letters in his hand,
but, to his aftonifhment, found it only a blank.
The torrent of his indignation bore down all decorum : he broke out into the moft violent invec-
tives and menaces, which the pope, after a while
indulging his humour, could fcarce put a ftop to
by very condefcending excufes, and returning him
the real volume. He daily received books from
all parts of Europe; and the contents of every
invoice, Giacomino, his librarian, ufed to lay
on a table appointed for that purpofe in the firft
room of his library. His firft bufinefs, on rifing,
was to look into thefe books, and put them up
in their proper places. In the height of Bufem-
baum's affair, the pope found means to convey a
copy of the Jefuit's work among the books which
the cardinal was to look into. On the fight of
this work, the cardinal

Improvifum afpris veluti qui fentibus anguem
Preffit humi nitens . . . .
Obftupuit, retròque pedem cum voce repreffit.

Being a little recovered from the tumult of
paffion, which fuch a hateful object had excited in
him, he rings, and calls his librarian : Giacomino
haftening to him, he orders him to open the window, and with all his force throws poor Bufem-
baum

baum down into Monte-Cavallo's fquare. In the midft of this tranfaction the pope appears, and gives him a very formal benediction. I have been told, that the cardinal anfwered this benediction with a gefture, which completed the diverfion the pope had promifed himfelf from this fcene.

The diftinguifhed manner, in which his eminence received madame du Boccage, his affiduous attendance on her, his eagernefs to bring her into the beft companies, had fet all Rome in a wonder. The Roman ladies were not a little piqued at feeing a French woman thus leading in triumph, one who never had fhewn them the leaft regard, and who, in no very obliging manner, roundly made known to them the reafon of fuch a preference. The pope did not fail of availing himfelf of this metamorphofis : when the cardinal went out in a coach with madame du Boccage, he took care to be at his window, and give them a double benediction, faying he had even declared himfelf the cardinal's rival, pretending to be as good a judge of the lady's merit as himfelf. The eagernefs with which thefe two octogenarians vied with each other in this intercourfe, rendered it fomething more than entertaining to the charming object of it, who, both in the regard fhewn to her every where, and in the prefents fhe received from the pope at her departure, was treated as a princefs. The cardinal has more than once faid to me in our airings in St. Peter's area, " Here madame du " Boccage and I have often taken an airing toge-" ther ; I was her fquire. All thefe fcoundrels " faid that I was in love with her ; and indeed they " faid no more than what was true : but it was
" not

" not the beauty and attractives of the fex which I
" loved in her ; no, it was the amiable qualities of
" her nation, heightened by a noble affemblage of
" various learning and exquifite talents."

With a greater compafs of learning, a longer
ftay at Rome might have given me a confiderable
infight into the prefent ftate of the fciences and
literature in this city. I inquired after fome circumftances of the author of *Ricciardetto*'s life; the
laft epic poem that Italy has produced, and wherein is revived all that natural turn and fprightlinefs, which procured fuch reputation to the *Mor-
gante*, the *Furiofo*, and other Italian mafter-pieces
of that kind. I very innocently met with an opportunity of being convinced, that the poet had
taken the originals of moft of the characters in his
poem from nature, and from perfons known to him.
The capital of them all is, according to the liberty
taken by the Italians, not the hero whofe name the
poem bears, but one *Ferrau*, or *Ferragus*, a giant,
whofe character is a ftrange but natural medley,
with all the good and bad qualities common to one
of ftrong paffions, and a ftranger to the yoke of
education. Being full of this character, as we
read the book every night, it came into my head
one day to afk a perfon of the firft rank in Rome
who the original of *Ferrau* might be: " Fie! fir,"
anfwered he fupercilioufly, " fie! mere ftuff and
" trafh." On that very day I happened to hear
that this perfonage was himfelf the original, which
I had been inquiring after.

The author of this poem, MonfignorFortinguerra,
has concealed his name under the Greek difguife
of *Carteromaco*. He had gradually rifen to the
upper

upper prelacy. His poem, which, after taking him up a long time, undoubtedly fhortened his life, would have raifed him to the purple in the age when the Bembos, the La Cafas, the Bibienas, obtained it by the florid fhrubberies of an entertaining literature; but different times, different cuftoms. Clement XI. was very fond of M. Fortinguerra; and, as he made him the companion of his chearful intervals, had contributed to his promotion. Clement XII. found him engaged in his *Ricciardetto*, urged him to continue it, and gave him expectations of the purple: however, he failed of it in a promotion, at which it had been formerly promifed him. The pope excufed himfelf, but with the ftrongeft affurances of his fucceeding in the next: ftill he met with a fecond difappointment; and this neglect throwing him into defpair, he gave himfelf up to vexation, fo that a lingering difeafe, its confequence, carried him to the grave. When he was very near it, the pope fent one of his chamberlains with a compliment to encourage him, and with a firm promife of granting him this long-wifhed-for purple. At this promife, the fick perfon turning about, and lifting up the fheet which covered him, made an explofion like that of Horace's *truncus ficulnus*, and faid to the meffenger, *Eccovi la rifpofta : bon viaggio e per lei e per mi.** After M. Fortinguerra had begun his *Ricciardetto* he ufed to carry it about with him, and all places were alike for his working at it. In vifits, which run away with a great part of a prelate's time, and in the various *functions*

* " That's your anfwer; there will foon be an end to us " both."

which

which take up the remainder, he would be drawing up a battle, a nocturnal meeting, or be describing a noon, a dawn, and all thofe vague pieces which form the *borra* of Italian poems. Could he have imagined that cardinal Lambertini was to have fucceeded Clement XII. that hope would have fupported him, as, from a friendfhip founded on a conformity of temper, difpofition and talents, and cemented by a familiar acquaintance, there was nothing which he might not have expected.

Italy always had, and Rome ftill has, *improvifatori*; that is, poets, who, like Alexander's Cherilus, compofe and repeat two or three hundred extempore verfes on any fubject; a talent, which however is not fo much to the praife of thofe who pride themfelves in it, as of the language which is fo copious and verfatile as to anfwer all the varieties of fuch a knack, which Cicero has termed *audax negotium & impudens*. There is reafon to hope, that the prefent prevalence of a juft tafte, and a fpirit of confiftence in the republic of letters, will at length profcribe the frivoloufnefs of thefe *improvifatori*, which too much abounds in moft literary differtations of Italian growth; and that thefe differtations will keep to what they promife to treat of, and for the future not fo eafily admit common-place, parade of fcience, and things trite and vulgar.

Latinity at Rome fhines in all its ancient luftre. The *Coriphæi* in this kind are M. Buonamici, whofe Latin hiftory of the two laft Italian wars is known to every body; Monfignor Giacomelli, the author of two or three excellent pieces worthy of the age

of the Bembos and Sadolets; father Serrai, of the
oratory of St. Jerome, &c. At my leaving Rome,
I was favoured with the firft copy of the Life of
the Illuftrious Gravina, which the latter was publifhing. The Latinity of this Life does honour to
the literary hero whom it celebrates.

Natural hiftory has long been cultivated in
Italy, where the learned Aldrovandus opened a
fchool to which Europe owes its firft inclination to
phyfical inquiries.

Rome was the centre of feveral of thofe branches
of fcience, which Italy communicated to the
reft of Europe. There is now a complaint, that
fome communities, who are particularly invefted
with the education of youth, feem not fo much to
mind training them to the fciences and literature,
as to infinuate themfelves into their good opinion
and efteem, and inftil into them a blind devotednefs to their mafters; in a word, to hood-wink parents from feeing the errors of this futile education,
and miflead them in their ideas of their children's
progrefs, by acting plays, which only exercife
the memory, without inftructing the mind, or
mending the heart.

I happened to be at the acts of the profeffors of
the Roman college, on opening their claffes in
1758. The rhetorician made a Latin fpeech in
profe, and then proceeded to a declamation, in
Alexandrine verfes, againft fonnet-makers and
poets, who conceit themfelves Horaces and Vir-
gils, without any previous trial of genius, or fund
of literature. The logician, after a long dif-
courfe, in bad profe, on the intenfe labour which
philofophy requires, on the diforders, and particularly

cularly the head-achs, occafioned by fuch labour, repeated a long poem, in hexameters and pentameters, on the remedy of thofe diforders; that is, coffee, and the beft way of making it: above fifty of the pentameters ended in the word *Cibus* in all its cafes, plural and fingular, which form an iambic. The jejunenefs of this compofition, with the poet's fnuffling monotony, were more than I could ftand, fo that I took myfelf away.

Cardinal Cavalchini, whom his devotednefs to the directors of this college, has put by the *tiara*, had two nephews there, in one of the upper forms. One day it came into his mind to examine them about literature and religion *(t)*; and he found them both fo very ignorant, that, to the great furprife of all Rome, he fent them away to the univerfity of Turin. A very fignal, but fruitlefs fatisfaction, was given to him in difmiffing from the college father Carraffa, his nephews immediate preceptor.

POPULATION and TRADE.—Rome in circumference is not lefs than three French leagues : it contains three hundred and fixty-feven churches, convents, chapels, &c. Of thefe are feventy-five parochial, eleven having chapters, a hundred convents of men, in fome of which are no lefs than three hundred religious, forty-fix nunneries, eleven confervatories, twenty-eight hofpitals, twenty-four colleges, and the remainder chapels, either belonging to fraternities, or for fome particular devotion. If to fuch as live in thefe places, or who officiate at them, you add the ecclefiaftics depending on the pope, the *caftrati*, the numerous retinue of the

(t) This happened fince Clement the XIIIth's exaltation.

court, of the cardinals and prelates; you at once conceive how Rome is peopled; the total of its inhabitants being only about a hundred and twenty, or a hundred and fifty thoufand fouls.

This number is kept up, not by the children born there, but by Italians, and people of all nations, flocking thither; of whom not a few fettle, on account of the many helps and conveniencies the place affords to lazinefs. Thefe reliefs cannot be fuppofed very inviting to thofe *quibus eft domus, & pater, & res*; fo that, in this refpect, it is as if Romulus's afylum ftill continued open.

Rome has fome manufactures, but which do not anfwer for exportation: the filken material of thefe manufactures is generally but bad; and the ftuffs made of it, though neither fightly nor ferviceable, are as dear as the beft and the moft beautiful of foreign manufactures. This exorbitant price is chiefly owing to the long credit which the Roman tradefmen are obliged to give, the *buona mancias* and the prefents required of them by the domeftics of the houfes which they ferve.

The only articles which Rome exports are artificial fiowers, pomatums, gloves, &c. but thefe conftitute a trade of great profit.

It has feveral confiderable houfes for banking, and bills of exchange; and the nature of the money affairs, which Rome deals in, puts it in their power to keep the courfe of exchange very high.

Holland and Swifferland fupply it with linen; England, with cloth: all it takes from France is the ftuffs of Mans: this is the only article of trade in this country, of which the Englifh have not yet been able to deprive the French.

JOURNEY TO NAPLES

BY MONT CASSINO.

WE set out from Rome for Naples in the beginning of October. There are two parallel roads leading to it : that by Veletri and Terracina is the most frequented ; the other goes through Cignani and near Mont Caffino, which we were for seeing: both are equally a destruction to carriages ; and they who ride post have frequent occasion to remember Horace's *minùs est gravis Appia tardis.* We followed his counsel, and put ourselves in the hands of the *procaccio*, who at a settled rate carries you in a *vis-à-vis* to Naples, provides your meals, and defrays all other customary expences ; but at your journey's end you find yourself sufficiently *laffatus, fed non fatiatus.*

We took Mont Caffino road, making part of a caravan of five or six such carriages. This way runs along the country of the ancient Hernici, which now separates the Campania of Rome from the kingdom of Naples.

ANAGNI.

Anagni was one of the most confiderable towns of this rocky country ; and Virgil has faid of it, *Hernica faxa colunt quos dives Anagnia pafcit*.* How this town, fince its inhabitants delivered up their countryman Boniface VIII. to the French and Sciara Colonna, is fallen from fuch an epithet (if it ever was worthy of it) is well known. The curfe which that pope thundered out againft it for

* Æn. L. vii.

fuch an injury, ftill purfues it, though the Anag-
nians procured a formal repeal of it by Clement VII. It is a general notion through Italy,
that in this place and its territory, fince that male-
diction, fo far from having the plenteous crops of
their neighbours, their profits do not anfwer their
charges and labour.

At the foot of the mountain on whofe fummit
ftands the town, our *procaccio* had prepared a
dinner for us, fuch as Boniface might have ordered
for the accurfed objects of his refentment. I perfuaded my fellow travellers, moftly French, to
go up to the town, and take our chance of faring
no better, and at our own expence. After an
afcent of an hour through very fine olive planta-
tions, we reached the town. The appearance
immediately confirmed the difadvantageous accounts we had heard of it. No fhelter for us but
a frightful cabaret, where fome goats livers, lights,
&c. were cooking for half-naked ill-looking vin-
tagers, who came in fucceffively, and fat down, in
clubs of four or five, at a great table without any
table-cloth. Of this table, and two forms along
the fides, confifted all the furniture of this delightful receptacle : they were as old as Boniface VIII.
and the naftinefs of them was of a piece with their
ancientnefs. We fat down however, heartily lamenting the *proccacio*'s dinner. The jargon which
our meffmates fpoke, being fo unintelligible as not
to admit of any talk with them, deprived us of
the only amends we could expect.

The people whom we afterwards faw in the
ftreets, gave us to underftand that we had the
honour of dining with the heads of the place :

yet

yet has it a bifhop ; and the cathedral and palace were both rebuilding, indeed in a tafte quite anfwerable to the condition of the fee. The cathedral piazza is a platform of earth, from whence one has a fight, as far as the eye can reach, of the feveral countries fouth of Anagni (u). The view of fuch a rich and variegated landfcape was fome comfort to us under our difafter, reminding us, that in the phyfical as in the moral world, even the worft fituations are not without fome bright fide to a reflective mind.

From Anagni, ftill fkirting the *Saxa Hernica*, we went along the foot of the mountain, on which is fituated Ferentino, the conqueft of which fignalifed the reign of Servius Tullius. We lay that night at Frufinone, the capital of the Campania of Rome. Neither this road, nor the town, afford a fingle monument of antiquity. The walls of the houfes are only heaps of rubbifh and pebbles, of a prodigious thicknefs, with two low narrow voids for a door and a window to each apartment : a manner of building, which, though it be a comfortable fence againft the exceffive heats, makes the rooms extremely damp, and gives them the appearance of vaults.

It was then vintage-time at Frufinone. They brought the grapes in bafkets and hampers ; and having crufhed them with their feet in a kind of

(u) It gives you a fight of the *rudera* of Fumone caftle, where Boniface VIII. confined his predeceffor Celeftin V. after compelling him to abdicate the papacy : but Boniface VIII. himfelf, when delivered up to the revenge of the French and the Colonnas, muft, on feeing that caftle, have been reminded of the fcriptural maxim, " With what meafure " ye mete, it fhall be meted to you."

bathing-tubs, they tumbled the wine into large coppers, where it boiled very violently. Thefe coppers were fet up in the very ftreet, at the door of every houfe, the brick work joining with the wall. This mirthful fcene, befides exhibiting in reality the vintages as defcribed by the authors, or reprefented by the artifts, of antiquity, was a fight which we had not yet met with in any part of Italy. All this work was done only by the men. At our arrival we had met a whole tribe of girls and women carrying home water, from a little ftream at the foot of the eminence on which Frufinone ftands. In the attitude of thefe women, the fhape of the veffels which they carried on their head, and fome refting in their way up the hill, we faw the originals of thofe fcenes, with which the learned Pouffin was fo fond of enlivening his landfcapes.

The next day's journey carried us through a country moft delightfully watered, through rich paftures and grounds abounding in variety of exquifite products; yet this fo delicious country wants inhabitants and hufbandmen. Here anciently ended Latium, and here began the populous and martial nation of the Samnites; now here end the papal dominions, and here the kingdom of Naples begins.

After croffing the Garigliano, which is enlarged by feveral ftreams running into it through the above-mentioned country, we paffed clofe by the ruins of Aquino, famous as the birth-place of the angelic doctor who adopted its name. Of this place, which ftill bears the title of County and Bifhoprick, all that remains is a mill on the fide of of a brook, which skirts the ruins of the city. The statelinefs and extent of the ruins are a melancholy proof of its former largenefs and fplendor, and imprefs on a reflective mind all the fentiments which it feels at the fight of a corpfe : *Hem ! nos homunculi indignamur fi quis noftrûm interiit, quorum vita brevior effe debet, cùm tot oppidorum cadavera proftrata jaceant ! Vifne tu te cohibere, & meminiffe hominem te effe natum ?**

This city, as I was informed, owes its ruin, and the emigration of its inhabitants, 1. to its being a thoroughfare for the troops in all the expeditions againft the kingdom of Naples; 2. to the diforders committed by thofe troops in a place defencelefs of itfelf, and deftitute of fuccors from thofe who defended the kingdom, on account of its being a very difadvantageous poft; 3. to the nearnefs of St. Germano, which, being under the aufpices, and defended by the money, of the Benedictins, has drawn within its circuit fuch of the inhabitants of Aquino, Cafino, and other neighbouring places, who were not difpofed to feek a more diftant retreat from the calamities of war.

C A S I N O.

In approaching St. Germano we paffed clofe by the fpot on which ftood the town of Cafino, the former magnificence of which is ftill feen in three monuments. 1. An amphi-theatre the moft intire of any edifice of that kind: the entrance into it was through five doors, ftill ftanding except one ; and the ruins of this, by the vaft blocks of which it was made, and the careful conftruction of the

* Sulpit. Epift. ad Cic.

N 3

sides, shew the grandeur of the edifice to which they belonged. The proportion of these doors is twenty-four king's feet to twelve. Time has spared the network veneering with which the whole circumference is covered; as likewise a projecting range of stones, forming, at about two thirds of its height, a kind of dentilated frieze : these stones, being all perforated perpendicularly, were undoubtedly intended for the lower end of the poles or rafters ; the upper ends of which, reaching beyond the body of the edifice, were to support, by means of transversal ropes, the canvas which sheltered the spectators. This amphi-theatre is at the hill's foot, and seems to have stood in the centre of the city. It is exactly round ; its height fifty feet, the diameter thirty.

2. A theatre, with only the scene remaining, and that leaning against the very side of the mountain, in a semi-circular form of two hundred and sixty feet diameter.

3. An ancient temple, with all its parts in good preservation. This temple stands on the brow of the hill, in the form of a Latin crofs ; which might bring a doubt on its antiquity, were it not evidenced from its being built without lime or cement. It is now a chapel to a hermitage.

On a level in an interval of the mountain stood Varro's country house and gardens. Cicero, reproaching Antony for profaning these places with his debaucheries, has these words: *Studiorum suorum M. Varro illud voluit diversorium. Quæ in illâ villâ dicebantur ! Quæ cogitabantur ! Quæ literis mandabantur ! Jura P. R. monumenta majorum, omnis sapientiæ ratio, omnisque doctrina*.

* Philipp. ii.

Of

Of all that immenfe erudition nothing has reached us but Varro's Treatife on Agriculture, which he compofed at the extremity of his advanced age. The beft fituation for a farm, which he there delineates from Cato, is exactly that of his country houfe near Cafino : *Optimus ager eft qui fub radice montis fitus fpectat ad meridiem.* This treatife is not a collection of Varro's leffons to cultivators, but an account of the feveral methods and proceedings of farmers for making the moft of different foils, and turning the feveral parts of hufbandry to the beft advantage.

Varro undoubtedly had truth on his fide, in faying that no part of the world was in his time fo well cultivated as Italy ; *nullam quæ tam tota fit culta.* Things are fadly altered. To mention only a diftrict, the cultivation of which Varro was the moft able to judge of ; that admirable fpot which we had paffed over from Frufinone, is fcarce tilled ; and particularly that, where Varro's own farm ftood, is partly forfaken.

The whole of this tract indeed is not eafy to cultivate ; the fatnefs of the foil makes it very difficult to manage ; fo that, to bring it into heart again, it fhould be divided into farms, and not worked, as it is, by a few ploughmen, who, living in the fmall towns above the plain, are at too a great a diftance from their work.

We faw thefe ploughmen at their bufinefs : their ploughs, which have only a fhare without wheels or fore part, are drawn by four, five, or fix pair of oxen *(v)*,

(v) When two pair are fufficient, they yoke them in front. Thefe oxen do not belong to the ploughmen, they only hiring them as wanted. N 4 oxen, with only one man, who ftands upright on a little ftool fitted to the head of the fhare, with his weight helps the action of the coulter, and finging or playing on a pipe, ftill keeps this poft, even on returning to a frefh furrow. By this odd procedure, where the field is inclofed by a ditch, a hedge, or bufhes, as much ground is loft, all along the circumference, as the file of oxen take up; a trifling lofs indeed in fuch a defert country, but which, in thofe that are well inhabited, and where ground is more valuable, would occafion a multitude of endlefs law-fuits.

MONT CASSINO.

This fpot, where we were furprifed to fee people fowing linfeed (in October) is a part of the immenfe eftates belonging to the abbey of Mont Caffino. St. Benedict founded this abbey in 525; or, in other words, that faint, attended by two difciples, and preceded by two angels, with three ravens, behind him, came and fettled in an hermitage, at that time poffeffed by a good anchoret, whom he perfuaded to give it up to him. Though this was in the fixth century, and at the gates of Rome, part of the town of Caffino was ftill idolatrous, worfhipping an Apollo who had a famous temple on the hill where now ftands the abbey. St. Benedict threw down the idol, demolifhed the temple, replacing it with the convent, converted the idolaters, and preached to the Chriftians, whom their bifhop had forfaken, and died lord temporal and fpiritual of the country and its inhabitants. All this was done at the time when Italy, a prey to barbarians, was fubject to

the

the Goths, to Theodat, to Vitiges, and Totila. Mont Caſſino was deſtroyed in 589 by the Lombards, rebuilt in 660, pillaged in 884 by the Saracens, but found means to improve its private misfortunes and the general deſolation into an enlargement of its poſſeſſions and increaſe of its opulence: *crevit ruinis.* This appears from its chronicles, and from the hiſtory which had been compoſed from thoſe vouchers.

The popes heaped immunities on it ; and, by an unparalleled privilege, its abbots, in 1326, obtained the title of Biſhops, and performed all paſtoral functions, till in 1367 Urban V. was obliged, for the good of the houſe, to reſtore things to their original footing.

Urban II. had, by a bull of 1092, conferred on the abbey the title of *Caput omnium Monaſteriorum, quia ex eodem loco, de Benedicti pectore monaſtici ordinis veneranda religio, quaſi de Paradiſi fonte manavit.*

The abbot, at preſent a regular, and whoſe dignity is only triennial, in all inſtruments ſtyles himſelf Patriarch of the Holy Religion, Abbot of the Sacred Monaſtery of Caſſino, Chancellor and Premier Chaplain of the Roman Empire, Abbot of the Abbots, Chief of the Benedictin Hierarchy, Chancellor and Collateral of the Kingdom of Sicily, Count and Governor of Campania, of the Terra de Labrador, and the Maritime Province, Prince of Peace.

The perſon of the preſent abbot, to whom we were introduced on our arrival at St. Germano, has nothing of the faſtuouſneſs of ſuch titles, being a young man of a noble, mild, and engaging countenance, heightened by a candour more common

in a novice than an abbot, and an eafy and natural politenefs.   I was recommended to Don Pepe,
one of the procurators general of the houfe by
his brother, procurator general to the order of
Malta in Sicily.   Don Pepe fhewed the greateft
regard to this recommendation, giving me at the
fame time to underftand, that he never heard from
his family but by fuch recommendations ; that he
had no knowledge of it, nor had he ever known
it, having, from the age of ten years, no other
father, no other relation, no other guardian and
benefactor, than St. Benedict ; and that this was
the cafe of far the greater part of the perfons of
birth, who wore the Benedictin habit.

I faid that we faw the abbot at St. Germano, a
fmall town of about four thoufand inhabitants,
infenfibly formed at the foot of Mont Caffino, out
of the ruins of neighbouring places.   Here the
abbot refides, with part of his officers, in a houfe
large enough to receive all paffengers, from the
pope to the beggar; and every one is treated according to his rank or recommendations.   The
abbot daily vifits all the guefts, who fometimes
amount to two or three hundred.   Such an exercife of hofpitality was the beft contrivance imagi-
nable, for reconciling envy with St. Benedict's immenfe riches.

The day after our arrival, we fet out for Mont
Caffino, but firft waited on the abbot to receive his
commands : he defired us to defer our journey till
the afternoon, apprehending that we fhould fare
but difagreeably in a houfe where they live only on
herbs and pulfe dreffed with oil.   Seeing us determined to ftand this meager dinner, that our jaunt
might be the eafier, he informed us where we
                                                    fhould

ſhould meet with muletiers, who, having ſtables on the top and at the foot of the hill, carry and bring back the pilgrims, and who, depending upon their word, never fail immediately returning from one ſtable to the other, when their departures exceed the returns.

We could not but be charmed with the abbot's courteouſneſs ; however, being in ſight of the monaſtery, which ſeemed at no great diſtance, and encouraged by the freſhneſs of the air and beauty of the ſky, we ſet out on foot. The ſteepneſs of the mountain is ſomething abated by a well-paved zig-zag road, which, in the plan and execution, is very like the preſent road from France into Alſace over Saverne hill.

We had been climbing a full hour ; yet Mont Caſſino appeared to be further off ; and the heat of the ſun, now aſcending the horizon, was increaſed by the reflexion of the immenſe rock which we were ſkirting. We began to repent of our undertaking, when we perceived a muletier upon his return : we would fain have perſuaded him to go back to Mont Caſſino ; but he went on.

At length we came to a place of the mountain, where, in the bare rock, is a cavity ſaid to be the impreſſion of one of St. Benedict's knees, when, proſtrating himſelf in this place, he called on God for ſtrength to deſtroy Apollo's temple, and overthrow the idol *(w)*. The heat made us ſo faint

(w) We had already ſeen, lower down, ſuch a cavity, ſaid to be the impreſſion of a mule's thigh, which the devil cauſed to fall under St. Benedict. The ſcrapings of the edges of this impreſſion were held by the country people to be an approved febrifuge.

that

that we began to be out of hopes, when we were overtaken by a muletier, who was returning upwards. This man very readily allowed us to get upon his beaft in turns; and this, at laft, brought us to Mont Caffino, after two hours continual walking in a bath of fweat, and quite foundered with hunger and wearinefs.

The entrance is through a long dark arched place, like a vault ; and this is all that remains of the original houfe built by St. Benedict : it indeed little fuits fuch a houfe, but may be of great ufe in cafe of a fudden attack. The other buildings, which ftand on a continued counterfcarp of eighteen feet elevation, have only a fcalade to fear. Thefe buildings outwardly form a vaft oblong fquare, of feveral ftories diftinguifhed in an elegant manner ; the whole crowned by a grand cornice fupporting the roof. The infide is divided into numberlefs courts, porticos, and colonades, fuited to the offices, wants, and conveniences, of a community which is always very numerous.

On our entrance, chance threw us into the bake-houfe, where they were drawing a prodigious quantity of fmall oil-cakes, in themfelves not over good ; but we, being very fharp fet, thought them admirable. As we were regaling ourfelves with the monaftical paftry, we made ufe of the conveniency of the place for drying our clothes. One of the bakers kindly lent us a hand, fmiling, and faying from time to time, *Ah ! Francefi !*

In going to the church we croffed three courts : in the middle of the two firft are two *fruftums* of columns ; one of granite, the other of exceeding fine porphyry: they are nine feet in circumference ;
. which

which fpeaks the height of thefe columns when intire, the grandeur of the edifice for the decoration of which they were brought hither, and the difficulty of bringing them to fuch a height.

You afcend from one court to the other by ftairs, the difpofition and ornaments of which fhow equal judgment, delicacy, and magnificence. The third, by way of excellence called *Paradife*, is fronted, all along its breadth, with a ftair-cafe of forty fteps, and two large marble ftatues on it, reprefenting St. Benedict and St. Scholaftica. It is crowned with a periftyle of granite pillars ; and this is terminated by a fplendid baluftrade, on the mafonry work of which ftand four antique bufts. This periftyle ferves as a front to a portico ftill more brilliant, forming the church's lobby, and refting on twenty columns moft of oriental granite. Under this grand portico are difpofed feventeen marble ftatues, as big as life, with this infcription :

HEROIBUS BENE MERENTIBUS

CASINATES

PROPRIAE PIETATIS ARGUMENTUM

MONIMENTUM ALIENÆ.

MDCXLVI.

The firft rank of this auguft affembly confifts of eight popes, moft of the order of St. Benedict ; St. Gregory leading, and Benedict XIV. clofing the file. Next appear fix fovereigns, of whom the firft is Charlemagne, and the laft Don Carlos king of Naples, and now king of Spain ; but the workmanfhip of this ftatue does no great

honour

honour to the subject of it. St. Benedict's father and mother, and the first benefactor to Mont Cassino, complete the group; among which the statues of St. Gregory and St. Henry, by the ce-lebrated Le Gros, are eminently diltinguished.

In one of the inward corners of the portico stands an ancient column of transparent alabaster, cut spiral-wise; its height six feet, and surmounted with a crofs. A similar pillar is likewise one of the ornaments of the Vatican library.

The inside of the church eclipses all the splen-dor and richnefs bestowed on the avenues. It is an assemblage of the finest performances in paint-ing, marble, and metals, without the least void for the eye to rest on. The paintings, which re-present the miracles and visions of St. Benedict and his primitive disciples, are for the most part by Lanfranc, Luca Giordano, Muro, Solimene, and Conca. The architecture is not so much in the Roman as the Neapolitan taste, too profuse of ornaments; a profusion more especially appa-rent in the columns along the insides of the arcades of the nave; which makes this superb edifice look more like a theatre than a temple.

This edifice, after being successively destroyed by the Lombards and the Saracens, and totally overthrown by an earthquake in 1349, under-went the same disaster in the sixteenth century. Till that time it had been in the form of the Ro-man basilics; that is, the whole fore part of it, as far as the sanctuary, was a nave with two colla-terals, supported and separated by a double row of columns. These were the beautiful columns

of

of oriental granite, which the architect has difpofed under the arcade in the nave of the new church, which was begun in the year 1649.

The altar, done from defigns of Michael Angelo, exhibits the moft exquifite marbles, moft of them antique. At the foot of the altar is the tomb of St. Benedict and St. Scholaftica, which is alfo fhewn in France, in the abbey of St. Benoit fur Loire. The two ends of the crofs, in the centre of which ftands the altar, are filled with two monuments, one of Peter de Medicis, brother to Leo X. the other of captain Ferramofca; in both which, the execution, and the grandeur and majefty of the defign, are equally admired.

The choir, a great part of which was painted by Solimene, and its ftalls of the moft delicate fculpture, take up the lower end of the church. The ftately organ-loft is loaded, as it were, with figures and decorations, all over gilt with gold.

Going out of the church, we could not but take notice of the doors: they are covered with compartments of bronze, containing, in filver letters, an enumeration of the fiefs, eftates, and dependences, belonging to Mont Caffino. Thefe immenfe poffeffions lie chiefly in the territories of Naples and the Two Sicilies. The lordfhips are always in the hands of the fovereign, to whom the abbey furnifhes, what is called in France, *homme vivant et meurent*; with this difference, that a man is reprefented by a whole family, the perpetuity of which, how long foever it lafts, excludes all change and right of relief. The laft living and dying family failed in the reign

reign of Don Carlos, the prefent king of Spain. It is in acknowledgment of the indulgence fhewn to Mont Caffino, on that occafion, that his ftatue in the lobby of the church was erected. To reprefent the *living and dying man*, he accepted of a woman, who had twelve fons married, and heads of families. This woman was ftill living in 1758, with the title of St. Benedict's Mother ; and by a very fpecial favour, fhe was allowed admiffion into the monaftery of Mont Caffino.

The facrifty, for ornaments, vies with the church to which it is contiguous. Thefe confift in ftatues, paintings, and baffo relievos, all worthy of, and fuitable to, the place. The like ornaments adorn the chapter; and indeed every clauftral piece.

No where have I feen the records fo fplendidly lodged, and fo well kept, as thofe of Mont Caffino. They take up three large rooms ornamented with paintings and other curiofities. Among the paintings are St. Peter and St. Paul, by a Greek artift, who flourifhed in the ninth century ; and an original picture of Dante. Among the antiques we obferved a Grecian-marble clofe-ftool, of the moft exquifite figure, in fine prefervation, and all its projectures adorned with flourifhes, the whole in fuch a tafte, and fuch delicacy of workmanfhip, that I could not believe it had been made, as we were told, for the ufe of the houfe, at a time when baths were more ufual than at prefent. The two utenfils of this kind at Rome, in the convent of St. John de Lateran, have no other likenefs to this than in the general figure : on comparing the defign and execution, thofe of Rome feem to have been for

the

the ufe of the populace; and that at Mont Caffino, for fome prince, no lefs magnificent than curious in the choice of whatever was for his perfonal ufe.

In all thefe records, every thing is diftributed with fuch judgment and precifion, that there is not a document, a claim, a voucher, nor the leaft paper, which is not ready at hand. The keeper of the records bears the title of Apoftolical Pro-thonotary; and any briefs, or warrants from him, are received as authentic in all the courts of Rome and the Two Sicilies. He has a fmall li-brary for his own private ufe, in which are fome books, printed when that art was in its infancy. I obferved, among others, the *Rationale Divinorum Officiorum*, publifhed *per Johannem Fuft, civem Mo-guntinum, & Petrum Gernzheim, clericum diæcefis ejufdem, anno millefimo quadringentefimo quinqua-gefimo nono, fexto die Octobris.*

We concluded our view of the houfe with St. Benedict's library and tower. As to the library, it would little become me to fpeak of it after father Mabillon's account (x). The tower is over the firft entrance. It was from this tower that St. Benedict faw the foul of St. Germain bi-fhop of Capua, and that of St. Scholaftica, flying to heaven in a fiery whirlwind: here likewife was his cell, in which he died. Time and the barba-rians having fpared this tower, it has fince been connected with the body of the edifice : no traces

(x) I fhall only take notice, that the *Defenfor*, which the learned Benedictin places at the head of the *Inedita* of this library, has been printed fix times between 1544 and 1560. *Iter Italic.* pag. 123.

of its original form remain, except in the infide of St. Benedict's apartment.

This apartment confifts of three rooms, one converted into a chapel, but crowded with fmall paintings by the beft mafters ancient and modern. I have already obferved, in the article of Rome, fpeaking of the chambers where St. Philip Neri, St. Ignatius, St. Staniflaus Kofka, breathed their laft, that it is cuftomary in Italy to embellifh, with fuch valuable pieces, the places where cano-nifed faints expired. To give fome idea of St. Benedict's collection, it is fufficient to name the principal mafters whofe performances are to be feen here: Raphael, Julio Romano, Albert Durer, Luke of Holland, Mark Anthony Ca-ravagio, Jofepino, Hannibal Carraccio, Guido, Dominichini, Guerchini, Lanfranc, L' Efpag-noletto, the Calabrian, the Baffans, Salviati, Salvator Rofa, Claude Lorrain, Luke Giordano, and Solimene: of the three laft there are fome ineftimable pieces.

On going out of the abbey, we took notice of a ftatue of St. Benedict, with an open book in his hand, in which is written a fingular privilege mentioned by St. Gregory to have been divinely conferred on this patriarch. It is exprefled in thefe words: *Vix obtinere potui ut ex hoc loco animæ mihi cederentur* ; that is, according to the explanation given us, that all the Benedictins dying at Mont Caffino are faved. It is, to be fure, by an exten-fion of this privilege, that the Benedictin nuns in France believe, that before any of them is near dying, the founder of Mont Caffino gives the
houfe

house notice of it by some noises in the night, which they call *St. Benedict's strokes.*

We had with astonishment seen, from the highest apartments which faced the north, that the monastery is but two thirds of the height of the mountain whose name it bears. The part above it seemed to us a bare rock, the peak of which is generally either covered with snow, or hid in clouds.

From the same apartments we were also shewn Albanetta, a small house, in a very delightful situation, west of the monastery, and not above five or six hundred paces distant. Its air is accounted so salubrious, that all the patients in the monastery, on their recovery are removed thither. Albanetta is famous for being the recess of Ignatius Loyola, who, in 1538, withdrew thither for some months, and composed his rule : *Montem illum contemplationis,* says a Dominican in a work intitled *Turtur Animæ, aliquot mensibus inhabitavit S. Ignatius, ibique, velut alter Moses & legislator, secundas religiosarum legum tabulas fabricavit, primis non absimiles.* Unhappily for the Jesuits, he did not find the Benedictins so pliable as St. Benedict found the anchoret, who on his coming to Mont Cassino readily gave up to him the hermitage, of which he had long been in possession.

After spending the day most pleasantly, amidst so many fine things, we returned to St. Germano. On giving an account of our expedition, the abbot said, like the baker, but in a manner rather courteous than sly, *Ah! Francesi!* and was for having us stay till the next day, to rest from our fatigues.

From St. Germano we went and lay at Ca-

pua,

pua, acrofs a wild, and almoft defert country, which feems to afford many lurking-places for robbers. The flope of the mountains on our left, is that fine country which was watered by the Volturnus; a country fo celebrated in antiquity for the Venafran oil, the Falernian and Maffican wines; for the inexhauftible abundance of the tract called Campus Stellatus, which Cicero ufed to call *agrum orbis terræ pulcherrimum*; laftly, for the expedition of the Romans againft the Samnites, and againft Hannibal.

We could not prevail on our *procaccio* to take his way through this fine country. The roads, he faid, were fo bad and fo broken, that for travellers the wildernefs was to be preferred to the promifed land. He was continually talking to us of the pleafure he fhould foon have in welcoming us to Capua, how glorioufly we fhould live there, what good beds we fhould have, and what a number of fine things he would fhew us.

C A P U A.

Capua, where we arrived early, is no longer the ancient Capua, that celebrated rival of Rome: the latter, which is full half a league from the former, now lies buried under the ruins of its ancient grandeur. A great quantity of thefe ruins have been removed into the new town: the walls of the town-houfe are lined with them, and exhibit gigantic grotefque heads, which adorned the keyftones of the amphitheatre: porticos, baffo relievos, are found in its galleries; befides infcriptions without number, among which I obferved one of the Upper Empire, confecrated to S. C. in honour

of

of one *Pefcennius*, for having, with his own money, redeemed, for the good of his fellow citizens, a field, the name of which is effaced. This Redemption is expreffed by the word *reciperavit* (y).

Private houfes are likewife enriched with fragments of thefe ruins. The two uprights at our *procaccio*'s gate were two blocks of marble, with a confular figure on each, as big as life. Facing this houfe was a church, the conftruction of which, like that of the temple of Cafino and the cathedral of Terracina, feem to fpeak it an ancient temple.

The infide of the cathedral, like a bafilic, is fupported and divided by twenty-four granite columns, of different modules, and confequently collected by chance. This church receives a confiderable air of grandeur from the portico, confifting of twenty columns of unequal dimenfions.

After gratifying our curiofity, we returned to our quarters, heartily difpofed to do honour to the glorious living which the *procaccio* had given us to expect. The preparations confifted in a very foul table-cloth, laid over three boards fupported by two benches, with two old *bicchieri*, or earthen ewers, full of very bad wine. They told us that glaffes were not ufed in that country, but we fhould drink round in the *bicchieri*. The repaft itfelf was a leg of an old he-goat, a fricaffee with lamp-oil, and a fallad, with bread as bad as the wine. Such fare we could not touch ; fo we made our fupper of fome fruit, and this we devoured without bread.

(y) It is there ufed in the fenfe annexed to it by Verrius Flaccus,

As

As to the excellent beds, thefe were three ftraw matreffes, each within a fort of an old bag. My fellow travellers ventured to lay themfelves down, but the vermin foon made them repent of their haftinefs. I, in this more wary than they, had betaken myfelf to a loft, where, on frefh ftraw, I had a pretty good night of it. Such to us were the delights of Capua.

NAPLES.

A fhort day's journey brought us from Capua to Naples, acrofs that admirable country, of which Pliny fpeaks, under the name of *Campi Leborini* ;* from whence, I fuppofe, has corruptively been formed its modern appellation of *Terra di Lavoro*. From this tract, as the fineft, the moft fertile, and moft delightful of all Italy, Virgil took the model of his Elyfian fields :

Ver ibi perpetuum, atque alienis meffibus æftas.

Naples is the queen of this fine country. We had inadvertently relied on our *procaccio* for the choice of an inn in this city ; and he fet us down at an old Calabrian's, in a ftreet, the inhabitants of which were all fhoe-makers and coblers. There however we ftayed, apprehending we fhould be no gainers by a removal.

Naples is at prefent the only confiderable place in a ftate, which formerly was covered with towns and inhabitants. The Greater Greece, the ruins of which are part of this ftate, had feen its period fo early as Cicero's time : *Magna Græcia*

* Hift. L. iii.

nuns

nunc non eſt (z). This country, which was governed by the laws of Pythagoras, of Zaleucus,
Carondas, Architas, Parmenides, Zeno; which was
honoured with the preſence of Homer, Simonides,
Pindar, Plato, and Virgil ; the aſylum of arts
and philoſophy ; the theatre of induſtry and commerce, by its many ports on the two ſeas ; the
centre of the moſt ingenious magnificence, and
of the moſt curious luxury ; this country now
ſcarce affords inhabitants to carry on a very ſuper-
ficial cultivation of it.

The invaſions of barbarians, the revolutions in
government, the claims of the popes, the frequent change of its ſovereigns, the extinction of the
trade to the Levant and Africa, are the moſt palpable cauſes of the low condition, into which this
ſtate is ſunk, yet from which it may not be im-
poſſible to raiſe it. Don Carlos, when ſovereign
here, had actually begun this glorious work, by
clearing the revenue farms alienated by the Spaniſh viceroys ; by freeing the country people from
ſlavery to the nobility and clergy, who had power
of life and death over theſe poor wretches ; and
by granting to ſuch places, as were moſt advanta-
geouſly ſituated, proper privileges for increaſing
their population, and animating induſtry.

The concentration of the kingdom of Naples

(z) *Pro S. Roſcio.* To which he adds, *Qui in Salentinis
aut in Brutiis habitant, unde vix ter in anno nuntiam audire
poſſunt :* which proves that, in point of communication and
intercourſe, this country was as bad off as at preſent ; but it
proves nothing againſt the environs of Naples, in which
were finer towns than in the environs of Rome, as the ſame
Cicero informs us, *Orat. contra Rullum ad Quirites, verſ.
medium ;* Labicos, Fidenas, &c.

Q 4 within

within its metropolis, like the monftrous enlargement of the capitals of the principal ftates of Europe, was originally derived from the fchemes of the
farmers of the public revenues, for molefting the
ruftics and country gentlemen; for putting them
out of conceit with a rural life ; for alluring them
into the centre of peace, plenty, and pleafure;
and thus getting them together, under their hand,
like pigeons in a cot, or fifhes in a pond.

Cruftis
*Excipiunt homines quos in vivaria mittant.**

Rome, under the emperors, had fwallowed up
Italy. After the conqueft of the Turks, Conftantinople abforbed Greece and part of Afia. Since
the reign of Lewis XIV. Paris has been ingulphing
France. Thus the capitals of moft ftates in Europe are become the deftruction of the human fpecies, as fo many abyffes into which they irretrie-
vably precipitate themfelves.

After the deftructive wars of Francis I. and
Henry II. in the midft of the flame of civil com-
buftions, France was in a ftate of population
which it never could recover fince the enlargement
of Paris. If, of the million of inhabitants, which
this city has contained for a century paft, every
twenty years thofe had been driven out whofe
fathers were not born there, fcarce a fourth part
would have remained at each mufter: the furplus
France has furnifhed, and thus has thinned itfelf.
Every town, in proportion to its largenefs, fuftains
the fame lofs ; and there is not one, even of the
fecond clafs, which is not a ftanding proof that
the common duration of families in them fcarce

* Hor. Ep. I. L. i.

amounts

amounts to a century, when they fail, and make room for new colonies.

The primitive Greeks, the Gauls, the Scythians, whose numerous swarms have covered and renewed the universe, lived in villages: their frequent emigrations proclaim a lage excess of population, which has ceased since cities took place in the countries where those vigorous people dwelled.

> *Campeſtres melius Scythæ,*
> *Quorum plauſtra vagas ritè trahunt domos.*

From these observations we may, by way of comfort, look on Peterſburgh and Pekin, as the fureſt barriers which Europe could defire againſt northern emigrations.

Let us return to Naples, which, together with its environs, prefents the traveller with a fight abfolutely new; neither the inhabitants nor the arts being there like thofe in the other parts of Italy.

The people, both of city and country, are vigorous, robuſt, raw-boned, full of fire and fprightlinefs, active, indefatigably laborious, in a word, cut out for war; and thus, it is only in fobriety that they are any thing like thofe Italians which we had feen fince our leaving Turin.

This breed of men glory in being defcended from the Greeks, and refembling them: they are broad and full chefted, with a fhort thick neck; flefhy, with a fine complexion, and a very brifk eye. They who are better acquainted with ancient and modern Greece, than I pretend to be, may from this picture decide how far the Neapolitans refemble either the ancient or the prefent Greeks. Their apparel will likewife furnifh them with
another

another article for comparison : the Neapolitans go with the neck and shoulders, the breast and arms, almost naked ; whilst the other Italians, and especially the Lombards, are very careful to keep those parts closely covered.   And here I am quite at a loss to find out on what foundation M. de Montesquieu says in his Persian Letters, that thirty or forty thousand men, of the very refuse of the Neapolitan people, live on dead, rotten, and dried fish, thrown up by the sea ; whereas all the fish this city consumes, is got by fishing.

It is certainly not a little strange, that such a people, almost ever looked upon as nothing, in the various revolutions which have so often changed its master, should never have joined in any but in that of Mazaniello *(a)*.   Could its indifference to political commotions be put to a stronger trial than when the unfortunate Conradin, aged only seventeen years, the last branch of a line hated and proscribed by the heads of the church, was publicly beheaded in the midst of the capital of his ancestors dominions ?   There is no viewing the place, where the vestiges of this horrid scene are still shewn, without various emotions.

This indifference *(b)*, however in appearance it may favour of stupidity, is the effect of instinct enlightened by experience : *Quid refert mea,* say they with the ass in the fable, *clitellas dum portem meas ?*   To finish the picture of this people, it

---

(a) Machiavel, in the 55th of his Discourses on Livy, Book i. had foretold to the Neapolitans what issue they had to expect from this revolution.

(b) On this indifference is doubtless founded the title of *Fideliſſima,* which the city of Naples every where assumes,

is fufficient only to add, that Naples, though without fo much as the fhadow of police, knows very
little of thofe diforders which all the magiftrate's
vigilance at Paris can hardly prevent.

In this picture I do not include the fubftantial
citizens, nor the lawyers, who are not lefs numerous
at Naples than at Paris; nor the nobility. Thefe
claffes, who are no lefs prudent from fyftem, than
the people from inftinct, devote to idlenefs (c),
and facrifice to pleafure, all the advantages of a
happy conftitution and a fiery temperament.
They are the moft voluptuous of men :

*In hos tota ruens Venus
Cyprum deferuit.*

Under an appearance of giddinefs, levity, and
merriment, the commonalty and citizens of Naples, amidft labour and pleafure, conceal deep
and well-conducted views, if not in every head,
at leaft as a body; and as a body they form a
democracy, independent of the king and the nobility, joining with the latter when their intereft fo
requires. The lower clergy, and the majority of
monks, with whom Naples fwarms, never fail
fiding with them.

The tribe laft mentioned are the populace's hereditary counfel; and to what a degree Naples is
ftocked with counfellors of this kind, appears
from the following correct lift.

17 Houfes of Francifcans of all colours.
15 Of Dominicans.

(c) *In otia natam Parthenopen.*   Ovid. Metam. L. xv.
    Otiofa Neapolis.   Horat. Epod. v.

8 Of

8 Of Carmelites.
9 Of Camaldulans, Carthufians, and Beno-
dictins.
4 Of Minims.
3 Of Servites.
9 Of Regular Canons.
2 Of Hieronimites and Bafilians.
5 Of Spaniards.
6 Of Jefuits.
6 Of Theatines.
3 Of Regular Priefts.
2 Of Barnabites.
1 Of the Oratory.
1 Of *Fate-Ben-Fratelli.*
3 Of Attendants on the Infirm.
3 Of *Scuole-Pie.*
2 Of Lucca Fathers.
33 Convents for Maidens.
33 Houfes of Retirement for Women.
6 Hofpitals for the ⎫
   Sick.   ⎪
1 For Pilgrims.   ⎪ The greater part under
4 For Orphans.   ⎬ the direction of Monks
1 For old Men.   ⎪ appointed for that pur-
1 For Poor who   ⎪ pofe.
   have no fhelter. ⎭
___
178

All thefe houfes are rich, either by ancient endowments or daily donations ; and, as every where
elfe, the richeft of all are thofe of the Jefuits.
   The monks, who converfe with the nobility and
the citizens, are very ftudious and artful in fcenting
inheritances, and leave no ftone unturned to procure

cure for their houfes either prefents, or partial le-
gacies, when they cannot get the whole into their
hands. It is to be obferved, however, that there
is the fame police among them as among the general lovers; when the object of their purfuit has
determined for any one of fuch an order, the other
orders never offer to intervene, unlefs a rupture
happens.

To the fuccefs of thefe practices are owing
thofe amazing riches which are difplayed in the
decoration of their churches; in the brilliant and
very coftly fpectacles frequently given there; and,
laftly, in the enormous quantities of plate with
which their facrifties are crowded. The churches
of Naples are perhaps as rich in this kind, as all
the churches of Italy put together.

Every monaftery has a good laboratory, which,
accordingly, brings in confiderably. Moft of the
monks practife phyfic; and it is the practice
of thefe phyficians that conftitutes the fund for
the laboratory of their houfe, the current expences of which arife from the families who come
thither to confeffion.

Farther, every laboratory is known by fome
medicament, or conferve, which is not made fo
well any where elfe; and for thefe it has a fure
demand, at leaft among ftrangers, and thofe who
are not flaves either to their phyfician or their confeffor. The Minims, for inftance, whofe houfe
faces the palace, have the run for *diabolos*; a kind
of anife-feed comfits for the ufe of old men who
retain a colt's tooth. This reftorative bears a moft
extravagant price. I am apt to think that the
faculty even of Montpelier are not acquainted with
the

the receipt, having feen a canon of that city pay down five louis-d'ors only for a fmall quantity.

The nobility conftitute a body united by common views and interefts; and which, from being formerly diftributed into thirty courts, confifts at prefent only of five; the deputies of which fhare the municipal government with a magiftrate, who reprefents, and is chofen by the people.

Thefe courts are large infulated falons, and inclofed with iron grates, that every thing done there may be feen. Whether this uncommon difpofition was by the nobility's choice, or directed by the fovereign, or required by the people, I know not.

Cardinal Spinelli, in 1750, experienced the power of thefe two fo different factions, when they happened to be combined. Befides his being of one of the firft families in Naples, he was a perfon of extraordinary parts and abilities, intimately in favour with Benedict XIV. and, as archbifhop of Naples, regarded beyond any of his predeceffors; fo that his fovereign was beginning to admit him into his confidence. The minifters, fearing this confidence might be carried too far, laid hold of a fentence of that prelate's court, by which a prieft was condemned to retract fome pofitions which had an ill found, and made ufe of it to frighten the people, as the forerunner of an inquifition, which they have never known but by name, and which they look on as the main inftrument of tyranny. A fchedule on this head being fent to a trufty notary, kindled a flame, which in a few days fpread throughout the whole kingdom. The populace, alarmed by the dread of the *Holy Office*, as they call

call the inquifition, was continually reinforced by droves of peafants, who on the fame account were flocking from all parts of the kingdom, and came to ftand by their lords and patrons. All this angry multitude furrounded the palace; and the king, who, defignedly, had not been advifed of this commotion, coming abroad as ufual, the whole fquare at once rang, as had been agreed on, with the cry of *No Holy Office! No Holy Office!*

His majefty ordered notice to be given to the people, that he would inquire into the matter, and do them juftice. The affair being brought before an extraordinary council, held at the king's return, was referred to the *courts,* who deliberated on it with great folemnity: the people in the mean time crowded about the grate, within which the nobility were fitting; and on the rifing of each court, gathering about the nobles, they coldly afked them *Metterem' in fuoco?* "Shall we fet it on fire?" This cool tumult caufed fuch a warm confternation, that the cardinal, being forfaken by the king, was obliged to quit Naples, deliver up his archbifhoprick to his majefty, and withdraw to Rome, where we have feen him in the tranquil poffeffion of honours, and thefe heightened by the public efteem.

The prejudice of the people againft the inquifition, kept up by its fear of coming under the papal dominion, is to this ftate what the liberties of the Gallican church are to France. It is certainly a little furprifing, that at the gates of Rome, in a ftate not only catholic, but a feudatory of Rome, and for a long time ruled by the catholic kings, this falutary fear has had its effect:

but

but it is ftill more fo, that this prejudice, like the
liberties of the Gallican church, fhould owe its
eftablifhment and permanency, not fo much to
the fovereigns as to the nation ; that is, to divines
and civilians who have introduced and fomented it,
and often in oppofition to the fovereign, who fometimes, however, has found the advantage of it *(d)*.

An object of this kind, ftill more remarkable,
is the tribunal of the monarchy of Sicily. It
is known, that by this tribunal the king exercifes
over Sicily the authority which he claims as hereditary legate of the holy fee, and perpetual repre-
fentative of the pope. By virtue of this authority,
which refts on a very uncertain bull of Urban II.
and which Leibnitz has placed at the head of his
Diplomatic Collection, his Sicilian majefty, by himfelf or his delegates, tries and punifhes, excommu-
nicates and abfolves, all laymen, monks, priefts,
abbots, bifhops, archbifhops, and even cardinals.
His decrees, in all ecclefiaftical matters, are without
appeal, no more than a preventive power remaining
to the court of Rome; and this it makes ufe of only
in troublefome times. In a word, the prefident
of the monarchical tribunal, is, in all petitions and
reprefentations, ftyled *Beatiffimo Padre*, a title
ftill more ftrange than the authority fignified by it.

It is eafily conceived, that the popes have not
been wanting in their endeavours to procure the
fuppreffion of a *monarchy*, more odious to them

(d) Thus the moft important difcoveries in government, owe their origin, their progrefs, and their eftablifhment, not to place-men, but to perfons unconnected,
and who, labouring only for themfelves and pofterity,
have oppofed the judgment, and often braved the perfecutions, of their age.

in a catholic king, owning himself their feudatory, and in queens, to whom, of their own right, the kingdom of Sicily may devolve, than the supremacy of the kings and queens of England. The nation, often assisted, and sometimes forsaken by the sovereign, has, by its lawyers and its divines, constantly either eluded or warded off the strokes of the most enterprising or most turbulent popes (e), against a prerogative, which the most easy popes look upon as heretical, schismatical, and execrable.

Under these predicaments it was, that in 1715, Clement XI. abolished the tribunal of the monarchy. Victor Amedeus had been made king of Sicily at the treaty of Utrecht. It was apprehended, that this kingdom would soon slip through his fingers, and return to the house of Austria; and it might be supposed, that a temporary sovereign would not concern himself much in support of a prerogative which others were to enjoy: but the tribunal did for itself all that could have been done by a sovereign the most jealous of his authority. Amidst a continual succession of

(e) Paul V. made a smart attack on this privilege by the pen of cardinal Baronius, who in vol. xi. inserts a long discussion on this point. It was answered by cardinal Ascanio Colonna; and Baronius replied. As to the question of Fact, the advantage seemed on Baronius's side; but, concerning the question of Right, his arguments were the less conclusive, the far greater part of them being drawn from the pope's supremacy over the temporalities of kings; which was bringing for proof what was to be proved. This supremacy was both the sword and buckler to the same Paul V. in the quarrels which he was then engaged in against Venice, against England, against the commons of France, and likewise against Spain on account of Sicily.

bulls, briefs, refcripts, monitory letters, and mandates, it found means to draw into its quarrel fome powers, whofe rights were indirectly affected by it: accordingly the parliament of Paris fuppreffed the abolitory bull.

The affair at length was terminated under Benedict XIII. by the famous cardinal Cofcia, who in confirming the title to the emperor, as king of the Two Sicilies, contrived for his court an ultimate fubterfuge, by caufing the bull of Transfer to be figned by two fubdataries, the datary and vice-chancellor having refufed to fet their hands to an act, which fanctified an authority till then looked on at Rome as the *abomination of defolation in the holy place.*

The Neapolitan commonalty begin, in favour of Don Carlos, to lay afide their indifference about what fovereign they are under: not that there is, between this prince and his fubjects of all ranks, any intercourfe or familiarity; never was fovereign lefs obfervant of fuch a behaviour than Don Carlos. All the time he fpends in the palace, the queen has: in the forenoon he amufes himfelf with fifhing, and in the afternoon he hunts: the intermediate hours are what he gives to his council. When in town, he goes through Naples four times a day, and always full gallop. Concerning this the Neapolitans fay, that when Philip V. went into Spain, Lewis XIV. advifed him to this impetuous pace; and his children have retained it. Thefe exercifes are regularly continued all weathers, rain or heat; fo that the king has now a conftitution which can bear any thing.

It is by the choice of his minifters, by his doing
bufinefs

bufinefs along with them, by the habit he has acquired of feeing every thing at once, and feeing it
as it fhould be, that this prince has won the confidence and hearts of his fubjects. They perceive
in him the whole of what the *Protocol* of Italian
policy requires in the choice of minifters, and the
fovereigns employment of them.

* *La prima conjettura*, fays this *Protocol* †, *che fi
fa d'un Principe e del cervel fuo è vedere gli huomini
che lui a d'intorno : quando fono fufficienti e fideli,
fempre fi può reputarlo favio.... Ma come il Principe poffa conofcere il Miniftro, ci è quefto modo che
non falla mai. Quando tu vedi il Miniftro penfar
più à fe che a te, e che in tutte le attioni vi ricerca
l'utile fuo, quefto tal così fatto mas non fia buon miniftro, né mai te ne potrai fidare.... D'altra parte,
il Principe per mantenerfi buon il buono, deve penfare
à lui, honorandolo, facendolo ricco, obligandofelo,
participandogli li honori e carichi, &c.*

Such is the king of Naples's behaviour towards
his minifters; and his fubjects judge of him by them.

The prince royal, prefumptive heir to the
crown, has reached his thirteenth year; but in a

* " The firft conjecture formed of a prince and his capacity,
" is from a view of the perfons about him : if they are men
" of abilities and faithful, he may be concluded wife; ....
" and an infallible way for a prince to know a minifter is, If
" you fee he minds himfelf more than you, and that the
" drift of all his proceedings is his own advantage ; fuch a
" one will never prove a good minifter ; no confidence is to
" be placed in him..... On the other hand, that a good mi-
" nifter may continue fuch, the prince is to fhew a regard for
" him, and confer honours and lucrative employments on
" him, &c.

† Cap. xxii.

ftate

ftate of imbecillity, which age, far from diminifh-
ing, increafes.   Every afternoon the queen comes
to his apartment, embraces him, kiffes him, and
withdraws all in tears.   Amidft all the events,
which may call him to the throne, will it be conferred on this prince, notwithftanding his condition ?   Should this condition exclude him, what
form can be given to an exclufion quite unprece-
dented, and which, by referring the nomination
of the fucceffor to the choice of the reigning king,
or of the nation, will open a vaft field for dif-
cuffions and inferences ?

An Italian poet faid of the Neapolitans in his
times,

> *In Napoli il dir molto e l'haver poco.*
> In Naples, great cry and little wool.

My ftay at Naples was not long enough to be
thoroughly acquainted with their manner of living,
whether private or focial.   I only know, that
there is more fleeping here than in any other country in Italy ; that they confume an amazing quantity of chocolate, which every private perfon has
made in his own houfe, as he likes beft ; that the
converfazioni, or affemblies, are like thofe of other
cities of Italy ; that the chat in private companies is quite Grecian, that is, very free, and very
merry ; that gallantry is in high life as common,
and with as little caution, as it is rare and clofe
among the citizens ; and that, tracing it down to
the commonalty, the extremities are found to join ;
that, in general, continency is, at Naples, the
moft fcarce virtue ; that love, which elfewhere
is often no more than affectation and fantaftical-

nefs,

nefs, is there one of the moft ftimulating wants ;
in a word, that Mount Vefuvius, which overlooks
this city, is the neareft emblem under which it
can be reprefented in this refpect.

Other neceffities, which the police and fome remains of fhame reftrain in other parts, efpecially
in cities, are at Naples above all the controul of
laws. The fulphur, with which their vegetables
and food are impregnated; the continual ufe of
chocolate, of the ftrongeft liquors, and of the
moft inflammative drugs, occafion eruptions and
explofions, which will not bear either delay or circumfpection : the court-yards of palaces and hô-
tels, the porches of private houfes, the ftairs and
landing-places, are fo many receptacles for the neceffities of all paffengers. Perfons fhall often
throw themfelves out of their coach, and mingle
among the foot people; every one taking, within
the walls of others, that liberty which he allows
within his own :

Veniam petimufque damufque viciffim.

From this general liberty, and the little care taken
by an owner or tenant about the cleanlinefs of his
hôtel, his houfe or landing-place, you may think
what filthinefs and infection there muft be in a city,
which is reckoned to contain between five and fix
hundred thoufand fouls.

I have faid, that at Naples men and arts are not
the men and arts of the other parts of Italy. As to
the men, I believe I have made my affertion good :
as to arts, I fhall now, if not prove it, at leaft
point out wherein they differ, with appeal, however, to connoiffeurs.

The architecture of both sacred and civil, public and private edifices, is no longer the architecture of Rome. It is every where crowded with bosses and prominences of a gigantic proportion, and a heaviness, which strikes the eye the more disagreeably, as all these jetties are either of a brown stone, like the body of the buildings; or, in those where they are only stucco, besmeared over with a coarse dirty brown colour in imitation of the stone. All the gates and doors, besides their enormous height, are loaded with balconies supported by brackets larger than what they bear, or suspended as by a miracle: so unsightly are all the particulars of their construction.

The outside of most of the churches, even the most stately and splendid, is, as all over Italy, only a bare wall, standing, as it were, in expectation of a portal; and these *expecting* walls are an eternal pretence for begging in behalf of the poor church, as wanting a necessary decoration: in a word, these churches will always be in want of a portal, for the same reasons that the church of saint Sulpice at Paris has already been forty years a building.

As to the inside of these churches, it is rather rich and glaring than fine; the decorations and distribution every where uniform, being two crosses interfected at the junction by a cupola. Seeing one is seeing all.

The finest marbles and paintings are crowded in those churches; and where these are replaced or divided by gilding, it is with a profuseness which tires the eye without entertaining it. Such was the new decoration of the old church of the nuns of St. Clare, which I saw finished during my stay at Naples.

Naples. In order to find a ground for the gilding, which was by no means to be omitted, part of the church was incumbered with pieces of lattice-work, in the form of a lozenge, originally an Arabian invention; and thefe lattices, with their lozenges, befides the heavinefs of their relievo, were charged with moft dazzling and laboured gildings : a decoration fuitable to the times of king Robert, from which this edifice dates its erection.

Not that architects have wanted opportunities of difplaying their talents in a city, which has above three hundred churches, including chapels belonging to brotherhoods, affociations, and congregations, which, as at Rome, are in higher efteem and more frequented than the parifh churches, the number of which is thirty.

The fountains in feveral parts of the city, and even thofe in the fpacious fquare before the harbour, bear the marks of this bad tafte, contrary to the intention of thofe, at whofe expence they were made ; but which is feen only in the choice of the marbles.

It is the fame with the plate of all kinds in the churches. It is all in *laminæ*, and mirrors executed with the moft exquifite attention, from defigns where real beauty is facrificed to fhow.

But no where does the Neapolitan tafte *(f)* fhine with fo much luftre as in the pyramids, or obelifks, erected in fquares fronting the principal churches. In the monftrous expence of them, in the uncouth

(f) The authors of the Defcriptions of Naples, to praife a piece well executed in their tafte, fay, *Cofa ftravagamente lavorata.*

affem-

affemblage of the various marbles, they exceed all the enormities of Gothic rudenefs. Such an obelifk was finifhing before the great church of the Jefuits, and only from money raifed by a father of the houfe, univerfally known at Naples, for felling to the country people little prayers, making them believe that the bits of paper, on which thefe prayers were printed, when fwallowed by hens had a wonderful virtue for increafing their fecundity. This new obelifk is more crowded with decorations, and more glaringly fet off, than all the ancient : it is the very triumph of bad tafte. Round thefe monuments is celebrated the feftival of the faints to which they are confecrated, and this for feveral nights, with illuminations, ferenades, and fire-works ; all the people of Naples flocking to thofe nocturnal exhibitions.

The new caftle, begun by Charles of Anjou, is one of the oldeft buildings in Naples. The main gate, which is confined, and as it were buried between two enormous baftions, was a marble triumphal arch, erected in 1494, to celebrate king Alphonfo of Arragon's entry into Naples. It is covered with trophies and baffo-relievos, of fuch workmanfhip that the Lombards and Florentines conteft the honour of it : it is one of the fineft things in Naples, and at the fame time, the moft difadvantageoufly placed. A baftion in this caftle which faces the harbour, was built in the laft century, by a Spanifh viceroy, with the monies arifing from a tax levied on proftitutes for that very purpofe ; and the ftone-cutters, that pofterity might know how much the ftate owed to that clafs of females, chiffeled out an oblong oval on the

facing

facing of every ſtone in the front of this baſtion, which is likewiſe of a great height.

The king's palace, built by the Spaniſh vice-roys from a plan of the celebrated Fontana, diſtinguiſhes itſelf from the generality of the Neapolitan ſtructures. It would be admired even at Rome. Oppoſite to this palace, one of theſe viceroys had a marble Coloſſus made, to which has been fitted a coloſſal head of Jupiter, found in the ruins of Puzzolo : the fore part of this ſtatue is covered with an eagle's ſkin, on which is a very prolix inſcription, in honour of the viceroy to which Naples is obliged for this decoration, when in reality it is a mere fright. Another of the ſame kind, is a coloſſal virgin in the Carthuſian monaſtery, near the prior's apartment. If, as ſaid, it be the work of the famous Bernini, I am inclined to think he did not ground his reputation on it.

This Carthuſian monaſtery lies at the foot of the caſtle St. Elmo. Under it one ſees the fineſt part of Naples. There are few religious houſes in Italy ſo well endowed, ſo delightfully ſituated, and ſo rich in maſterly paintings of all the ſchools. Foreigners are generally well received there. We ſpent a whole day at this place, and had a dinner of excellent ſea-fiſh, which we paid for as at a tavern ; neither the prior, nor any of the officers of the houſe, having honoured us with their preſence. In the part of this houſe which projects moſt over the city, is a belvedere, where, to our very great amazement, we partly heard all that was ſaid in the ſquares and ſtreets : not indeed any connected tale, but a clatter of very diſtinct words ; which brought to my mind Rabelais's iſland, where

the

the words freeze, and on a thaw make a like clatter.

I fhall take my leave of the Neapolitan architecture with a word about the houfes. They are built of a kind of very light fand-ftone, to the height of feven or eight ftories, and all terminate in a platform without roof or covering; a conftruction fo far from giving them the appearance of the Louvre, the Palais-Bourbon, or the Paris obfervatory, that it makes them look like houfes, the top of which had been confumed by fire; and the more, as the upper part of thefe houfes is blackened by the fmoke and the vapours of the air, more than the middle parts. This conftruction, however, does not fo much arife from the climate, it raining here as much as in other parts; but from the conveniency of the puzzolana, of which the neighbourhood affords plenty. It is compofed of metallic particles, and minute fharp cryftals, and, when mixed with the calx of marble or fhells, it makes a mortar, which water rather confolidates than weakens. It is even neceffary, on laying it over a platform, to keep it under water for fome days, that it may be proof againft the fun, which otherwife would foon reduce it to duft. Had this fand been made ufe of, inftead of cement, for binding the flints with which the platform of the Paris obfervatory is paved, that magnificent monument of Lewis the XIVth's reign would, very probably, have lafted above a century, in the fame condition as it came out of Mr. Perrault's hands.

Naples has been infinitely more happy in painters than in architects. Befides, being a colony of the Bologna fchool, by the works with which

Lan-

Lanfranc, Dominichini, Guido, &c. have enriched it, it has itself produced artifts, who, in many refpects, would have done honour to their metropolis, had not the national tafte for brilliancy and the *ftravagante* led them out of the circle, to which the Caracci had limited their art.

Agreeably to the method I laid down to myfelf, and which I have hitherto obferved, I fhall only take notice of fome of thofe paintings, with which, amidft the multitude of mafter-pieces to be feen in Naples, I was moft taken.

In the van of thefe I fhall place the Twelve Prophets, by Efpagnoletto, in the curves of the arches along the nave of the Carthufian church. The want of room in the feveral fpaces obliged the painter to reprefent them as half reclined ; but this neceffity he has improved into a variety of attitudes, and each correfponding with the character of the prophet. They are all melancholy, thoughtful, extafied old men. Here was a frefh difficulty to overcome ; and fo ingenioufly has this been done, that they fhew the fame difference of countenance, air, and difpofition, as of attitude ; a difference allufive to the genius of their refpective writings. Never have fublime fouls been expreffed with fuch force and truth. The admirable artift has furpaffed himfelf in the colouring, which has, and ftill retains, all the energy fuch fubjects require. To conclude this account, I own, and doubtlefs to my fhame, that with nothing, even in the very Vatican, was I fo much taken as with thefe prophets.

To thefe may be joined a Saint Francis by Guido, in the houfe of the fathers of the Oratory,

together

together with a picture by the fame hand, reprefenting Jefus Chrift and St. John naked, in the
bloom of youth.

The fecond age of the Neapolitan fchool is
filled up by Luca Giordano. From this painter
alone we have as many good pieces in all kinds,
as fome fchools have produced : *Solus academiam
facit.* The only Neapolitan rival, who came
any thing near him, was Maffimo. The legif-
lators in painting charge him with incorrectnefs,
improper freedoms, and other faults; and bringing in with him Solimene, and the mafters of the
third age, they fay to them, *Vos primi picturam
perdidiftis.* I fhall only mention one piece of
his, a Virgin del Rofario in the church of the Dominicans near the palace, and into which I followed a *novena* which was celebrating by a band of
the fineft hands in mufic that Naples afforded:
but I was more taken up with this painting than
all the mufic. Giordano has there reprefented the
virgin amidft angels carrying her in triumph under a canopy which projects from the canvas, and
indeed feems detached from it. Saint Dominic
and a Jacobine nun attend on her. The perfons,
the canopy, the valences of it, feem as waving in
the air; every thing is in motion. Such indeed are
moft of this great mafter's works. So vivid, fo
varied are his colourings, that every thing lives
and acts : fo that the freedoms which Giordano has
allowed himfelf, in order to affect fo powerfully,
are eafily excufed : *dulcibus abundat vitiis.*

In a church, near the *Seggia* joining to the great
fquare, I faw a picture of Solimene's, of which I
fhall take notice, not fo much for the beauty of
the

the execution, as the oddity of the subject. It represents Jesus Christ and St. Francis. Jesus Christ opens his breast, where, on his heart, as in a looking-glass, is seen St. Francis: St. Francis returns the compliment to Jesus Christ, the portrait of whom is seen on the saint's heart. Italy is full of such extravagant representations, often executed by the greatest masters, in little pictures bespoke by enthusiastic beldams. I know one by Dominichini, a foot and a half to six inches, on brass, of St. Catherine of Sienna. Two youthful angels support her; and Jesus Christ, in the habit of a Jacobine nun, standing on a thin cloud, draws her heart out of her breast, through his monachal habit. The ground of this painting is a most delightful landscape. Dominichini never did any thing finer in little. The heads are all most exquisitely finished, and speak the admirable hand from whence they came. All the several particulars are in the most precise truth. As to the colouring, never did any more soft and mellow come from Dominichini's pencil. What a pity that such perfections should be wasted on such a subject!

In paintings, Naples offers a vast field to the lamentations of the artists and *dilettanti*. All the world has heard of the great and valuable collections made in this kind by the house of Farnese, which, during half the finest age Italy ever saw, had reigned over arts, sciences, and talents, as sovereigns, and as intelligent sovereigns. The princes of that house were no less careful of those riches, than of their sovereignty itself; and their palaces at Parma and Placentia were full of them.

The last of these princes dying lately without issue,

iffue, his dominions have fucceffively devolved to Don Carlos and Don Philip, in right of their mother, the queen of Spain, Elizabeth Farnefe, the laft of that illuftrious name. Conformably to the treaty of Vienna, Don Carlos, in 1739, delivered them up to Don Philip, but, by a cuftom in law, referved to himfelf the moveables. Of thefe the moft valuable part were the collections of paintings, medals, books, &c. The whole was packed up in a hurry, and fent away to Naples, where the king's palaces, being already full, could not receive thofe ineftimable collections. This prince was then building, at Capo di Monte, (a delicious eminence, commanding part of Naples, its harbour, and its two bays) a moft ftately palace, from a plan of Van-Vitelli, a Roman architect. This palace was intended to be furnifhed with the Parma moveables; and till they could be properly diftributed, the cafes of books and paintings were heaped together in the ground-floor apartments, thefe being finifhed. When the palace came to be nearly completed, it was perceived that it would want water, and no hydraulic invention could fupply it, though all the feats, of which there are fo many in that delightful fpot, have plenty; and though Tofcanella, which overlooks it, is famous for an inexhauftible well of very fine water. On this pretence, or for fome reafons hidden under it, the palace of Capo di Monte was given over.

Ferramenta cafertam
*Gefferunt fabri.**

.* Hor. Ep. I. L. i.

This

. This new palace now became the great object of attention, and the cases of books and paintings remained where they had been thrown when brought from Parma. The paintings had been lately unpacked when we saw them at Capo di Monte ; in which interval they suffered extremely, and there was no appearance of any happier fate; for, being thrown confusedly into uninhabited apartments, exposed to the moisture and the injuries of the air, in a ruinous palace, nothing can save them from a destruction to which, for these twenty years past, so many causes concur. The library we may conclude to be irretrievable. I was told, that it is still lying in the bales as it came from Parma.

Naples affords few antiquities. Nothing is known of the situation of Paleopolis and Neapolis, between which, according to Livy, the consul Publius posted himself in his campaign against Hannibal. Of the ancient monuments at Naples the most intire, and unquestionably the most curious, is Virgil's tomb.

This monument, which in Misson and father Montfaucon is represented as a pyramid almost ruined, is a lantern or turret, about twenty feet high, on open arcades, the solid parts of which were formerly adorned with pillars. This structure stands on a platform cut in the eastern side of the hill of Pausilipo, in sight of the two bays of Naples, the harbour, the castles, part of the city lengthwise, and fronting Mount Vesuvius. Unquestionably it was in order to make it so conspicuous, that its elevation so much exceeds the proportion of its base. It commands the entrance of the famous

grotto

grotto at Paufilipo; and by the excavations daily carrying on in this part of the mountain, commands it fo, that at prefent it is fcarce two feet from the brink of a precipice a hundred and eighty feet deep ; and if thefe excavations be continued, they muft certainly undermine this venerable monument.

On the external furface of the cupola in which it terminates, is a prodigy much celebrated by the Neapolitan poets : I mean its being exactly crowned with a laurel, though the tree's only nourifhment muft be what its roots meet with in the joining of the ftones. All travellers are fure to have a pluck at this tree, which they do by means of a rope with a ftone at the end of it. Farther, the fide of the mountain where the tomb ftands, inftead of any trees of this kind, is covered with yews and firs. Virgil's laurel however recruits its daily loffes, and perpetuates itfelf with renovating vigour. In the fixteenth century there was only one ftem, which ftood in the centre of the cupola, where we will fuppofe it to have been planted by fome Neapolitan, a warm admirer of Virgil. About the beginning of the laft century, a fir, blown by the wind from a collateral part of the mountain, fell with its top on the ftem, thus choaking it ; but nature itfelf repaired the accident, fetting as layers the compreffed ramifications of the root, which now have fpread over the cupola's whole furface.

The learned Cluvier*, on explaining fome verfes of Statius with geographical ftrictnefs, has advanced

* Ital. Antiq.

vanced

vanced, that the monument in queſtion is not
Virgil's tomb, and that this ſhould be ſought for
eaſt of Naples, near Veſuvius (an opinion, in
which Mr. Addiſon joins); but Statius † meant only
to indicate Naples by Virgil's Tomb, and by Mount
Veſuvius, oppoſite to which it ſtands, and which
makes the direct point of view to it.

Maronei ſedens in margine templi,
Sumo animum ac magni tumulis acanto Magiſtri . . .
. . . . . Fractas ubi Veſbius egerit undas.

Farther, Donatus, in his Life of Virgil, for-
mally ſays, that his bones were carried to Naples,
and by Auguſtus's order, *ſepulta fuêre in via*
Puteolanâ, intrà lapidem ſecundum.

As to the den or cavern, which, running
through Pauſilipo to the extent of half a mile,
brings the ſhore of Chiaïa to a level with that of
Puzzolo, the uncertainty of the monuments and
writers on the date of this great undertaking, ſeems
to warrant me in referring it, together with the
catacombs under the mountains eaſt of Naples,
to thoſe ages which have left amazing ſpe-
cimens of ſuch works (g) in Magna Græcia,
Sicily, Phœnicia, and moſt of the Mediterranean
iſlands. [See *Obſervations on the* CLOACÆ *in the*
article of ROME]. Farther, the grotto or cave
of

† Syl. iv.

(g) Varro, *de Re Ruſt.* L. iii. c. 17, ſeems to attribute it
to Lucullus; Strabo, L. v. to one Cocceius, but at the
ſame time ſpeaks with high commendations of the firſt Grecian colonies for works of this kind. John Villani, Chron.
I. i. c. 30, ſays that Virgil opened this cavern with the
ſtroke of a magic wand. Laſtly, Benjamin de Tudella,

of Paulilipo is drawn in an exact right line. Towards the end of October, placing myſelf at its eaſtern aperture, I ſaw the ſun filled its weſtern aperture for the ſpace of two minutes ; the grotto in the mean time forming, in its whole length, a tube of light : and by this phænomenon aſtronomers may readily determine the grotto's projection.

To avoid repetitions, I ſhall ſay nothing of Cuma, Puzzolo, or even of Herculanum itſelf. Among the ruins of this city I ventured into a defile newly opened, and carried pretty far. I led the way to ſeveral, and each with a lighted candle. In the part where the excavation was freſheſt, I perceived the aſhes, which conſtitute the whole ground hereabouts, looſening from the upper part of the gut, drop on my head, and run down along the walls like corn through a hopper : this alarmed me ; and I communicating my apprehenſions to the company, we all, without any long deliberation, made off faſter than we had come in. In this gut we ſaw a moſaic floor, and the walls of a houſe through which the ſearch was carried in a breadth of about four feet : a wall which it ſkirted was built of turf or pumice ſtone, with coins of brick, from whence

Itin. Hieroſol. gives the honour of it to Romulus, " by way," ſays he, " of providing a ſhelter againſt the invaſion with " which he was threatened by David's army under Joab." After all, this grotto is only child's-play, if compared to the catacombs : there is no conceiving their immenſity without ſeeing them. Theſe countries being at that time covered with inhabitants, and for that very reaſon having very few woods, the want of ſtones for building was the firſt motive for theſe excavations ; of which, afterwards, a farther public advantage was taken, by making, as the proverb ſays, a ditch of the earth. I muſt add, that the poſition of the catacombs ſeems to point out that of Paleopolis, which, according to Diodorus Siculus, was founded by Hercules.

pro-

projected, to about two thirds of their diameter, columns of the same substance; the whole covered over with a strong lay of puzzolana whitewashed with lime; so that Herculanum was built as Naples is at present.

The discoveries made by these searches are owing to chance; the laxity of the ground not admitting them to be extended throughout all the parts of the subterraneous city. The dangers consequential to such a laxity are easily conceived, amidst frequent disruptions which there is no preventing. Notwithstanding these obstacles, every day affords riches; the value of which they who have not seen Portici will not be able to judge of, till the engravers employed by the king of Naples, after finishing the paintings, will exercise themselves on the sculptures. The latter are what will especially shew the grandeur and the magnificence of the ancients, and their taste for the fine arts. Considering the known effects of air on paintings after being buried sixteen hundred years, it was prudently determined to begin the description of the monuments of Herculanum with these paintings. On the recommendation of count Gazzola, master of the ordnance, and the marquis of Fraggiani, president of the tribunal of the monarchy, his Sicilian majesty was pleased to make me a present of this most valuable collection.

The principal pieces of sculpture taken out of the ruins of Herculanum are already pretty well known by the several accounts which have been published of them; but I cannot omit a Mercury, which I saw in one of the guts. This statue, which is of bronze, and as big as life, represents

Q 2   the

the meſſenger of the gods juſt alighted from a long journey, and taking off his talaries. Extreme fatigue is expreſſed in his attitude, and every part of his body, which is without any covering: it is ſeen even in his flagging eyebrows, the frontal muſcles not being able to keep them up. Concerning beauties of this kind Pliny the younger uſed to ſay, *De illis judico quantum ego ſapio, qui fortaſſis in omni re, in hac certe perquam exiguum ſapio**. Applying to myſelf what Pliny ſaid of himſelf, I ſhall, with the public, wait the deſcription of Herculanum: it will furniſh me with the reaſons of my admiration of many pieces, which every body may admire, but which artiſts alone can deſcribe.

From the ſame motives I ſhall give only the bare hiſtory of the late diſcovery of the remains of the ancient Pœſtum. This city, built, according to Solinus, by the ancient Dorians, and, according to Strabo, by the Sybarites, ſtood at the end of a ſmall bay, now part of that of Salerno, at a league eaſtward from the mouth of the river Silo or Silaro; a ſituation, on account of which the Greeks afterwards gave it the name of *Poſidonia*. It was famous in the Roman times for its roſes; Virgil, Ovid, and Propertius, having taken notice of them. Its edifices, which proclaim the magnificence of its firſt founders, were unqueſtionably cotemporary with a famous temple dedicated to Juno Argiva, which Strabo places at the very mouth of the Silo, and makes Jaſon its founder. The cauſes of the depopulation and extinction of Magna Græcia reached this city; ſo that, for ſeveral centuries, its

* Severo, L. iii.

walls

walls and territory were become a wafte, known neither to mariners, nor the inhabitants of the neighbouring country.

About the year 1755, a difciple of a painter at Naples being in holiday time at Capaccio, the place of his birth, as he was walking, a fancy took him to go upon the rifing grounds which border on the ancient territory of Pœftum. The only dwelling which he could perceive there, was a thatched farm-houfe : the beft parts of the ground the farmer cultivated ; the others he referved for his cattle to feed in, and the ruins of the ancient city were a part of the latter. The young painter, on the heights from whence they were perceivable, had been ftruck with the fight, and on going up was amazed to fee ramparts and gates ftill partly fubfifting ; ftreets, the direction of which was vifible ; public buildings and temples. All thofe edifices, unqueftionably built by the Dorians, the founders of Pœftum, fpoke the moft remote antiquity, both in the refemblance of their conftruction, and proportions, with thofe remains of ancient Egyptian architecture ftill to be feen in Upper Egypt.

The artift, on his return to Capaccio, inquired of his neighbours about thofe monuments, and was informed, that this country had from time immemorial been a defert ; that about ten or twelve years ago the farmer, whofe dwelling he had feen, took it into his head to remove thither ; and that, fearching the ruins about his dwelling, he had found fome things which had turned to fo good account, as to put him into a condition of renting that wild and uninhabited fpot. The young difciple haftened away to Naples, to communicate this difcovery to his mafter. The rapture with which he fpoke of it, fo excited the painter's curiofity, that he repaired thither, and found a gratification the more ample and exquifite, as his eyes were converfant with fuch objects. Pœftum now rofe from its long obfcurity. The curious flocked thither; the moft inviting reprefentations were made of its ruins; the count de Gazzola, having plans and elevations taken of them in his prefence, employed the beft artifts in Naples in engraving them at his own houfe; and, in a word, at his requeft the king himfelf came in perfon to fee thefe ruins, and appointed them for the rendezvous of a great hunt.

I fhall mention Vefuvius, only in commemoration of the exquifitenefs of the grapes which, growing among the ravages of its eruptions, yield the wine known by the name of *Lacryma Chrifti.* And here let me gratefully remember the generous courtefy of an old man, to whom we owed the regale : he lived half way up the hill, in a cavern formed by irregular congeftions of *lava.* In going up towards him without feeing him, we were eating the grapes with all the appetency which heat and fatigue can excite for a very palatable refrefhment. His fudden appearance had fufpended our voracity, till he faid to us with an afpect which confirmed the kindnefs of his words, *Mangiate, fiòli, mangiate:* "Eat, children, eat." We imagined that the expectation of the *buona mancia* was at the bottom of this courtefy, and accordingly behaved like perfons accuftomed to fuch mercenary civilities; but, to our no fmall furprife, the good old man would **hear of no fuch** thing;

thing; and it was only at our repeated inftances that he accepted of a carlin, which he faid he would keep very charily, as a token of the happinefs he had to ferve Frenchmen.

A tafte for the higher fciences has got footing at Naples. We were prefent at a private exercife, where the prince de La Rocella's eldeft fon, who was fcarce entered into his fifteenth year, explained Newton's Trajectories with the profoundnefs of a great geometrician, the perfpicuity and eafe of a man of wit, and all the gracefulnefs and vivacity of his age.

Another prince has made great advancements in chemiftry and difcoveries analogous to that fcience; particularly, he gives to white marble a fixed tincture of any colour whatever, and penetrating through the whole mafs however large. We faw a cardinal's hat of this kind; and near it was a rough piece of equal bulk, which had gone through the like operation: it was broken before our eyes, and the whole infide was of as fine a red as the fuperficies. Something ftill more wonderful is a cube, likewife of white marble, with its furface two feet fquare every way: on one is painted a virgin, and all the *laminæ* which are fawed away from the cube, fhew the like image. It is this prince of San-Severo who has recovered the ancient fecret of inextinguifhable lamps. We faw one burning in a vault hermetically fhut; and we were affured it had been there eighteen months, without any fupply to the fubftance which feeds its light. This lamp illuminates the vault of a chapel in which lie the prince's anceftors; and the fcope of all his chemical difcoveries is to

increafe

increase the ornaments of this chapel, which already is but too full of them. Among those which he intends to add, we saw, in his palace, a white marble statue, as big as life, representing Man in the bands of Sin. These bands are a large net inclosing the figure, which is struggling in it. This net, with its numberless mashes and knots, was made out of the same block; an immense labour, which might have been much better employed. After all, it is a mere Gothic piece, and the more such, as the figure is nothing near so fine as it might, had not the net ingroffed all the artist's attention. This odd piece, at Rome would scarcely be looked on; but Naples reckons it among its wonders.

I shall not repeat, what is known to all the world, that Naples is the centre of the best music in Italy, and the *non plus ultra* in execution. It is to all Italy, in music, what Athens was to Greece in eloquence and philosophy; but its music, like the other arts, favours a little of the national fondness for the *capricciofo* and the *stravagante*.

The emulation of musicians at Naples shows itself most distinguishably at the opera, which is the most splendid, the most grand and magnificent dramatic exhibition in Italy, and, it may be suppofed, in all Europe.

The theatre is of an astonishing spaciousness, having six rows of boxes, each of which, like a room, is furnished with tables, pier-glaffes, tapestry, canopies, branches, &c. the king's is a salon fronting the stage, and of such a size as very conveniently to hold the royal family and part of the court: the orchestra has room for two hundred

perfons:

perfons: the pit is full of fixed benches, like thofe of our amphitheatres, which are not ufed in Italy: the decorations, inftead of being like fcreens, reprefent fome public place, the infide of a temple, or of a palace; the whole in three large pieces, two along the fides, and one filling up the end of the ftage, and in which painters difplay all the magic of perfpective.

The exhibition is variegated by marches, battles, triumphs, all in the moft grand execution : battles are fought between numerous bodies of fencing-mafters in rich uniforms, and who appear to be really fighting, the clafhing of their weapons keeping time with the orcheftra: thefe battles are not without their cavalry, and mounted on horfes from the king's ftables, or thofe of the firft nobility. In triumphs the car is drawn by the king's fineft horfes, caparifoned at the expence of the undertakers. The intervals between the acts are filled up with ballets in no wife relating to the play, and the more out of the way by being executed on French airs, as fitter for this purpofe than the Italian, by reafon of their quicker meafure.

The theatrical undertakers are a fociety of creditable perfons of all ranks, who, with the approbation of the court, are renewed annually. The piece for the year is fold in print; and at the beginning of it are the names of the poet, the mufician, the actors, the principal fymphonifts, the decorator, and even the taylor.

The opera for 1758 was Metaftafio's *Demophoön*, fet to mufic for that year by the celebrated Saffone; for operas in Italy are like the motets in France, muficians compofing, by way of emulation, from

the

the fame words. It was the opinion of all Naples, that all the former mufical compofitions on Demophoön fell fhort of Saffone's. This play is known, both in its fubject and bufinefs, to be very near a-kin to the French *Agnes de Caftro*. The *duetto* clofing the fecond act, with other pieces of that kind, was generally applauded; but at the arietta *Mifero Pargoletto*, in which Timante fpeaks to his fon, whom he holds in his arms, there was not a dry eye in the houfe: the whole expreffion of this *arietta* was that of nature : the very French who were prefent overlooked the aukward phyz of the Soprano, who acted Timante, and the difagreement of his voice with the enormity of his ftature, of his arms and his legs, and wept as cordially as the Neapolitans themfelves. At the operas in Italy, clapping an *arietta* is a fignal for an *encore*. The orcheftra then returns to the prelude, and the *caftrato* walks about in a circle, and fings the favourite *arietta* the fecond time. This is fometimes repeated even to the fifth or fixth time; and in thefe repetitions it is, that the finger exerts every refource of nature and art, to furpafs himfelf in each repetition, by the variety of gradations which he introduces into the trills, modulations, and whatever belongs to the expreffion.   Slight and quick as fome of thefe gradations may be, not one of them efcapes an Italian ear: they perceive them, they feel them, they relifh them with a delight, which in Italy is called the *foretafte of the joys of Paradife*, where, we may hope, there will be others equivalent, for thofe nations whofe organs are lefs fenfible to the powers of harmony.

The

The opera at Naples acts from St. Charles's day to Lent, and three times a week : the other parts of the year are left to the comic opera, and a play not like that of the other parts of Italy, which is also acted by Italian players in foreign countries. Most of the arguments of the Neapolitan drama are a mixture of tragi-comedy, like those of Lopez de Vega, and Spanish play-wrights; a manner which, like many of the other customs and modes, is a relique of the long dominion of the Spaniards at Naples. The principal characters in these compositions are kings and queens, princes and princesses : the droll parts are a *Dianina, Polichinello,* and *Don Fastidio de Fastidii.*

All the intrigues are carried on by *Dianina*: she who acted that part during my stay at Naples, was a handsome young woman about seventeen, danced and sang very prettily, and had all the cunning, readiness of wit, and sprightliness of a chamber-maid.

Polichinello is a Calabrian peasant, become a footman in the decline of life, but still retaining all his former bluntness and stupidity. Instead of a hat, he has an old cap, like that of a charity-boy; and a bag, with an opening at the bottom, serves him for a cloak, which is tied about the waist with a cord : his stockings are sack-cloth guetres, with large wooden shoes : his speech consists of a jargon of the Neapolitan and Calabrian; and this coarse idiom, the vehicle of all the obscenity belonging to his part, makes Naples laugh more in one evening, than all the rest of Italy in a whole twelvemonth. Foreigners, who cannot join in the laugh, are easily known by their seriousness. The first time I was at this play,

I hap-

I happened to be among fix, who gravely kept
their countenance. I took the liberty of afking
them how they could fit fo compofed; and I had
for anfwer, that it was their misfortune to be,
fome Tufcans, others Romans and Venetians.

Don Faftidio de Faftidii was admirably acted
by a man with fpindle fhanks, tun belly, long
fcraggy neck, large mouth, lantern jaws, and a
nofe of an enormous length : being in a Spanifh
drefs, he has on a black wig, with the two fhort
ties continually flapping his ears before and behind, and thus filling up the void which his bare
neck leaves between his broad fhoulders and his
head. A more drole mafque certainly was never
contrived. All great concerns are conducted by this
perfonage, who, abounding in folemn fentences,
turgid phrafes, and pompous words, always opens
his opinion with a *Con-cio-fia-cofa-che*, and a prolix
period of four claufes, but which he never finifhes,
either being impertinently interrupted by *Polichinello*, or bewildering himfelf in the ideas by the
connexion of which his period is to be formed.
When out, he continues chewing high, with increafed gravity. He is generally counfellor of
ftate, hufband and father, and gets frequent drub-
bings ; he is a cuckold on record ; his precious
daughter proves with child, and is run away with;
yet all thefe difagreeable accidents do not abate
his felf-conceit, his confidence in his fagacity, and
his inexhauftible loquacity.

The Neapolitan actors, like thofe of moft of
the cities in Italy, do not make a living by the
ftage; they are either artificers or tradefmen.
Don Faftidio was a creditable goldfmith: I have
seen

feen him at work in his fhop, as if he had never trod the ftage. *Dianina* was to have been married to a jeweller in the beginning of November. The houfes being open only at certain times in the year, the ftage is but a temporary ftation, which would not maintain idlers who fhould wholly give themfelves to it. The public morality is a gainer by this difpofition, and the theatre is no lofer, all who appear on it acting for themfelves no lefs than for the public. Our Neapolitan players ufed to perform their rehearfals in a fmall theatre, near the new-caftle fquare, called *il Teatro della Cava:* it was indeed in a real vault, very damp, and offenfive to the fmell. The price of the boxes was about ten fous French money. Thefe rehearfals were crowded by the commonalty, who thus faw a play for two or three fous; and by fuch foreigners, who were for feeing both the people and the actors in a half undrefs; they themfelves laughing at the jokes arifing from the occafion, or which incidents fuggefted.

I have already obferved, that, in all the theatres of Italy, the parts of men, and efpecially of gallants, are acted by women; whereas at Rome, according to the cuftom of the ancient Romans, all the female parts are performed by men; which is called *far da Donna.*

From what I have already faid of the richnefs of the churches at Naples in plate, in paintings, and in decorations fhewing more oftentation than tafte, it may have been concluded that Naples, even relatively to religion, affects fingularity. No where are feftivals attended with fuch pomp and buftle. The moft brilliant part of thefe fefti-

vals is the octaves. The eight days following the
festival of the patron saint of every church, whether regular or secular, are a continual solemnity,
at which the finest voices and best hands attend,
both morning and evening. Such is the number
of churches within Naples, that the octaves make
the whole year one continued entertainment for the
devout, the lovers of music, and likewise for the
musicians, being the main source of their sub-
fistence.

The feast of Corpus Christi eclipses these
hebdomadary solemnities : at that season, the
richest churches ingross the whole opera, its
voices, instruments, machines, decorations, and
illuminations ; and the octave of this feast not
sufficing for the number of exhibitions, and the
curiofity of the people, it is prolonged, so that one
exhibition is not a disadvantage to another. I saw,
in the Jesuits great college, the store-house of the
machines which they set up in their church on this
festival : few opera-houses can shew the like. To
give me an idea of this spectacle, I was told that
the *Santiſſimo*, being carried up on clouds almost to
the roof of the church, descends of itself for the
benediction, making its way through the clouds,
which separate, and receiving in its passage the
veneration of angels and other beings, part of
whom leave their station to attend on it. What
can the Greeks think at the sight of spectacles like
these ; they, who have no better way of keeping
the Eucharift than in a leathern purse hung up
against the wall in the sacrifty of their churches ?

The news-papers mention no other liquefaction
than that of the blood of St. Januarius : but this
miracle

miracle is common at Naples; it is repeated there
at feveral times, and in feveral churches, on St.
Stephen's blood, on St. Pantaleon's, St. Patrizia's,
St. Vitus's, St. John the Baptiſt's ; and likewiſe
on ſome milk of the Virgin Mary's, of which the
Minims have two phials liquefying every Lady-
day(*b*). Mr. Addiſon in his Travels through Italy,
and afterwards Mr. Voltaire in his Univerſal Hiſtory, apply to theſe liquefactions the paſſage of the
fifth Satire of Horace, book i. where the poet
relates a miracle of the ſame kind, ſhewn him in
the ſame country :

Ignatia limphis
Iratis extructa dedit riſuſque jocoſque,
Dum flamma ſine thura liqueſcere limine ſacro
Perſuadere cupit.

The Neapolitans, and the Italians in general,
who have had any education, are in Horace's way
of thinking, but without allowing themſelves his
way of talking : their behaviour and converſation
on any thing relative to belief, even the moſt popular, are regulated by the danger, in Italy, of
being reckoned a miſbeliever, and the little inconveniency they find in appearing too credulous.
The ſame Mr. Addiſon, above quoted, ſaw
the harbour of Naples in Virgil's beautiful deſcription of that of Carthage :

Eſt in ſeceſſu longo locus, inſula portum
Efficit objectu laterum, &c. *

(*b*) Concerning theſe miracles, ſee the Jeſuit Pietra Santa's
Thaumaſia.

* Æneid. Lib. i.

The

The refemblance is indeed ftriking. Virgil, in this defcription, might have in his eye the two bays of Naples: in a word, the *Sylvæ, decora alta, corufcæ*, give a natural reprefentation of the fite of the poet's tomb; but Macrobius will have this defcription to be merely an imitation of that which Homer,* in the thirteenth book of the Odyffee, has drawn of the harbour of Ithaca. Both defcriptions indeed offer the fame objects; fome more particularifed in Virgil; others, fuch as the famous Grotto of the Nymphs, more clearly delineated in Homer.

The air of Naples, the bad fare at our inn, and the wine which we were in fome meafure obliged to fight for, (though at Naples the very beft is fold at a low rate) affected my health. The air and aliments, which in the Neapolitans caufed the explofions and eruptions taken notice of above, operating on me only by halves, had the effect of a medicament, which, its action being concentrated, would torment a patient inftead of relieving him. The captain of an Englifh privateer very obligingly told us, we fhould be extremely welcome to a paffage over to Sicily; but a conveniency unexpectedly offering, I returned to Rome, and even without taking leave of the count di Gazzola, who, on hearing of my departure, commended my prudence; adding, that, of twenty foreigners, who in fpight of the intimations of nature would continue at Naples, fix or feven generally loft their lives. Two of the French abbots, who had come to Rome on account of the conclave, lay danger-

* Saturn. L. v. c. 3.

oufly ill at Naples; and, however alluring this city is to a foreigner, the dangers of making any ftay here may well make him fay, *Tanti pœnitere non emo.*

It remains to be obferved concerning Naples, 1. That princes are as common there as marquifes at Paris; that the nobility's luxury lies chiefly in equipages, coaches and four or fix being much more common at Naples than at Paris; that the mules, or horfes, are the very fineft which can be got; that the length of the traces is one of the chief marks of grandeur and diftinction; laftly, that the lackeys are very handfome well-made fellows, in rich liveries, trailing fwords of an enormous length; whereas the mafter's, which is more like a poniard, is carried by the firft lackey at a button-hole.

2. That the kingdom of Naples is ftill governed by laws which the Normans introduced in the eleventh century. Thefe laws are to the common law of Italy, what the cuftom of Normandy is to the common law of France: it is the ancient feudal law in all its purity, or rather in all its rigour, with regard to younger brothers and daughters, in fucceffions and all difpofals of poffeffions. This law being equally common to Normandy and the kingdom of Naples, is fo unexceptionable a mo- nument of the Norman conqueft, that the principal articles of the *confuetudines Napolitanæ*, and of the Norman cuftom, are explained by one another, in the Neapolitan and Norman Commentaries; and Banage is as well known and as much con- fulted at Naples, as *Matthæus de Afflictis* at Rouen.

This refemblance, this affinity, this family-look, ftill difcernible between the laws of the conquer-ors and thofe of a country conquered feven hun-dred years ago, feem to me a proof that, at the time of the conqueft, thefe laws and cuftoms, commonly thought to proceed from caprice, ig-norance, and barbarifm, were founded on rational and fixed principles; and, though not digefted into books, were fafely preferved in the memory of thofe whofe welfare depended on the prefervation of them; and this the more eafily, the articles being but few. Such was the Roman law itfelf in its origin, and fuch the Twelve Tables of which Cicero * has faid, *Fremant omnes licet, dicam quod fentio, Bibliothecas mehercule omnium philofophorum omnes, mihi videtur* XII. *Tab. Libellus, fi quis legum fontes & capita viderit, & autoritatis pondere, et utilitatis ubertate fuperare.*

The Two Sicilies, as governed by the feudal law in all its ftrictnefs, offer to the nobility of thofe ftates of Italy, where the laws have eftablifhed an equality, fuch as Genoa, Venice, Milan, &c. an advantage, which in France Normandy offers to the Parifians and inhabitants of the common-law provinces, where equality is fettled by the municipal law, fiefs are purchafed, and go with-out any divifion or difmemberment to the purcha-fer's eldeft fon. A great part of the Sicilian fiefs are, accordingly, in the hands of Venetians, Ge-noefe, &c. and it is fomething ftrange to me, that the fovereigns of this kingdom have never thought of prohibiting, or at leaft of caufing to be pur-chafed, a conveniency, which, befides its detri-

* De Orat. L. i. N. 195.

ment

ment to cultivation, throws the principal fruits of their subjects industry into foreign hands.

A litigious disposition, if not introduced, has been perpetuated at Naples, jointly with the Norman laws; so that there are few countries which have so many law-courts, and people living by the law. This is the greatest, and perhaps the only change, that has happened in the Neapolitan manners, as exhibited in the picture given of them by Statius, who wrote under Domitian. He says of Naples,

Nulla foro rabies, aut strictæ jurgia legis,
*Moris jura viris solum & sine fascibus æquum.**

3. In all the countries which I have seen, there is not a town, Langres in France excepted, where the walls of churches are so crowded with epitaphs and funerary inscriptions as Naples; and they generally favour very strongly of the country : grief expresses itself in epigrams, antitheses, and puns; a diction quite opposite to the style used by the ancients on these lugubrious objects. Misson has inserted a great many of those Neapolitan epitaphs, taken as they came. I shall mention two, which he should not have omitted. The first is a distich on a stone sarcophagus, surmounted with a little Bacchus, in a chapel of the Mount of Olives church : it was composed by king Alphonso the Magnanimous, in honour of a favourite called Maffimo.

Qui fuit Alfonsi quondam pars maxima regis
Maximus, hâc tenui nunc tumulatur humo.

* Sylv. L. iii.

The second, which affects both by the subject and the turn of it, heightens the beauty of the monument erected by the great Gonsalvo's grandson, in the church of Santa Maria la-Nuova, to the memory of M. de Lautrec, who died before Naples, which he was besieging for Francis I.. This monument is of the last century:

ODETTO FUXIO LAUTRECO,
FERDINANDUS CONSALVUS, F. FILIUS
LUD. MAGNI CONSALVI NEPOS,
CUM EJUS OSSA, LICET HOSTIS,
UT BELLI FORTUNA TULERAT,
SINE HONORE JACERE COMPERISSET
HUMANARUM MISERIARUM MEMOR,
IN AVITO SACELLO,
GALLO DUCI,
HISPANUS PRINCEPS
POSUIT.

At Naples, opposite to the Carmelites and the Torrion, so famous by Guise's Memoirs, is seen another monument, but of less honour to human nature, the pillar at the foot of which the unfortunate Conradin was beheaded and interred *(i)* by order of Charles of Anjou, who had wrested the kingdom of Naples from him. On this pillar is a distich in Gothic characters, containing a taunt not less shocking than the event it commemorates.

Asturis ungue Leo pullum rapiens Aquilinum,
Hic deplumavit, Acephalumque dedit.

(i) In the middle of the very square where he was executed, he being at that time under excommunication.

The

The emprefs Margaret, dowager of the emperor Conradin, had flown from the heart of Germany to Naples, to ranfom her fon's life ; but fhe came too late, and all her comfort was her being permitted to remove his corpfe from the unhallowed place where it had been put into the ground, to the Carmelite church. A private perfon afterwards erected, at his own expence, a little chapel on the very fpot, and about the pillar, on the top of which he had a crofs fet up. The floor of this chapel, lying lower than the ground of the fquare about it, is, excepting the middle, (which is a thoroughfare from one part of the fquare to the other) always damp, from a caufe manifeftly natural ; but the Neapolitans look on this moiftnefs as a miraculous and perpetual teftimony of the innocence of Conradin, and his coufin Frederic duke of Auftria, who had been involved in his misfortunes and cataftrophe : this is a refpectable prejudice, deferving to be kept up in fupport of humanity, and the right of nations.

Naples, by its fituation and harbour, has always been the centre of a commerce, which it lies in its own breaft to enlarge, and very confiderably. Its exports are hemp, flax, goats hair, filk, dried fruits, manna, horfes, excellent fhip-timber, and different kinds of grain. The imports are cloth, linen, and filk ftuffs. The importation of cloth is intirely in the hands of the Englifh, in oppofition to the French, in confequence of a wrong meafure which I fhall briefly fet forth. The French had for a long time the exclufive monopoly of fupplying Naples with cloth ; and thefe cloths, moft of which are fuperfine, paid a duty *ad valorem*. The Englifh began the fame trade with low-priced

R 3

cloths,

cloths, either as meaning thereby only to fill up the void left them by the finer cloths of the French, or that their manufactures were not yet in a condition to enter into an open competition with them. However it be, having long traded on this footing, and thus paying very low duties, and from time to time renewing treaties in which the tariff of the former duties was ftill retained, they are gradually come to fupply Naples with the fuperfine cloths, and without any variation of the ancient tariff. The French, efpecially fince the acceffion of Don Carlos to the crown, might certainly claim equal indulgence; but, whether from forgetfulnefs or mifmanagement on their fide, or good luck and addrefs on that of the Englifh, things ftill continue to the prejudice of France, all whofe trade in this country is now dwindled to camblets and Picardy lawns.

Naples, being a long time under the dominion of the Spaniards, had imbibed their difpofition: it paid tribute to the trading nations for all its wants, without knowing how to go about leffening thofe wants by induftry, or fo much as furnifhing fome returns by the mere natural productions of its foil. Don Carlos and his miniftry have made it one of their principal objects, to raife the nation from fuch a fituation, equally fcandalous and detrimental, by fetting up new manufactures, and reviving thofe which were declining under the want of protection.

For fome years, the manufacture of linens had confifted only of what was made by the country people for their own ufe; whereas it now begins to fupply the towns-people with houfhold linen;

and

and from the profitable fale of them they will naturally receive a farther improvement. Manufactories of velvets, half velvets, handkerchiefs, filk ftockings, &c. increafe, and produce goods which recommend themfelves to foreigners. Great quantities of fpun cotton, befides fupplying the national manufactures, are exported to Germany and Swifferland. Laftly, commerce has even a profefforfhip in the univerfity: it had been originally founded by a private perfon for morality; but being difcontinued for want of an audience, the government have applied it to the explanation of the principles and particulars of trade, which at leaft proves the miniftry's great attention to that part of adminiftration.

From my account of the prefent ftate of mufic at Naples, it is eafily conceived to form no inconfiderable branch of trade. The marble flabs for veneering, in working of which the Neapolitans excel; the macaroons and other paftry works, of which the Italians are fo fond, and for which Naples is particularly famous; horfes and mules of the Neapolitan breed, the like of which no part of Italy affords; together with jewelry and the book trade, which flourifh greatly at Naples; make fo many branches of the trade which fupports this great city, and, if the government continues its protection, will enrich it.

When thefe matters are come to a kind of confiftency, it is thought the duties on exportation, and the embargo on ftuds, will be taken off. This confiftency is the king's view in the reimburfement of the capitals, for the intereft of which moft of thofe duties, alienated by the Spanifh viceroys, are

ftill

ftill levied for certain companies on account of former loans.

Till that liberty, which commerce requires, fhall take place, thefe duties are collected with a rigour not known in any other country. This I experienced at my leaving Naples : I was fearched in fuch a manner, that I could fcarce help thinking that even a Triorches would be feizable, and fubject to a fine for having more than he fhould. By their very narrow infpection of my clothes, which was the next article they proceeded to, I was quite amazed to find that linen, ftuffs, and ftockings, though made at Naples, paid a confiderable export duty.

If any thing obftructs the employment of induftry, on which the government is fo intent, and which clogs the refources in view for it, it will perhaps be the refolution taken by the fame government to fet up Naples as a military power, and keep it on that footing. In confequence of this refolution it is, that the king of Naples, in a profound peace, keeps a body of between forty and fifty thoufand men. Population indeed is no great fufferer by it, the far greater part of the foot confifting of French deferters drawn hither by the large pay, but ftill given to defert; which is the more extraordinary, as no difcharge is to be hoped for, but by death, or when irrecoverably difabled by illnefs. We were continually accofted, in the ftreets of Naples, by one or other of thefe foldiers, who, taking us to be French, talked to us of their hardfhips, and their forrow for ever having lifted in that fervice ; but their forrow fignified nothing, the frontiers being too well fecured for any of them to efcape. One

act

act of humanity in the government, however, deserves notice; that, on deserters being brought back to their corps, they are only put in prison and kept on bread and water for a few days : on a second crime the punishment is something heavier, but never death.

In our return to France, we met on the Leghorn heaths some French soldiers, who were come so far as from Westphalia to shut themselves up in that mouse-trap. We told them, as pathetically as we could, the conditions and the lamentations of those who had been caught in it : they said they would try, and walked on.

RETURN from NAPLES to ROME.

IN this return, I followed, from Capua to Terracina, part of the way which Horace took in that journey from Rome to Brundusium, which, in imitation of Lucilius, he describes with equal beauty and simplicity in the fifth Satire of his first book : my eyes were then in that state of *lippitude*, with which Horace was troubled on this journey.

Reading that satire with close attention, I discovered a fact which has escaped the commentators and translators, viz. that Horace performed this long journey on foot. This may be concluded, 1. from the word *repere* (k), which occurs twice; and from *altius præcinctis*, all terms agreeing only with persons on foot : 2. from the distance of the places where they put up at night : 3. from the express mention he makes of his travelling part

(k) Dacier, after explaining in a note that *repere*, the same as ἑρπειν in Greek, to *slide*, to *creep*, to *crawl*, signifies to go, concludes from it, that Horace travelled on horseback.

of

of the road in a carriage, and not faying a word about his beaft when he took boat for Forum Appii: 4. from the age and circumftances of the poet, who was in the twenty-third year of his age, having, the year before, ferved the campaign of Philippi in the foot: 5. from the rhetorician Heliodorus being of the company, and who, Greek like, was a mighty walker, both from choice and œconomy, and likewife in confequence of the Grecian education. The illuftration of this difcovery I leave to the firft Capuchin who, in tranflating Horace, or commenting on him, will be pleafed to obferve, that the wits of Auguftus's court ftill retained, with this ancient way of travelling, the fimplicity and plainnefs of manners which it feems to indicate.

I have faid, that the fatire in queftion is written with equal beauty and fimplicity: but here I muft except the epifode of Meffius and Sarmentus: it is in the low vulgar ftyle, which had over-run Paris at our coming thither in 1755, and which we may fuppofe Horace to have brought with him from the army. He makes ufe of it again in the fatire *profcripti regis Rupili*, which he wrote the year following. His converfation in high life, his connexions with Auguftus's friends, the manners of a court equally polite and learned, foon made him lay afide that ribaldry, which accordingly is no longer feen in his works, and which he left to *lippis atque tonforibus*; though Lambinus, and moft of the commentators, pronounce it to be *urbaniffimum et feftiviffimum (l).*

(l) M. Dacier's note on this ribaldry is rather more ridiculous than that on *repere*.

The

The curiofities in the feveral places along the
main road from Naples to Rome, are to be met
with in all books of travels ; fo that I fhall only
fpeak of the non-defcripts.

At the diftance of three leagues from Capua we
croffed the Garigliano, the Liris of the ancients.
This river, which was a boundary to Latium, waters a very fruitful country, bordered by thofe
rifings which produced the famous Falernian
wine. Here are feen the ruins of the town of
Minturnum and its marfhes, where Marius fought
fhelter from Sylla's revenge. Speaking of this
country, fo often imbrued with French blood, Brantome* breaks out into this lamentation : " Alas !
" I have feen thofe very places ; I have even been
" on the Garigliano. It was at fun-fet, more than
" at any other time of the day, that the fhades
" and *manes* began to appear like ghofts : the no-
" ble fouls of our brave French who expired there,
" feemed to rife from the earth to fpeak to me,
" and, as it were, anfwered me, talking of their
" battles and their glorious death."

M O L A.

Mola, the next place on the road, is the ancient
Formiæ, built by the Leftrigones, who were accounted men-eaters. All that remains of this
town is a fingle ftreet at the bottom of the bay,
which is covered towards the weft by the promontory of Gaeta. The hill where Formiæ ftood, is
now covered with excellent vineyards. As I was
walking among them, I perceived the remains of a
wall of a prodigious thicknefs, confifting of very

* Life of Confalvo.

large

large ftones uniformly cut in embofments. This embellifhment muft have been a tedious work, the ftones being a compound of extremely hard *filex*, joined together by a natural cement, to which naturalifts give the Englifh name of *pudding :* the whole promontory of Gaeta is one intire mafs of this kind.

The hills, of which this promontory is a continuance, were for a long time the haunt of gangs of *banditti*, deferters from the armies, which, for a great part of the fixteenth century, had been fighting againft one another for the kingdom of Naples. Thefe *banditti*, who lived by pillage, and were true fucceffors to the Leftrigones, had formed themfelves into a kind of republic, which the Spanifh viceroys little difturbed, if, as is faid, they did not tolerate it. Whilft they held this poft, travellers never ventured near them, except in numerous caravans completely armed. I was told that one of thefe caravans, with which Taffo was going to Naples, being attacked, defeated, and pillaged, one of the *banditti*, hearing, on the field of battle, the name of the author of *Jerufalem*, took no fmall pains to find him out, and prefented him to the commander of the troop, who received him with refpect, and even a kind of veneration : all his baggage was returned, with the addition of a prefent ; and the commander himfelf, at the head of a detachment, efcorted him out of all danger: thus providence is frequently pleafed to alleviate the afflictions with which fome cotemporary jealoufy embitters the life of illuftrious perfons, who, like Taffo,

> *Ploravere fuis non refpondere favorem*
> *Speratum meritis.*

The

The frontiers of the kingdom of Naples were at length cleared of thefe robbers, towards the clofe of the laft century, by the marquis de Carpi. Father Mabillon, Miffon, Burnet, and all travellers who have made the tour of Italy fince that happy expedition, join in commemorating the brave marquis de Carpi.

At Mola I afked for a barber: immediately after, comes in a tall, fwarthy, meager man with whifkers, a coat all in tatters, and a fpada of an enormous length; in a word, he appeared to be a brave defcendant from the ancient Leftrigones: after all the Italian ceremonies previous to this operation, he fhaved me with fuch dexterity and difpatch, that I never before nor fince met with the like. I did not forget to afk him what countryman he was, and where he had learned his trade: he told me that he was a Catalonian, and was juft come from Conftantinople, where for fix years he had practifed fhaving, but could hardly keep life and foul together, being but a bungler in comparifon with the Turkifh barbers.

Beyond Mola, fronting a bay formed by the fea in the hinder part of the promontory of Gaeta, the Appian road is lined with fome houfes, one of which is fuppofed to be Cicero's *Formianum*. Thefe houfes, ftill partly fubfifting, fhew the antiquity of their conftruction, in the very fmall, and very elegant rooms, windows, and doors: every thing is faced with marble, and the decorations are diftributed with equal moderation and tafte. Facing thefe houfes, a gentle flope full of olive-yards leads to the fea. There it was, that, according to tradition, Cicero fell a victim to the refentment

of

of Antony and Fulvia; and this fpot, Appian fays, travellers ufed to vifit with a veneration little fhort of religious worfhip.

F O N D I.

I faw at Fondi, the laft place in the kingdom of Naples, St. Thomas d'Aquinas's fchool and chamber: it is only from a refpect to thefe monuments, that the Dominicans abide in a houfe of a very forlorn appearance, and in which St. Thomas's chamber itfelf is a neft of rats. Between this town and the ruins of the caftle, which is famous for a princefs of the houfe of Colonna being carried away by the noted corfair Barbaroffa, runs a very fine brook, by the inhabitants called *Fontana di Petronio*. At the fource are ftill feen remains of apartments, which unqueftionably were baths. The pavement is in mofaic compartments. In one of the inward angles ftands part of a marble confular ftatue as big as life.

When I was at Fondi, it happened to be a fair or market day; at leaft the market-place fwarmed with men and women, buying, felling, talking, and all in their Sunday drefs. The women's apparel is perfectly like that of the country women about Bugey, and the maids at Lyons. The men wear a jacket, and a kind of feaman's watch-coat thrown over the fhoulders, both very coarfe and of a Capuchin colour: their legs favoured of the heroic times, having on the bufkin, in which our tragic actors figure; but the fole of it is only a piece of raw leather; the hair on the out or infide, according to the feafon, or the fancy of the wearer: and it is tied to the foot in three places with pieces of packthread, which are afterwards carried

carried crofs-wife about the leg, to above the calf.
In winter, they add woollen ftockings, or, in
their jargon, *cioccias*, which is pronounced like the
French word *chauffes :* fo, in the Calabrian jargon,
inftead of *camino* they fay *ciminiere*, which is precifely the French word *cheminée :* whether or no
the French carried thofe words to the fartheft part
of Italy, or whether they brought them from
thence, is not worth inquiry.

By means of the fair I had a fight of Mola court,
which was held under a fhed in a corner of the market-place. The judge's appearance put me in
mind of Horace's *Aufidius Lufcus*, and

Infani pramia fcribæ,
Prætextam et latum clavum prumæque batillum.

This magiftrate, without the awful *infignia* of
juftice, or richnefs of apparel, had all that fuper-
cilious ftiffnefs of deportment, which, in the petty
jurifdictions of every country, jufticiaries affect as
effential to their character.

TERRACINA.

Terracina is the firft place in the ecclefiaftical
ftate. Though the pope keeps a garrifon here, as
a frontier town, it is very thin of inhabitants,
and of courfe has no appearance of wealth. Its
houfes are little better than heaps of ftones and
rock, almoft without any opening for door or windows; and the ftreet door being of fuch an uncommon thicknefs, every houfe here might ftand
fomething of a fiege. The day I paffed through
this place being Friday, the ox, which was
to be eaten on the Sunday, ran about the ftreets
with

with the mob at its heels, hooting and harraffing him: this is the way in all little towns, where they fay that the flesh of thefe creatures, which are killed when fpent with fatigue and all over fweat, is made more tender and palatable by fuch exercife.

The cathedral of Terracina is in a great part the remainder of a temple : under the portico, which is fupported by very beautiful marble pillars, is a large vafe of white marble, adorned with relievos. The middle of the focle, on which the colonnade is raifed, exhibits a large and fine infcription in praife of Theodofius, who repaired the road from Rome to Naples, and all the cities on this road, with a magnificence which would have done honour to the firft ages of the empire.

The cathedral's fteeple to the north and eaft overlooks a country naturally very rich, and charmingly interfected with brooks and little ftreams; fo that nothing but hands is wanting for very advantageous improvements. The Pontine marfhes are a part of this country : weftward the profpect is bounded by the promontory *Circello*, famous in mythology as the manfion of *Circe*, and for the trick fhe put on Ulyffes's companions : the remainder of this delightful view is filled up by the main fea.

Having dined at Terracina, I fet out before moft of the carriages ; and, invited by the clearnefs of the fky, the mildnefs of the air, and the beauty of the Appian road, which hereabouts is as found and intire as the cenfor Appius left it, I walked on it to the length of about two leagues. All the ftones with which it was made, are of fuch a hardnefs, that nineteen centuries have not made

the

the leaſt impreſſion on them : they are all ſo irregular in their joinings, as if they had been laid
confuſedly, and as chance offered them ; but their
exact correſpondence both among themſelves, and
thoſe which form the borders and lining of the
cauſeway, indicates the moſt ſkilful combination
for the ſolidity of works of this kind. There are
ſtill ſome remains of thoſe *cippi (m)*, or joſſing-
blocks, for the more eaſy getting a horſeback or
alighting, the Romans riding without ſtirrups. I
have ſeen ſuch joſſing-blocks at Paris, at the gate
of the Pelletier hôtel in old Temple ſtreet, and at
the gate of the Urſins old hôtel. Theſe belong
to the time when the firſt officers of the parliament
had but a ſingle mule in their ſtable.

That part of the Appian road where I footed
it, has, both on the right and left, one continued
row of ruined palaces, temples, aqueducts, and
tombs. Theſe ruins raiſed in me a reflexion, what
a glorious ſight Italy muſt have afforded to northern
virtuoſi, who came to ſee it in the time of the Upper empire. Among theſe *rudera* I perceived, on
the right, amidſt a heap of buſhes, a piece which
appeared to me in better preſervation than any
thing I had yet ſeen in my walk. Towards the
road, it ſeemed only a bare wall ; but going round
it, I was ſurpriſed to find it a little temple, or
chapel, intirely of large ſlabs of white marble of
the moſt exquiſite workmanſhip, and in the fineſt
preſervation. The ornaments were only plain .
mouldings in the arch of the front, and a ſlight
entablature of a moſt delicate ſimplicity. If this

(m) Theſe Miſſon took for remains of walls running along
both ſides of the cauſeway.

temple, which refembles a vaft niche, was not a
tomb, it was doubtlefs a chapel, like that confecrated by Cicero to the memory of his dear Tul-
liola, fo often mentioned in his Letters to *Atticus*.
Whatever may have been its original defign and
ufe, it is now made a repofitory for dung and de-
cayed plants and vegetables, kept there to mace-
rate by the proprietor of a neighbouring fpot of
ground. The proportion of the door, being buried full one third of its height, fhews that the
whole furface of the Appian road is raifed at leaft
two feet, if, as is highly probable, fome fteps led
up to this temple *(n)* : it is enough, that I make
known this difcovery to artifts who are able to
clear it up. It would not become me to go beyond Cicero, when fpeaking of a monument of
this kind : *ibi capella quædam eft : ea quidem mirè,
ut etiam nos, qui harum rerum rudes fumus, intelligere
poffumus, fcitè facta et venuftè.* *

In my perambulation I met with fome gutters,
which enabled me to verify what is faid of the
conftruction of the Roman roads by thofe who have
beftowed their attention on thefe monuments, in
which the magnificence of the mafters of the
univerfe is perhaps moft auguftly difplayed. Thefe
gutters, by laying open perpendicularly the fide of
the caufeway, fhewed me that the pavement refted
all along on folid mafonry work, lined with fmall
ftones of equal bignefs, bound by a very ftrong
cement. Though the gutters in fome places were

(*n*) A farther confequence of this is, that originally the
via Appia was two or three feet above the level of the ground,
which at prefent is equal to it.

* Cic. in Verr. L. ii.

not

not much lefs than two feet in depth, I could not any where perceive where the mafonry begins. Its depth doubtlefs is in proportion to the laxity of the marfhy ground, which, all along this part, is its bafis.

On comparing roads of fuch a conftruction with the modern roads, now every where fo multiplied, the latter feem only as garden walks, in the keeping and annual repair of which

Et Dominum fallunt, & profunt Furibus ;*

whilft all that can be expected from them, in the revolutions and changes which the courfe of time brings with it, is to become mires quite impracticable to carriages.

PIPERNO.

Piperno, once a confiderable city, but now ruined, and the native place of Camilla, one of Virgil's heroines, I fhall remember for more fenfible reafons ; for, though I was in the beft inn, I had a moft wretched fupper ; and as to my bed, I very willingly ftarted from it at three o'clock in the morning (*o*). I dined ftill worfe, at an inn

(*o*) This city is very famous in Livy, by the name of *Privernum*, for its fortitude under the mifcarriages of a war, which it had declared againft the Romans. A fenator having in a full houfe afked the deputies of the vanquifhed, what punifhment they thought they deferved ; *That*, faid they, *due to men who ftill infift on freedom.* "But," added the conful, "fhould we condefcend to grant you a peace, will "you be fure to abide by the conditions ?" *For ever*, anfwered they, *if honourable ; as little as poffible, if difgraceful.* On thefe anfwers, the fenate declared the *Privernates* citizens of Rome. Of fuch men the wretched peafants, difperfed in the ecclefiaftical ftate, are the fucceffors.

* Hor. Ep. vi. Lib. i.

ftanding

ſtanding by itſelf in the front of a wood of holyoaks. On one ſide of this inn, in the midſt of a very even ſpot of ground, the earth has given way, and opened a circular gulph of about fifty feet diameter. At the depth of fifty or twenty feet, and through three ſucceſſive *ſtrata* of ſhells of different kinds, one ſees a water of a blackiſh green, and the depth of which, I was told, could not be found; with the addition, that an inn, where things *che non convenivano* were practiſed, had ſtood on that ſpot; and that St. Nicholas, in puniſhment of their profligacy, opened the gulph, which ſwallowed houſe, people, and all.

Some woods of tall trees, which I croſſed in this road, are as aukwardly felled as thoſe which I had ſeen in the kingdom of Naples. The wood-cutters, to ſave themſelves the trouble of ſtooping, do by theſe woods as the reapers do by the corn, cutting them at the height of the waiſt, leaving ſuch ſtandards as would not be thus neglected among more induſtrious, more active, and at the ſame time a more numerous people.

VELETRI.

The only entertainment my curioſity met with at Veletri, which I reached very early, was a fine palace, with a garden extremely ſpacious, and, like the palace, embelliſhed with ſtatues and antiques of all kinds, beſides the regularity of its diſpoſition, which ſurpaſſed any I ever ſaw in Italy. In Veletri ſquare ſtands a bronze ſtatue of Urban VIII. caſt by Bernini: it is exactly the ſame with that on his tomb in St. Peter's at Rome.

The Veletrians ſeem to want that regard in which
the

the Romans never fail towards mafterly performances. This ftatue has not only been placed in
a kind of enclofure on the fquare; but this place
is the receptacle of all the filth in the neighbourhood, befides the ordure of the populace.

It being All Saints eve, I faw vefpers pontifi-
cally celebrated in the cathedral by cardinal Delci,
dean of the facred college, and, as fuch, titu-
lary of the bifhoprick of Oftia, incorporated with
that of Veletri. What a difference between the
pomp and fplendor of Rome on fuch occafions,
and the plain, poor, and mean appearance of
religion at Veletri! In fhort, the dean of the facred college, when performing the moft brilliant
functions of the firft fee in the Roman church,
does not make the figure of the moft petty parochial prieft at Paris, at the head of his clergy.

Veletri ftands on a rifing ground, and is furrounded with vineyards and little gardens, which,
to the *curiali* at Rome, are as Tivoli, Frefcati, &c.
to the prelates and perfons of rank. This city,
though little better than a defert, has more fountains, and thefe yielding more water, than many
capitals in our country; and thefe fountains add
a new delight to that which Veletri receives from
the purity of its air.

This city gave birth to Auguftus, whofe father and anceftors had there performed the fame
functions, which appeared fo ridiculous to Horace in the perfon of the magiftrate of Fondi:
this magiftrate however was related to the celebrated Livia, confort to Auguftus, who in a
great meafure conducted himfelf by her councils.
Several fmall towns in the Campania of Rome

had

had the like honour of giving birth to emperors. Galba was born in a village within the diftrict of Fondi; Vefpafian, in a farm-houfe near Reate; Nerva, at Narni: and the inhabitants of thefe places, high and low, rich and poor, learned and unlearned, ftill call thofe mafters of the univerfe Coufins and Countrymen; and he who was born in their town, is with them the greateft emperor ever mentioned in hiftory.

JOURNEY from ROME to FLORENCE.

The rains which at Rome conclude the *influenza*, and to which September ufually puts a period, had continued to October: it poured down inceffantly day and night; and never was a feafon lefs fit for travelling. To this excufe my kind friends added the complaint of my eyes, that I might fpend the winter at Rome. "Are you "then," faid C. P. "for opening a fhop at Flo- "rence?" where dim-fightednefs is very common, and the inhabitants, being more or lefs afflicted with this diforder, fhew a predilection for the un- happy perfons who labour under it.

Amidft all thefe inftances, and my own inclina- tion to ftay, fome concerns of my fellow traveller preponderated for our departure. The deluge in- creafing, inftead of abating, we could not but expect as bad weather in our return, as it had been fine in our coming; and our domeftics, in going to the poft-houfe for horfes, were wet to the fkin. The rain however held up juft as we were getting into the chaife, after a focial dinner with our felect acquaintance; and to Florence we had very fine autumn weather.

At

At Baccano, the fecond ftage, a fine fpaniel of the large kind came up to us, and efcorted us to Florence, playing and eating with us, lying in our room, and attending us in all our walks about the towns on the road : in fhort, he was as fond of us as if born and bred amongft us. The mafter of the inn, where we alighted at Florence, knowing him again at firft fight, told us that this dog was ufed to run to and fro between Baccano or Viterbo and Florence : he faid, that he often came there with travellers, but that he never went farther than Florence, and, when a little refrefhed, he would fet off again for Viterbo : accordingly fo it was; for, after a ftay of four days, *Baccano*, the name we had given him, mingled with fome Eng-lifh gentlemen who fet out from our inn.

Night was coming on when we reached the third or fourth ftage, which was a lonely houfe in the midft of a wood, on a rifing ground, furrounded with ftreams, moft of which had overflowed. The place perfectly agreed with the account given of it at Rome : our fupper we could not complain of ; and we were attended by a young, fprightly, and courteous landlady, whofe behaviour, like that of her hufband, gave no room for fufpicion. Our only precaution was, that, when we were lighted up to our apartment, I called from the gallery to our domeftics, to fee that we might fet out early, and that, whenever they came to call us, they would find our chamber-door open : indeed we did not fhut it, and had a very quiet night; whereas, had we fhewn any fufpicion or fear, it might have been a night of difturbance, if not of bloodfhed.

This confidence is the fureft guard againft any bad defigns which may be apprehended in thefe parts. The villains, being the moft cowardly fcoundrels on earth, dread nothing fo much as coolnefs of temper: judging of others by themfelves, they imagine it muft be certainly backed by a magazine of arms; and fuch they account all the poftchaifes with Englifh or French paffengers; fo that a gentleman of either nation, alighting fword in hand, fhall drive a dozen of thefe rafcals with all their daggers and piftols about them. I myfelf, on the fudden appearance of a man bolting out of a corner of a wood with a gun, fword, dagger, ftiletto and piftols, have, as the beft way, leaped out of the chaife without any arms, gone up to him, and, looking him in the face, afked him, *Che hora é?* "What's o'clock?" and fent him away in a ftrong panic, fo that his many arms and weapons jingled.

What other travellers do, I know not; but certainly no traveller could be more poorly armed than we were. *Tutta Brefcia*, fay the Italians, *non armarebbe un cogl.....* "With all the arms in "Brefcia, a cowardly rafcal would not think he "had enough.."

VITERBO.

Viterbo, which we vifited the fecond day, is a very pretty place, with a cathedral, a guild-hall, a fquare, a palace, and beautiful fountains.

This city is moderately well peopled, and fhews itfelf at a diftance by fome very lofty towers, like thofe we had feen in Romania, and which, like thofe, had been ufed as fortreffes in the civil wars that harraffed Viterbo till the fixteenth century. All

All the public edifices in Viterbo are adorned
with infcriptions, fome ancient and fome of the
middle age, but forged by the famous Annius, a
Dominican, and by which Miffon was deceived,
and Gruter himfelf had adopted, but without having ever feen them. This fame Annius, who
died and was buried at Viterbo, where he was
likewife born, in the pontificate of Alexander VI.
had publifhed, under the name of *Philo*, *Berofus*,
Metafthenes, and feveral Greek and Latin authors,
of whom only the names now remain, feveral
pieces on antiquity and ancient geography, and
which for fome time had the run of the fpurious
decretals. They are cited as real by feveral writers of the fixteenth century, and among others by
Leandro Alberti, who maintained, as a French
Dominican has fince, in an apology of Annius,
that all thofe writings accounted fpurious had been
publifhed from ancient manufcripts, which, Leandro goes fo far as to fay, he had feen in Annius's
poffeffion: *Effendo io già molto giovine, ho veduto
gli anticki libri di detti autori.* It may be fuppofed,
that it was fuch kind of falfifications which put
father Hardouin on his fyftem concerning the
falfity of almoft all the monuments both of civil
and ecclefiaftical antiquity.

The country about Viterbo is covered with feats
of the cardinals and firft families of Rome; but
the moft ftately and fplendid of all is Caprarola,
built by Vignola, for cardinal Farnefe, nephew
to Paul III. This palace, together with a part of
the country joining to Bolfena lake, ftill belongs
to the houfe of Farnefe and its reprefentatives:
formerly both were a part of the duchy of Caftro,
the

the annexment of which proved fo tedious and
difficult to the holy fee; yet to this fame fee,
foon or late, will revert thofe allodial lands,
which by the feudal laws have efcheated to
Don Carlos. After this reunion, nothing will
remain but the bare memory of a houfe, whofe
perpetuity feemed fecured by the immenfity of its
poffeffions.

The road which led us from Rome into Tufcany
is the *via Caffia* mentioned by Cicero, in his Phi-
lippics, as dividing Etruria. This road, which
croffes a hilly country, was, in itfelf the worft,
and kept in the worft repair, which we had yet
feen in Italy : according to appearances, no manner of care has been taken of it fince the time of
that Caffius whofe name it bears. Be it obferved,
that the towns along this road are all built on hills,
and were founded by the Etrufci, except Viterbo,
which ftands at the foot of a hill called *Cyminus*,
to which it has given its name. Viterbo indeed is
a modern city, made up of the remains of the
Etrufcan towns deftroyed by the Lombards.

MONTE FIASCONE.

Monte Fiafcone was the capital of the Falifci :
it is famous for its wine, and the numerous femi-
nary founded by cardinal Barbarigo, whofe canonifation is now in hand ; and laftly, by the famous
epitaph, *Eft, eft, eft ; propter nimium eft*, &c.
but without a date. The German prelate whom it
commemorates was one *Fugger*, of the family of
the celebrated Fuggers of Augfburg, bankers to
the emperor Maximilian, patrons of literature and
learned men, and fince honoured with the title

of

of Counts of the Empire. Their name in German is pronounced *Foucre*, which the valet de chambre, who conducted his master's funeral, has latinised by *De Fucris*. Out of his master's spoil this same valet instituted a yearly libation of two casks of Muscadello to be poured out on the German prelate's tomb every Tuesday in Whitsun week. This libation was daily observed till cardinal Barbarigo came to be bishop; but he converted it into bread, to be distributed to the poor on the same day.

The road from Aquapendente to Sienna is no better than a heap of large flints, thrown there by the cultivators of the neighbouring grounds. These stones lying loose, and rolling one on the other, make the road intolerable at all times. We were told at Radicofani, that about a month before, a young French abbé going this road in a crazy post-chaise, the bottom came out; and that the abbé had been obliged to travel on about a league in this plight, crying out and roaring all the way; but the noise of the stones drowned his lamentations.

RADICOFANI.

Radicofani, now the first stage within the Tuscan dominions, belonged for a considerable time to the pope. It is an immense and very lofty mountain, with a citadel on the top of it, which from beneath has the appearance of a town. This citadel is said to have been built by the Lombards, and was repaired at a great expence by Adrian IV. The dukes of Tuscany likewise, besides improving the old, added new works: but about the year 1740, a great part of it was destroyed by fire, and has

not

not yet been intirely rebuilt: the pope, indeed, is
not fo dangerous an enemy, that any great difpatch fhould be ufed in the repair.

Radicofani, towards the fouth, gives a view of
the fea, and the *Stati degli Prefidii*; and north-
wards, of the ancient Clufium, and that part of
Tufcany which is moft famous in the Roman hiftory. This fortrefs was the theatre of a very fingular adventure, which happened to an abbot of
Clugny in his way from Rome to Sienna, where
he was going for his health; and is the argument
of Boccaccio's ninety-fecond novel, where it is related with all the natural agreeablenefs for which
that writer is fo celebrated.

S I E N N A.

Sienna, which was founded by the Galli Senones
in Brennus's expedition, and long famous for its
numerous population, rich manufactories, large
trade, military feats and fignal victories over the
Florentines, has been continually on the decline
fince 1554, when the Spaniards fubjected it to the
dominion of the dukes of Tufcany.

The only veftiges of its ancient grandeur are
the turrets, with which the moft confiderable
houfes are flanked; its cathedral, which in the
whole and every part of it is a prodigy of magnificence, and kept with fuitable neatnefs; and a
great many churches and monafteries, which, with
a very rich and well-ferved hofpital, fhare what
remains of its former riches.

The moft fightly houfes have, in the ground
floor, and many in every ftory, in the piers between
the windows, large iron cramps, projecting about

a foot, with a thick ring at the end of them. I never could learn, either at Sienna, or at Florence, the prefent ufe, or the original meaning, of this odd decoration.

The large fquare, excavated in the figure of a fhell, environed with but ordinary buildings, and too large for Sienna in its prefent depopulation, is remarkable only for its fhape, and a fpring with water enough to make a little fea of the fquare. This fpring, which iflues from a fide of the fquare, has been celebrated by Dante, book xxx. of his *Hell.*

Per Fonte Branda non darei la vifta.

About the clofe of the fifteenth century, Pandulphus Petrucci had made himfelf mafter of Sienna, and governed the republic with the fame right and reputation as the firft Medicis governed Florence. This is the Pandulphus whom Machiavel fets as a pattern for ufurpers of the fovereignty in a free ftate; and to the minifters of thefe ufurpers he recommends, for their model, Antonio di Venafro, who ferved Pandulphus in that quality. Florence afforded the like copies and like models to Machiavel; but foreign inftances beft fuited his inftructions, which he intended for the Medicis, that a dominion, which his country was now unable to fhake off, might be directed to its greateft good.

Petrucci's character and high ftation procured the cardinalfhip to his fon Alphonfo, who, being promoted very young, imprudently put himfelf at the head of the faction, which, on the death of Julius II. entered into a kind of combination to exclude

exclude the ancient cardinals from the papacy: it
was indeed his misfortune to carry his point, procuring the young cardinal John de Medicis to be
fucceffor to Julius II. and he, being appointed to
proclaim this election, did it in thefe terms; " We
" have for pope, John de Medicis cardinal deacon,
" who has taken the name of Leo X. MAY THE
" YOUNG LIVE FOR EVER," *Vivano i Giovani*. But
Borghino his brother, who now filled the place of
their father Pandulphus, being foon after driven
out of Sienna by the intrigues of the Medicis, he
in revenge betook himfelf to intrigue, caballing
againft them, and againft Leo X. who, irritated at
fuch practices, confined him in the caftle of St.
Angelo, where he died during his imprifonment.

The territory of Sienna, and that part of Tufcany between Sienna and Florence, prefent the
traveller with a new heaven and a new earth. The
towns, the villages, and the farms, befides their
number, are better peopled than thofe in the ecclefiaftical ftate: the lands are better cultivated;
the men are more robuft, and, in their whole
carriage, fhew that chearfulnefs, vigour, and ala-
crity, which accompany eafe and plenty, and are
damped and extinguifhed by diftrefs. In the very
peafants are feen thofe fignificant phyfiognomies
which completely anfwer the pictures of Dante,
Boccace, Machiavel, &c. To this improvement
and extent of cultivation is certainly to be attributed the ferenity of the fky, which here is not
clogged with the fuliginous vapours exhaled from
the waftes of the ecclefiaftical ftate. In fhort, the
appearance of both countries is the very reverfe of
the defcription which two geographers, who do
not

not value themfelves on correctnefs, but are highly
entertaining, have drawn of the countries of Pa-
pimania and Pape Figuierra.

F L O R E N C E.

Florence, the capital of Tufcany, was lefs
known in antiquity than any of the cities now fubject to it.   Its firft inhabitants, being wholly given
up to the enjoyments of a delicious fituation, fell
an eafy prey to the feveral barbarians who ravaged
Italy, and were likewife victims to the jealoufy of
their neighbours, who, after driving them out of
their city, reduced it to a heap of ruins.   It owed
its reftoration to Charlemagne, who, on his return from Rome, in 802, rebuilt its walls, and
re-affembled the inhabitants, who had been difperfed in the country along the Arno.

   They availed themfelves of the anarchy, into
which Italy fell under Charlemagne's fucceffors,
to erect themfelves into a republic ; and the firft
exploit of this infant ftate was an act of revenge
againft the city of Fiefoli, which had deftroyed
Florence.   The Florentines, in their turn, pillaged and rafed it in 1010, and, to cut off all hopes
of its being rebuilt, like the Romans in their firft
conquefts, they removed the Fiefolefe to Florence,
and incorporated them with their republic.

   After this incorporation, Florence became to
Italy, what Naples was to Greece in thofe glorious
times of which Thucydides and Xenophon have
written the hiftory.   Profufe of the riches ac-
crueing to it from a large trade and flourifhing
manufactures, and ftimulated by that pride which
is the parent of vaft projects and noble enter-

prifes, it afpired to every kind of glory; and to this progreffive exertion of its genius Europe owed the revival of the patriotic, the political, and military virtues, and likewife of the fciences and arts, fo long fuppreffed by barbarifm.

Cofmo de Medicis, like a fecond Pififtratus, undertook to make himfelf mafter of a people who looked on liberty as the chief good. Immenfe riches, boundlefs liberality, popular manners, a latent and active policy, an intrepid courage and a patience ever uniform, the love of literature and the fine arts, much zeal for religion, an humble deference to all his minifters (o), were the inftruments of that tyranny, eftablifhed by one whofe grandfather was fcarce known; if the odious name of Tyranny may be given to a fovereignty which Cofmo exercifed, as he himfelf ufed to fay, *con capucchio*, "in a cowl," without any mark of diftinction from the other citizens. It was very fenfibly faid by an emperor, on feeing the palace which Cofmo built at Florence, "What croffes, "what uneafineffes, what oppofitions, what vexa- "tions, muft fuch an elevation have coft the man "who dared attempt it!"

However it be, Cofmo, to all the advantages which his country enjoyed, added inward tranquillity: he was a liberal patron of genius, and affifted the advancement of the fciences and arts, the hereditary tafte of which in his family

(o) *Con palefi e manifefte virtu, con fecreti e nafcofti vizzi fatto capo di una Republica piu tofto non ferva che libera.* Varchi. "With open and confpicuous virtues, clofe and fecret in "his vices, he became the head of a republic not under "flavery indeed, neither free."

did

did not a little contribute to perpetuate its sovereignty. In a word, he deserved that best of titles,
of Father of his Country, as it stands on his monument, and supplies the place of all the titles
and elogiums with which his descendants might
have loaded it.

COSMUS MEDICIS,

DECR. PUB.

PATER PATRI.

Laurence the Magnificent, his grandson, reigned
by the like claim, and in the like manner, over
Florence; of which the Medicis owed the sovereignty not so much to the labours of their ancestors, as to the intrigues of Leo X. and Clement VII. and the alliances which those popes procured to their family.

Laurence de Medicis, grandson to Laurence the
Magnificent, was indebted to Leo X. for his marriage with the heirefs of the house of Bologna, as
one of the secret articles of the *Concordat* made in
1515, between that pope and Francis I. Catharine de Medicis, the fruit of this marriage, was
in 1533 espoused to Henry II. son of the said
king, who came into this match in compliance
with the instances of Clement VII. Francis the
dauphin being poisoned in 1545, Henry, Catharine's husband, took the title of Dauphin, and
succeeded his father in 1547. Aretin, in a letter
to Catharine de Medicis, says, concerning Henry
the Second's accession to the crown, *Non si vanti
la Sorte d'averlo essunto in Rè con solenne misterio
del Fato.* In this match Francis I. must have
done no small violence to himself, if we may judge

by the ſtyle of a diſpatch of the 15th of April, 1532, in anſwer to the propoſal of pope Clement VII. of his ſending to the emperor a powerful ſuccour for the defence of Italy, then threatened by Soliman ; at the ſame time exhorting him to make uſe of this opportunity of reconciling him to the emperor : "I would have the holy father know," ſaid that prince, " that the king is neither a tradeſman, " nor a Florentine, nor ſo mean-ſpirited a creature, " that ranſoms, a priſon, and other ill treatments, " ſhould cow him, and make him act beneath his " duty, inſtead of ſtimulating him to reſent ſuch " wrongs," (alluding to the manner by which Clement VII. who had been priſoner of Charles V. procured his diſcharge) : " ſuch a puſillanimity his " holineſs may keep to himſelf, and not diſparage " a king of France ſo far as to think he would " do any thing like it : that, as for himſelf, he " had never given offence to the emperor ; but, " on the contrary, he had received ample matter " of offence from him ; that, if our ſaid holy fa- " ther found the emperor to be in ſuch a ferment, " he might, if he pleaſed, be his phyſician, and " give him rhubarb, or ſome ſuch phyſic as he " ſhould think fit for mollifying and cooling him ; " for, as to his part, the ſaid emperor might look " out for other phyſicians than him ; that he was " none of his domeſtics, or retainers, ſo as " to concern himſelf about curing his many " ailments ; and that he was very much ſurpriſed " the holy father ſhould think ſo ſlightly of him, " as to make uſe of ſuch words, &c. &c."

From the ſpirit and ſharpneſs of this letter, one would have little thought, that the following year
ſhould

ſhould ſee an alliance concluded between Francis I.
and Clement VII.

It is to the Medicis, and the two popes of
this houſe, that Florence owes thoſe edifices and
monuments which, diſtinguiſhing it from the
other cities of Europe, raiſe it to a rivalry with
the famous cities of ancient Greece.

Among the edifices of Florence, there are however ſome, which, though prior to the Medicis,
may be looked on as preludes to the Florentine
taſte for fine performances. Such are, the church
of St. Maria Novella, which, by reaſon of the
airineſs of the plan on which it was built in 1280,
Michael Angelo uſed to call *La Spoſa*, " The Bride;"
the great church of the Holy Croſs, built in 1294;
that of the Trinity ; that of Or-San-Michele, on
the outſide of which are fourteen niches, with ſtatues all maſter-pieces by the greateſt ſculptors of
Florence ; laſtly, the inward and outward decoration of the cathedral baptiſtery, and its bronze
doors, which Michael Angelo ſaid were fit to be
the doors of Paradiſe. The firſt of theſe doors
was finiſhed and put up in 1330, by Ugolin di
Piſa; and the two others in the following century,
by Laurence Ghiberti of Florence, who, in the
baſſo relievos, and other pieces of their accompaniments, has exhibited, both in the deſign and
execution, a perfection which art has never ſince
been able to ſurpaſs. Italy is full of Madonnas ſaid
to be done by angels. Had the workmanſhip of
theſe gates been attributed to angels, the connoiſſeurs themſelves, eſpecially on comparing it with
the taſte of the age when it was performed, would
have been the firſt to have believed the miracle.

The

The cathedral, the foundation of which was laid in 1296, faces the baptiftery : its vaftnefs, its height, its airinefs, and withal its folidity, are not fo much to be admired as its proportions, in the exquifitenefs and propriety of which the architects of the thirteenth century have anticipated the revival of the arts. Its dome was the work of the following age, and is fuch a work, that from it Michael Angelo took his model of St. Peter's dome ; and the more admirable is this work, the dome being double, and conftructed without a centre, or newel, and barely by means of a moft ingenious fcaffolding contrived by Brunelefco, who had planned this vaft machine, and who finifhed it by methods purely his own, without any traditionary precedent or information.

The cupola was fcarcely finifhed, when it raifed in Paul Tofcanelli, a Florentine phyfician, the notion of the firft dial, performed by modern aftronomy ; and the effay proved a mafter-piece : it is ftill the greateft monument of the kind in all Europe. This was likewife M. Condamine's opinion of it ; when at Florence he had urged the miniftry to repair it ; the approximation of the eclyptic, and perhaps the finking in of the cupola, having put it out of order. A Jefuit, to whom the repair was committed, had juft publifhed an account of his proceedings in a work printed at Florence in 1757.

Landini, in the *prolegomena* of his Commentary on Dante, fpeaks with the higheft praife of two geometricans whom Florence produced fo early as the fifteenth century. The name of both was Paul ; the firft celebrated for *immortal* writings, which

which however are not to be found in any catalogue of books printed ; the fecond not lefs profound in the higher fciences than the other ; and being ftill living in the beginning of the fixteenth century, he never looked on him without a refpectful complacency, as *una veneranda imagine d'antichità.*

The plan of Brunelefco's fcaffolding is among the pieces inferted in the Life of the Senator Nelli, publifhed by his fon, at Florence, in 1753. This fenator, who died in 1725, was likewife a great architect, and as fuch had a long time the fuperintendency of the cathedral. In the year 1692 fome fiffures were perceived in the calotte of the dome. The moft famous architects in Italy, being confulted by the great duke Cofmo III. gave it as their opinion, that the calotte was greatly impaired, and to be fecured only by girding it with ftrong iron chains. Thefe were accordingly prepared with all expedition; but Mr. Nelli having, under the authority of the celebrated Viviani, demonftrated that arcades like thofe of the dome were not liable to any lateral fpread, and that their confiftence depended on that of the foundations, the chains were laid afide as a mere dead weight, and only fome flight covering put on the fiffures, which were treated as an inconfiderable accident. The cathedral's great bell being broken in the time of Mr. Nelli's fuperintendency, he had it new caft, but without ears; inftead of which, it had a round aperture acrofs its upper part, and fitted with a great iron pin. In this pin, from whence hangs the clapper, is faftened an iron hood, which bearing up the calotte, and the whole weight of the bell,

caufes

caufes it to be eafily turned about the clapper, without any need of difmounting it to vary the clapper's points of incidence.

This operation reminds me of two authenticated certificates, mentioned in the hiftory of Mr. Nelli, from which it appears, that in 1658, one Jofeph Farnetti mended cracked bells without cafting them anew, fo that they founded *meglio che prima*, " better than at firft."

The mentioning Mr. Nelli, farther puts me in mind of one of thofe ftructures, by which the Florentine architects had anticipated the revival of the arts; I mean the German manfion, which, to this day, is an ornament of the palace fquare. This manfion is very large, all of ftone, and open towards the fquare, in arcades raifed by a continued focle about four feet above the ground: it was built in 1355, under the infpection, and from a plan, of Andrea Orgagnia, who, in oppofition to the ogives and tiers points ufual at that time, gave his arcades wide openings. In the beginning of this century, the focle, warping from its perpendicular towards the fquare, was drawing the arcades, fo that the whole manfion feemed in danger. The great duke, in 1715, was by all means for preventing it; and the architects could fee no remedy but building it wholly a-new, the expence of which they eftimated at thirty thoufand livres. Mr. Nelli however, alarmed at fuch an expence, undertook to underpin the focle, to preferve the arcades, and bring them again to their perpendicular pofition. The great duke, knowing his probity and fuperior fkill, fet him to work; and the whole was happily

pily finished, in 1716, at the small expence of two thousand livres.

I come now to the monuments of the magnificence of the Medicis, and their judicious taste for all the fine arts; mentioning however only those in which some particular circumstance struck me.

Of these the first is Donatello's *Judith*, standing under one of the arcades of the above-mentioned mansion, and by the Florentines called *Giulitta*. This exquisite piece is of bronze, and relates to the history of the Medicis, though, very probably, not set up by any of them. The Bithulian heroine is standing with a sabre raised up over Holofernes's throat: he lies as dead drunk, fallen down against a pedestal, round which is this inscription:

PUBLICÆ SALUTIS EXEMPLUM

CIV. POS.

I conclude from the inscription, that this monument was erected either before Cosmo de Medicis had seised on the government, or during his exile: but it is very strange, that, when the Medicis came to be fixed in the sovereignty, they allowed of such a monument, and with such an inscription; and that the people themselves never thought of paying their court to them, and manifesting their attachment, by pulling it down, or at least removing that perpetual signal to revolt and attempts on the sovereign's person. This forbearance of the Medicis may have proceeded from the reason, which induced them to prefer the modest title of Duchy to Kingdom, of which the opulence and

extent

extent of their dominions would have very well admitted. In the gallery of Pitti palace is to be seen the contre-part of this monument, an excellent head of Brutus by Michael Angelo, with this diftich on the pedeftal:

Dum Bruti effigiem Michael de marmore fingit,
In mentem fceleris venit & abftinuit.

Among the multitude of other mafterly pieces in the palace fquare, I obferved two coloffal ftatues of white marble; one of Hercules engaged with Cacus, by Bandinelli; the other, by Michael Angelo, reprefenting David making up to Goliah. Thefe ftatues, though highly valued, are expofed to the injuries of the air, fo that they are become unequally mouldy and rufty; which does not improve their appearance: but fuch is the refpect of the Florentines for monuments of this kind, that the care, taken every fpring in other places to have fuch ftatues, as ftand in the open air, cleanfed, rubbed, and fcraped, they look upon as a kind of facrilege.

The palace, in the court of which ftand thofe of Hercules and David, affords feveral ftatues very highly finifhed, as Bandinelli's *Adam* and *Eve,* and a *Victory* by Michael Angelo.

The *Adam* and *Eve,* though larger than nature, and quite naked, were for above a century an altarpiece in the cathedral: in this the good people of thofe days faw no immodefty or indecency; but they having fince been looked on with another eye, Cofmo III. ordered them to be removed.

Michael Angelo's *Victory,* a moft expreffive piece, though he did not put the finifhing hand to it, it, was defigned for the tomb of Julius II. On feeing Michael Angelo's maufoleum, I could not but think that this *Victory*, crowning his buft, would have been a more fuitable ornament to this maufoleum, than the three ftatues with which it has been decorated : they are indeed very correct, but fomething cold.

Without entering into any farther detail concerning the hundred and fixty public ftatues, (moft of which, being diftributed in the fquares, in the ftreets, and on the bridges, entertain the ftranger with a fpectacle fimilar to that which the moft flourifhing cities of Greece exhibited to the Paufaniases) I fhall only obferve, that thefe ftatues, though left open to the people, are refpected by them as facred ; and this refpect, which is inculcated from fathers to their children, has its rife in that tafte which the cuftom of feeing fine things, and hearing them praifed, naturally infpires.

This refpect is feen at Florence even in the peafants, and the very loweft people, and thus fupplies the place of rails, which in other countries can fcarce fecure the public monuments from that delight in mifchief, particularly natural to children, and of which, in the commonalty, education feldom gets the better. The Centaur, for inftance, a piece which may be compared to the moft valuable remains of antiquity, ftands in the centre of no fpacious fquare, and where, two or three days in a week, a market is kept. Paffing through it one morning in market-time, I afked a peafant why he did not make ufe of the pedeftal of the ftatue to hook on it feveral fmall flat bafkets of wares, with which he feemed pretty much incumbered.

Chiefa, voleffe attribuirfi quefto mio capriccio, come di molte altre mie invenzioni è accaduto, poffi reftare la teftimonianza di perfone maggiori, come io era ftato il primo à fognare quefta chimera. Quefta che li mando è veramente una abozzatura che fu da me frettelofamente fcritta, mentre fperavo che il Copernico non aveffe, ottant' anni dopo la fua publicazione, ad effer condannato per erroneo : fiche avevo in penfiero di amplificarmi con maggior commodità e tempo, apportandone altri rifcontri, riordinandolo e diftinguendolo in altra migliore forma e difpofizione. Ma una celefte voce mi rifvegliò e rifolvette in nebbia tutti li mei confufi ed avviluppati fantafmi, &c. i. e.

" I happened to compofe it whilft the thoughts of
" thofe reverend divines were taken up about
" fuppreffing Copernicus's book, and condemning
" the opinion of the motion of the earth, main-
" tained in the faid book, and which, at that
" time, I held to be true : and thofe gentlemen
" were pleafed to fupprefs the book, and declare
" the faid opinion falfe, and repugnant to the holy
" fcriptures. Senfible, at prefent, of the great
" duty and propriety of conforming to the deter-
" minations of our fuperiors, as guided by higher
" light and knowledge than my low genius can
" reach, I look on this compofition, which I now
" fend you, as only a fiction, or indeed a dream ;
" and as fuch your highnefs will receive it. How-
" ever, as poets fometimes place no little value on
" fome of their figments, fo I likewife found a com-
" placency in this trifle of mine. And as I had writ-
" ten it, and imparted it to cardinal Orfini and a few
" others, I afterwards gave a fmall number of co-
" pies of it to perfons of rank, left fome, and they
" perhaps

" perhaps diffident from our church, fhould be
" for affuming this whim of mine to themfelves,
" as has been the cafe of many of my inventions.
" Perfons of rank can teftify, that this chimera
" was firft hatched in my brain. This piece, which
" I fend your highnefs, is truly a fketch which I
" wrote in hafte, and when I hoped that Coperni-
" cus's book, fourfcore years after the publica-
" tion of it, would not have been condemned as
" erroneous; fo that I had fome thoughts of be-
" ftowing more time on it, enlarging it with frefh
" arguments, and digefting it into another form
" and a better difpofition ; but, as it were, a
" voice from heaven awakening me, all my
" fchemes and vifions vanifhed into air," &c.

The houfe of St. Mark, in the church of which
lie Galileo's remains, was the refidence of a perfon very famous in another kind, Jerome Savonarola. The nature of his cataftrophe, he having
been burned as a heretic, would not admit of
paying invocations to him ; but in refpect to his
memory, the chamber he lived in has been made a
chapel; and in a corner of this chapel is a picture of him, which, from a ftroke by a fabre on
his head, is miftaken for that of St. Peter the
Martyr; but we were apprifed that it reprefents
Savonarola. In going to this chapel, I was perfectly aftonifhed at feeing fome frefco paintings,
on old walls, performed in the fifteenth century, as
I was told, by one Fra. Angelico, a religious in
this houfe. This furname he had acquired by his
excellency in painting angels: his touch indeed
appeared to have all Barrocio and Guido's delicacy

U 3 and

architecture. The plan was fixed on by old Cofmo
de Medicis in the fifteenth century.

Florence every where exhibits ranges of palaces,
which at firft fight feem caft in the fame mould.
All the fronts perpendicular to the ftreets are,
at the gates and windows, loaded with boffages;
whilft the uppermoft ftories are only a plain wall,
but with windows, in the chambranles and accompaniments of which the architects may be faid to
have emulated each other in art and proportions.
Moft of thefe architects being likewife fculptors, thofe parts were often mafter-pieces in a
twofold refpect. This mafculine and correct tafte
derives both its rife and continuance at Florence
from the tenacious attachment of the inhabitants
to that order of architecture, which owes it
origin and name to the ancient Tufcans: from
it has been, and ftill daily is taken, whatever com-
ports with the ftrictnefs of its proportions *(p)*; and
this ftrictnefs is a fure prefervative againft the pre-
fumptions, the freedoms, and caprices, to which
the other orders can more eafily be accommodated.
The new fafhion for ornaments, which we found
on our return to prevail at Paris, under the name
of the *Grecian tafte*, is precifely, and in every particular, the manner of the Florentine architecture:
the tranfition of the Parifians from the *chantourné*
to the mafculine and grave, may be accounted for
by the fudden change of very large hats for very

___
(p) It was the fame with the ancient Egyptians. "They
"loved," fays the great Boffuet, "a regularity abfolutely
"plain. Is it not that nature of itfelf inclines us to fimpli-
"city, which is fo hard to be recovered when the tafte has
"been vitiated by novelties and capricious freedoms?"
Univerf. Hift.

fmall. Now fuch periodical variations from white
to black are unknown at Florence.

· Painting there is fubject to the like feverity in
the manner of handling the crayon and pencil,
yet without excluding the national gaiety, which
the Florentine painters have introduced into their
performances even on devout fubjects; and it is
principally in the painting of convents, that the
Florentine artifts have allowed themfelves the
greateft liberties. In thefe pictures, in which a
ftranger fees only edifying ftories, a Florentine, acquainted with tradition, difcovers the fecret hiftory
of the convent at the time when the painter
was employed. There are few, who in thefe
paintings do not meet with their neighbours,
their friends, their cronies of both fexes, their
miftreffes, &c. Thus in one of the fineft pieces
in Holy Crofs church, of the elder Bronzini, reprefenting Jefus Chrift drawing fouls out of the
lymbo, he has introduced all his neighbourhood.
The prettieft women among them were his models
for holy virgins and holy women of the Old Tefta-
ment, reprefented from head to foot in the ftate of
nature (*q*). The capital part, that of Eve, is his
miftrefs; and he himfelf is viewing her with a
look of paffion. This Bronzini is he who had a
confiderable hand in the collection of amorous
poems, fo well known in Italy by the name of
Opere Bernefche. It muft however be added, that,
in the painting in which he has taken all thefe
liberties, the expreffion of Adam, to whom Jefus

(*q*) Aretin, in Letter cxxxiii. Book v. tells us, that his
mother, when young, had fat for a very fine Annunciation
in St. Peter de Florence, or d'Arezzo.

Chrift

Chrift gives his hand, is quite fublime: the
afpect, the air, the whole phyfiognomy of this
general parent of mankind, fpeak fhame, repen-
tance, gratitude, confidence, and every fentiment
under which his foul muft have been labouring at
that fo long expected inftant.

All Florence is filled with excellent pieces in
this tafte ; moft of them the manufacture of the
country, that is, in general, more correct than
agreeable; the defign rather ftrong than pleafing,
and wrought from thofe robuft and vigorous perfons, whom Michael Angelo had daily before his
eyes, and which he had made the model of his
performances (r).

In imitation of him, and even before him, the
Florentine artifts, being at the fame time fculptors,
architects, and often painters, but all eminent
draughtfmen, had by the affemblage of thefe arts,
and the knowledge particular to each of them, a
facility, a correctnefs, an accuracy of fight, feldom obtained by the feparate ftudy of one of the
three.

This learned fchool, like the fchools of antiquity, owed its origin and progrefs to wealth and
liberty. Florence, wanton with the riches accruing to it from trade, and an induftry which declined
no object of gain, fet up for magnificence, and
plunged herfelf in enjoyments. Jealous of her liberty even to rage, perpetually diftracted at home

(r) Among the mafter-pieces of this kind, it gave me
fome difpleafure to fee feveral capital performances of Andrea
del Sarto piled up in the apartments of Pitti palace; having,
by order of the great dukes, been fucceffively taken out of
feveral churches, to which they were very valuable ornaments.

by

by that jealoufy, and victorious abroad (s), fhe affumed the fentiments of her fortune: that defire of glory, which prompted her to great things, infpired her with a love of the beautiful, the fources of which fhe laid open to her artifts. Opulence opened the workfhops. Freedom, which naturally enlarges the ideas, elevates the foul, and increafes its energy, warmed fuch geniufes as were born for arts: emulation, rivalry, and jealoufy, did what remained. Every artift, being judged by his peers, improved by the difcoveries, the faults, and works of his rivals. In this brilliant revolution, the analyfes of arts, obfervations, differtations, and fuch pofthumous fruits of genius, had no fhare. The curious, the patrons, were great contributors, not pretending to advife the artifts, but employing them; admiring, and not directing them. In a word, the moft fublime arts, together with the moft mechanical crafts, were created and improved by indefatigable hands, and not by idle reafoners.

The veneration of the Florentines for their great men contributed not a little to make them fuch. Florence is full of monuments confecrated to their memory, both by the fovereigns and private perfons. I fhall give a fhort account of thofe which came in my way.

The houfe built by the celebrated Vincent Viviani, in the neighbourhood of S. Maria Novella,

(s) In the hiftory of Florence, fays Varchi, we meet with *tutte quelle varietà ed accidenti che in un Popolo non meno ambiziofo e fottile che avaro, ne meno ricco che nobile ed induftriofo, poffono occorrere,* "all thofe viciffitudes and incidents which can fall "out among a people no lefs ambitious and fubtile, than "avaricious, and equally rich, fplendid, and ingenious."

is a monument of his gratitude towards Galileo, whofe laft pupil he was, as he ufed every where to call himfelf. In the front of the houfe is a bronze bufto of this reftorer of the fublime fciences; and fcrolls in the outward piers, between the cafements, fhew the detail and epochas of thofe admirable difcoveries with which he has enriched thofe fciences. Viviani's gratitude went ftill farther: on his fubftituting, by his will, his difciple the fenator Nelli joint executor to the abbé Panzanini his nephew, whom he made his heir, he appointed a magnificent maufoleum, fuitable to his regard, to be erected to his mafter, which was performed in 1733.

This monument, which ftands in Holy Crofs church, fronting Michael Angelo's maufoleum, and was executed in marble from a drawing of Julius Foggini, is a large farcophagus furmounted with a buft of Galileo, excellently wrought by John Foggini: Aftronomy and Geometry, both bigger than nature; the former, executed by Vincent Foggini (t), and the other, by Jerome Ticciati, ftand on each end of the farcophagus (u).

The

(t) To this family the republic of letters is indebted for the abbé Foggini, one of the fub-librarians in the Vatican, known by the Medicis edition of Virgil, and other works tranflated into French from editions publifhed by him according to Vatican manufcripts.

(u) In the fame church lies buried the famous St. Antonine. Among the paintings reprefenting his miracles, I met with one fomething fingular, and which I had before feen in a little church at Dijon. The archbifhop is holding a balance: in one of the fcales is a bafket of fruit, and in the other a bit of paper with *Deo gratias* written on it: afide ftands

The execution of Viviani's intentions had been intermitted by a difficulty confecutive to thofe which had difturbed Galileo's life and ftudies. This truly philofophic man, if ever mortal could claim that title, had undergone all the perfecutions and moleftations, which ever have been the portion of men fuperior to their times *(w)*. His works had been condemned by the inquifition, and he himfelf thrown into the prifon of that dreadful tribunal, where he remained about fix years; and at length, to obtain his releafe, was compelled to abjure what all the world now believes and maintains, the motion of the earth round the fun *(x)*. After furviving this misfortune eighteen years, he died in 1642, aged feventy-eight. His labours, his difcoveries, the eminent merit of the greater part of his difciples, the favour with which his fovereign honoured him, his very fufferings, were of no avail for the tranquil-

ftands a peafant in a ftupid amazement. The ftory is this: A peafant brought a bafket of fruit to St. Antonine; but, inftead of a good equivalent, which he expected, St. Antonine only faid to him, *Deo gratias:* the peafant fell a muttering, that he could not live by *Deo gratias,* and it was not equal to his fruit. St. Antonine, to fhew him the worth and weight of it, ordered a pair of fcales to be brought, in which the *Deo gratias* made his fruit kick the beam.

(w) *Urit enim fulgore fuo qui prægravat artes*
  Infra fe pofitas.   Horat.

(x) He was hunted out, and tried at the inquifition at Rome, who threw him into prifon. Florence had then, and ftill has, only one Francifcan for its inquifitor, to whom the emperor, fince his being fovereign of Tufcany, has added fome counfellors of the regency; without whofe concurrence the Francifcan cannot act. The inquifitors of Rome had Galileo's affair brought before them, as of very high moment.

lity of his latter years. I have feen in Mr. Nelli's
library the originals of letters and inftruments, by
which it appears that monks, priefts, and prelates, inveighed againſt him from the pulpit. It was
even debated, whether he could difpofe of his goods
by will, and whether the church ought to allow him
ecclefiaftical burial. The latter article had been
decided in the negative; and accordingly, on his
death, he had been buried as a heretic, ftrongly
fufpected of relapfing, in profane ground, facing
the gate of the Dominican novitiate, in St. Mark's
fquare.

Viviani ftood in need of all the weight accruing to him from the efteem of Lewis XIV. and
the penfion with which that prince honoured him,
to dare undertake erecting to his mafter, in the
middle of Florence, the monument above mentioned. The maufoleum directed by his will met
with the greateft oppofition : it was decided by
grave divines, that the very utmoft which could be
allowed was the removing of Galileo's bones into
holy ground; but there to be left, without any
honour or diftinction. I have feen the original of
the confultation on this head. The abbé Panzanini, Viviani's heir, endeavoured, but without
effect, to overcome that difficulty. Mr. Nelli's
executors were obliged to ufe all their intereft, and
even juridical means, by which they at length
prevailed, and, after taking up what remained of
Galileo, depofited him in the maufoleum.

The only monument of theological hatred againſt
this great philofopher, is now the Index of Prohibited Books, which was renewed and corrected,
in 1758, by Benedict XIV. The Dialogue, in
which

which lay his capital crime, is again proscribed (y) without any lenitive.

It would be a mistake, to imagine that Galileo had drawn such persecution on himself by indiscretion, pride, and sallies of defiance. That he may be tried on his own writings, I shall insert, from the original, part of the letter he wrote, in 1618, to archduke Leopold, along with the first telescope he had invented, and a memoir on the causes of the tides according to the Copernican system, which was afterwards condemned by the inquisition. Touching this memoir he says, *Mi è occorso di farlo mentre che frà questi Signori Teologi si andava pensando intorno alla probibizione del libro di Nic. Copernico, e della opinione della mobilità della terra posta in detto libro e da me creduta per vera in quel tempo: si chè piacque a questi signori di sospendere il libro e dichiarare per falsa e repugnante à le scritture sacre, la detta opinione. Hora, perche io so quanto convenga ubidire e credere alle determinazioni de' superiori come quelli che sono scorti da più alte cognizioni, alle quali la bassezza del mio ingegno per se stesso non arriva, reputo questa presente scrittura, che gli mando, come una Poesia overo un sogno, e per tale la riceva l'Altezza Vostra. Tuttavia, perche anco i Poeti apprezzano talvolte alcuna delle loro fantasie, io parimente fo qualche stima di questa mia vanità. E giache mi ritrovavo averla scritta & lasciatala vedere dal Cardinale Orsino e da alcuni altri pochi, ne ho poi lasciato andare alcune copie in mano di altri Signori Grandi; e questo, affinche, in ogni evento, che altri, forse separato della nostra*

(y) Together with the works of Bacon, Copernicus, Kepler, Descartes, and Foscarini.

Chiefa, voleſſe attribuirſi queſto mio capriccio, come di molte altre mie invenzioni è accaduto, poſſi reſtare la teſtimonianza di perſone maggiori, come io era ſtato il primo à ſognare queſta chimera. Queſta che li mando è veramente una abozzatura che fu da me fretteloſamente ſcritta, mentre ſperavo che il Copernico non aveſſe, ottant' anni dopo la ſua publicazione, ad eſſer condannato per erroneo : ſiche avevo in penſiero di amplificarmi con maggior commodità e tempo, apportandone altri riſcontri, riordinandolo e diſtinguendolo in altra migliore forma e diſpoſizione. Ma una celeſte voce mi riſvegliò e riſolvette in nebbia tutti li mei confuſi ed avviluppati fantaſmi, &c. i. e.

" I happened to compoſe it whilſt the thoughts of
" thoſe reverend divines were taken up about
" ſuppreſſing Copernicus's book, and condemning
" the opinion of the motion of the earth, main-
" tained in the ſaid book, and which, at that
" time, I held to be true : and thoſe gentlemen
" were pleaſed to ſuppreſs the book, and declare
" the ſaid opinion falſe, and repugnant to the holy
" ſcriptures. Senſible, at preſent, of the great
" duty and propriety of conforming to the deter-
" minations of our ſuperiors, as guided by higher
" light and knowledge than my low genius can
" reach, I look on this compoſition, which I now
" ſend you, as only a fiction, or indeed a dream ;
" and as ſuch your highneſs will receive it. How-
" ever, as poets ſometimes place no little value on
" ſome of their figments, ſo I likewiſe found a com-
" placency in this trifle of mine. And as I had writ-
" ten it, and imparted it to cardinal Orſini and a few
" others, I afterwards gave a ſmall number of co-
" pies of it to perſons of rank, leſt ſome, and they
" perhaps

" perhaps diffident from our church, should be
" for affuming this whim of mine to themfelves,
" as has been the cafe of many of my inventions.
" Perfons of rank can teftify, that this chimera
" was firft hatched in my brain. This piece, which
" I fend your highnefs, is truly a fketch which I
" wrote in hafte, and when I hoped that Coperni-
" cus's book, fourfcore years after the publica-
" tion of it, would not have been condemned as
" erroneous; fo that I had fome thoughts of be-
" ftowing more time on it, enlarging it with frefh
" arguments, and digefting it into another form
" and a better difpofition; but, as it were, a
" voice from heaven awakening me, all my
" fchemes and vifions vanifhed into air," &c.

The houfe of St. Mark, in the church of which
lie Galileo's remains, was the refidence of a perfon very famous in another kind, Jerome Savonarola. The nature of his cataftrophe, he having
been burned as a heretic, would not admit of
paying invocations to him; but in refpect to his
memory, the chamber he lived in has been made a
chapel; and in a corner of this chapel is a picture of him, which, from a ftroke by a fabre on
his head, is miftaken for that of St. Peter the
Martyr; but we were apprifed that it reprefents
Savonarola. In going to this chapel, I was perfectly aftonifhed at feeing fome frefco paintings,
on old walls, performed in the fifteenth century, as
I was told, by one Fra. Angelico, a religious in
this houfe. This furname he had acquired by his
excellency in painting angels: his touch indeed
appeared to have all Barrocio and Guido's delicacy

and

and beauty. An original letter from Bruzzini to Varchi, in Magliabechi's library, relates, that as Bruzzini was returning from Rome with Machiavel, they were told of Savonarola's being put to death ; and that Machiavel thereupon cried out, *Non fapeva il povero uomo che gli profeti difarmati capitano tutti male,* &c. " The poor man did not " know that all prophets, if not feconded by arms, " come to an unfortunate end," &c. I have read elfewhere, that Savonarola, challenging, in full fenate, one of his adverfaries to pafs through a large fire with him, that it might be feen, by a divine judgment, which fide was in the right ; a fenator, John Canacci by name, moved, that it would be better to make the trial in a large veffel full of water, as attended with no danger ; and the miracle would not be lefs decifive in favour of him who fhould come out without being wetted.

The cathedral's fteeple, built from a defign of Giotto, is at the lower part adorned with four ftatues of Donatello, reprefenting four eminent perfons his cotemporaries, whofe names however are loft. That of a little bald-headed old man, he always looked on as his mafter-piece ; and indeed it wants only fpeech.

The walls along both fides of the nave of the cathedral are, like thofe of the Pritaneum of Athens, covered with portraits, epitaphs, and infcriptions, in honour of perfons diftinguifhed in arts, arms, and literature, though the greater part of them be not buried in the church. On one fide is a marble buft of Brunelefco, who was the architect in building the dome. Next to that, the

the picture of Giotto, with two panegyrics, in one of which, by Politianus, is this fine verse:

Naturæ deerat noſtræ quod defuit arti.

Then some inscriptions in honour of generals, who distinguished themselves in the service of the republic: and this respectable file is closed by the busto of Marcilius Ficinus, the reviver of the Platonic philosophy. The opposite side exhibits the portraits of warriors, and that of Dante by Giotto his cotemporary, whose talents occasioned that fine reflexion which the poet has introduced in the eleventh Canto of his *Purgatory*.

> *O vana gloria dell' humane poſſe,*
> *Com' poco verde in ſu la cima dura,*
> *Se non è giunta dall' etati groſſe !*
> *Credette Cimabue nella pintura*
> *Tener lo campo ; ed ora ha Giotto il grido,*
> *Si che la fama di colui oſcura.*
> *Così ha tolto l'uno all' altro Guido*
> *La gloria della lingua ; e forſe è nato*
> *Chi l'uno e l'altro caccerà di nido.*

This portrait of Dante is an homage which the republic of Florence, by a public decree, paid to the memory of one whom it had banished, and who died in exile*. The decree even ordered, that out of the public money should be erected to him, in the cathedral, *& in luogo honorato, un marmoreo, et artificioſamente ſculto ſepulchro, con quelle ſtatue e ſegni che lo poteſſero rendere ornatiſſimo,* i. e. "and in some honourable place, a marble

---

* See the article of FERRARA.

" tomb,

" tomb, of a fine fculpture, and with ftatues and
" emblems, fo as to render it a very ornamental
" piece." This we are informed of by Landini
in his *prolegomena* on Dante's poem, where he
ftrongly urges the execution of the decree in every
point.

To this poet Florence has paid a farther mark
of refpect, by inftituting in its univerfity a profefforfhip, whofe province is to explain his work, the public veneration for which feems to have been heightened by its antiquated ftyle and obfcure phrafes.

This regard of the Florentines is the more
eftimable, as having prevailed over their perfonal
reafons for refentment againft a poem, which, in
the author's intention, was a downright fatire on the
government and its principal members, and a
caricatura of the manners of his compatriots of
both fexes. This was doubtlefs his meaning in
giving his poem the name of a *Comedy*; whereas
he calls Virgil's Æneid a *Tragedy*, though his
argument be infinitely more tragical than that of
the Æneid.

Hell, of which he had compofed the feven firft
cantos before his banifhment, certainly contributed no lefs to it, than the haughtinefs (z) with
which he rejected the public's choice of him for
an embaffy to Boniface VIII. It is highly probable,
that this beginning of his work had tranfpired. He
finifhed it in his exile, with the addition of *Purgatory*
and *Paradife*, which, from a neceffity of employing himfelf, he added to his firft plan, without
departing from his original intention, which he

(z) *S'io vo, anfwered he, chi fta: s'io fto, chi va.*

care-

carefully concealed under a multitude of theological and myftical queftions.

The part of the convent of St. Laurence, which
makes the firft lobby to the Medicean library, is
decorated with a marble ftatue of the famous
hiftorian Paulus Jovius, as big as life, and by
Francefco San-Gallo, one of the firft mafters of
the Florentine fchool. In the front of Guicchar-
dini, now Altoviti palace, are fifteen pilafters,
each bearing a bufto in the manner of the ancient
Hermeses.   Each of thefe buftos reprefents fome
illuftrious Florentine.   On the ground floor ftand
five lawyers, philofophers, or *literati :* the firft
ftory is filled by five hiftorians ; and in the fecond
are feen five poets, or polite writers ; Dante,
Petrach, Boccacio, Monfignor de la Cafa, and
Lewis Alamani.

The office-palace, where the feveral courts are
held, and which was built by the great Cofmo I.
from a plan of the celebrated Vafari, has niches
in all its piers, where the grand duke intended
to fet up ftatues of the moft celebrated Florentines.
His death defeated fo commendable a fcheme,
and the niches remain void.

Galileo's tomb is not the only proof of the Florentines conftant regard for the glory of their
worthies.   In Magliabechi's library is a marble
bufto of its founder, very well executed, and faid
to be a perfect likenefs : it looks however to be
rather the jole of fome wild beaft than the head of
a man ; though, amidft all the hideoufnefs of its
features, the countenance is full of expreffion.

The above monument is of our times, together
with that erected by the marquis Nicolini to
M.

M. Joſeph Avarani, one of the moſt learned lawyers
whom the univerſity of Piſa ever produced, and
whoſe works are not inferior to thoſe of Cujas
himſelf, uniting the embelliſhments of philology,
the gravity of hiſtory, the rigour of criticiſm, and
the preciſion of the higher ſciences, with a profound knowledge of the Roman laws, and of their
analogy with the law of nature and of nations.
He had been the marquis's preceptor; and his
grateful pupil has conſecrated his image in the
convent of Santa Croce in an excellent marble
medallion, which ſtruck me the more, as at the
very firſt ſight it ſhews the face, features, and
every particular of Mr. Voltaire, ſo that no picture
was ever ſo like him, as he is to this medallion.

The marquis Nicolini has carried his acknow-
ledgements ſtill farther. On the 18th of April,
1745, he delivered, before the academy de la
Cruſca, a panegyric on his maſter, containing
forty quarto pages of letter-preſs.

To this account of the monuments (a) which
gratitude has erected to merit, I muſt add,

1. That which decorates the porch of the hoſpital
of S. Maria Nuova. The firſt thought of this

(a) Among the ways of perpetuating the memory of its
great men, it will readily be thought, that Florence has not
omitted epitaphs: but I ſhall only ſet down that on Varchi,
as both true, and well expreſſed.

D. O. M.
BENED. VARCHIO, POETÆ, PHILOSOPHO, HISTORICO,
QUI CUM ANN. LXIII.
SUMMA ANIMI LIBERTATE,
SINE ULLA AVARITIA AUT AMBITIONE VIXISSET,
OBIIT NON INVITUS,
XVI. KAL. DECEMB. M.DC.LXVI.

foundation

foundation for the relief of diftrefs was owing to an aged fervant maid, who laid it before a rich widow of the Portinari family, with whom fhe lived. The widow clofed with the propofal, and immediately employed part of her eftate in beginning to carry it into execution *(b)*, publicly owning that it was the follicitations of her maid which had brought her to this difpofal of her fortune. On the death of the old fervant, the directors of this foundation buried her in their church, under a white marble tomb-ftone, on which was her image in relievo : but this in time wearing away by the continual friction of feet, it has been removed, and fet in the porch-wall of the houfe.

2. The image of a mule, at the end of the portico which forms the ground floor of Pitti palace, with a diftich on the bafe, importing that the mule reprefented by that ftatue ferved with remarkable vigour and diligence in building the palace, being never backward to whatever fervice it was put to. Of this kind is another infcription, confecrated by a Venetian, in one of the quays along the Arno, to the memory of a horfe killed under him at the fiege of Florence in the fixteenth century. Such monuments however are in fome degree culpable, if excefs of gratitude can be fo; though their founders may indeed plead the example of the Egyptians, Athenians, and of the emperor Adrian, who, according to Spartian, was fo fond of his horfes and dogs, as to erect monuments to them.

It is from this perpetual regard to pofterity, that the Florentines have for fome centuries paft invented a way for the prefervation of thofe inftru-

(b) In 1290.

ments, which relate to the fubſtance and ranks of the citizens, the want of which reflects an air of barbariſm on the moſt civilized northern countries.

For ſuch inſtruments there are two repoſitories; one, in the neighbourhood of the palace above the church of Or-San-Michele; the other, in the vaſt apartments over the new market built in 1548, and in that part of the city which the Arno ſeparates from the palace.

Every fourth year, the notaries of the city of Florence and all the Tuſcan territories are obliged to deliver in, at the firſt of theſe repoſitories, a duplicate of all their inſtruments. On the death of a notary, his *Protocol*, bound, numbered and ſigned, is tranſmitted to that in the new market. Thus, by means of the diſtance of the two repoſitories, the choice of inſulated places for them, and the moſt ſcrupulous precautions againſt any accident by fire, Florence has authenticated duplicates of all inſtruments and writings of any concern to ſociety; and in caſe one of the repoſitories ſhould be totally burned down, it would not affect the public.

The order in theſe repoſitories is excellently adapted to the ends of their eſtabliſhment : each has a double repertory; one of matters, the other of names ; and by means of theſe repertories, if a pedigree is to be drawn up, however long and complex, it is but one morning's work, and ſtands good in courts of law, on a bare certificate given by the minute-keeper who makes out the duplicate. With the like eaſe are procured juridical vouchers on all matters, where a recourſe to inſtruments is
neceſſary.

neceſſary. The finding of every inſtrument being very eaſy, and ſoon diſpatched, the fee for the certificate is very ſmall; but this is made up to the minute-keepers from the prodigious multitude of conſultations, occaſioned by the facility of being ſatisfied. Every private perſon, when he wants a connected indication of thoſe very vouchers which are in his poſſeſſion, immediately repairs to the repoſitory. In a word, this double repoſitory is a public ſanctuary, and a common record-office, where all families and every citizen have authenticated vouchers of their poſſeſſions and ſtations.

Whatever relates to the titles of families, is preſerved with no leſs care. The ſeveral quarters, and moſt of the ſtreets of the city of Florence, ſtill bear the name of the firſt families who lived in them. The palaces unalterably retain the names of thoſe who built them; and to the ſecond and third poſſeſſors they are, in ſome meaſure, but as inns. The manner of denoting is thus: *Palazzo di tal, poi di tal, oggi di tal*, i. e. " The " palace of ſuch a one, afterwards ſuch a one's, at " preſent ſuch a one's." This attention reaches to all monuments of the firſt owners; ſo that a front with their coat of arms on it cannot be pulled down, even though the ſecond owner ſhould intend to build a new front on a larger plan, unleſs he take care that the new front ſhall be in the beſt manner, agreeable to the former. A very ſtriking proof of the power of laws and cuſtom, in this reſpect, is Pitti palace: this immenſe building, of which the palace of Luxemburg at Paris is a copy, has for above two hundred years belonged

to the houfe of Medicis, and been the manfion of
all the Great Dukes, yet without any alteration of
the name; it is ftill Pitti palace.

By means of thefe precautions for the prefervation of family monuments and vouchers, the
defcent of the nobility of Florence is perhaps,
of all countries in Europe, the beft afcertained,
fome houfes excepted, which avail themfelves
of their antiquity to derive their origin fo far
back as Charlemagne. Every one knows the
beginning and rife of each, and the different
degrees of aggrandizement, fplendor, and de-
clenfion, which it has gone through. From
thefe common notions it is, that Landini, in
his notes on the fixteenth canto of Dante's *Paradife*, has given a large account of the ancient
houfes of Florence, even fo far as fpecifying the
quarters where ftood their principal refidence. Accordingly it is to Florence that all the favourites
of fortune in Italy, go to look out for anceftors
of repute. A refemblance of name immediately
concludes thefe contracts, where both fides are
gainers. This is matter of laughter at Florence;
but the adopted Florentine, in his own country,
plumes himfelf with a botched genealogy, in
which the feams are not vifible to every eye.

In the beft days of the republic of Florence,
trade, banking, and ever-active induftry, were
the nurture and fupport of the nobility. Old
Cofmo de Medicis came to be the chief man in the
ftate, becaufe he was the firft trader and the firft
banker of Florence, if not of all Europe. Peter
his fon, and Laurence his grandfon, continued
trade and banking. All the public and private
edifices

edifices of any note were built by merchants, and the greater part of them members of the *Arte della Lana*, or woollen trade. To this manufacture the republic of Florence chiefly owed its grandeur, and all its noble and ornamental undertakings. The names of the houses which were at the head of the paper trade, the linen, wood, tile, cheese, and coal trades, still subsist. In a word, N. Capponi, who, not longer ago than the sixteenth century, was Gonfalonier, and the first man in the republic then newly formed by the Florentines, during the imprisonment of Clement VII. *non aveva mai, non che lasciata, intermessa la mercatura,* " so far from going out of trade, never intermit-" ted trading." See the end of the ninth book of Varchi's history.

The permanency of the sovereignty in the Medicis family, and the alliances with German and Spanish princesses, gave a turn to their ideas of commerce. In imitation of the sovereign, the most opulent houses went out of trade, quitted manufactures, and preferred chivalry to wealth acquired and perpetuated by industry. In order to secure their commercial gains to their descendants, they availed themselves of the liberty allowed by the ancient Roman laws, to make perpetual and gradual intails *ad infinitum*; so that the relations did not succeed to the intails, as in common successions, but as in the order prescribed by the testator, which thus remained a perpetual law to his family. Cosmo I. opened a resource to younger brothers in the order of St. Stephen: the church offered others to those who
would

would enter into holy orders. Many went abroad, and rofe to confiderable fortunes. Still population was on the ebb ; and Florence's whole wealth not only was in the hands of a few houfes, but by law incommunicable to new-raifed families. Since the emperor's becoming fovereign of Tufcany, he has, agreeably to Juftinian's law, reduced intails to four degrees. What is to be expected from this new arrangement? *Ipfi viderint.*

Villani lays open to us a main fpring of the primitive riches of the Florentines in their way of living *(c)* in the thirteenth century: *Vivevano fobri,* fays he, *e di groffe vivande, e con piccole fpefe, e molti coftumi groffi e rudi ; e di groffi panni veftivano loro e loro donne. Molti portavano le pelle fcoperte fonza panno e con berrete in capo, e tutti con ufaiti in piede :* "They lived foberly, and with little "expence : their common fare was butchers "meat ; and many of their ways were homely, "and quite unpolifhed : both they and their wives "wore coarfe ftuffs, many round caps on their "heads, but all wore fpatterdafhes." He adds, that a hundred livres was a creditable portion, and three hundred a fortune ; and that daughters were never married till paft their twentieth year, being at that age acquainted with all the parts of houfe-wifery : *Con la loro groffa vita e povertà, faccienno maggiori piu virtudiofe cofe, che non fono fatte à tempi noftri, con più morbideffa e con più richeffa.* "Amidft this poverty and coarfe way of living, "they performed greater things, in the way of the "fine arts, than are done in our time, with all its

(c) Concerning this fee Canto XV. and XVI. of Dante's *Paradifi.*

"luxury

"luxury and riches." They were free; and, as among the firſt Romans, if individuals were poor, the republic was opulent:

Privatus illis cenſus erat brevis,
Commune magnum.

It was people living and clothed as above, who conquered Tuſcany, and embelliſhed Florence with ſo many ſtately and uſeful edifices.

The decreaſe of wealth has gradually brought Florence to its ancient temperance, and all the parſimony of the thirteenth century. Since its no longer being the reſidence of a ſovereign, or court, luxury has been ſuperſeded by a modeſt plainneſs in clothing; and ſome perſons in very good circumſtances, as at Rome, even wear an eccleſiaſtical garb, though not belonging to the church.

As to their table, I have often heard Lombards with a ſneer extol the Florentine ſuppers, which, ſay they, conſiſt of a few ſallad-leaves, gathered by the gueſts themſelves in pots ſtanding at the window, and garniſhed with a little wild endive. I have dined at ſome houſes in Florence, where, beſides plenty and goodneſs, every thing was ſerved up extremely neat; the wine excellent; and what improved the reliſh of the whole, was that feſtivity inherent in the Florentines. I muſt farther add, that, in the whole courſe of our travels, we never found an inn where we fared ſo well, were ſo well attended, and the bills ſo reaſonable, as at Florence: an evident proof of the plenty, and perhaps of the ſuperabundancy of proviſions.

Part of our evenings we uſed to ſpend at a coffeehouſe, among perſons whoſe acquaintance was of

great ufe to us, and whom it was highly entertaining to fee together. They divert themfelves with
banters of all kinds, giving and taking very gen-
teelly. The celebrated Dr. Lami, the greateft
fcholar in all Tufcany, ufed to come in for his
fhare, both actively and paffively, as if raillery
had been the fole bufinefs of his life.

Portions of young women are not yet reduced
.to what they were in the thirteenth century : I however knew a Florentine, a man of family and reputation, who chofe to marry on the ancient footing, faying he was for being mafter at home.

The theatres at Florence, as in the other parts of
Italy, are a party matter.   It has two droll-opera
houfes, which as rivals ftrive to furpafs each
other ; and an Italian play-houfe, the harlequin
of which was a creditable fhopkeeper dealing in
all kinds of millenery ware.   Mademoifelle Rad-
dicati, one of the firft dancers in Italy, gave us an
opportunity of paying tribute to Florence, which
we did by a glee addreffed to her in the name of a
doctor, who was one of the retinue of fome abbots of the firft diftinction, returning from the
conclave.   It was a dozen of verfes, none of the
beft, but the fofteft our mufe could produce.

Mentioning verfes puts me in mind of a converfation with a Florentine noble, a man of tafte,
and who, though he had never been at Paris,
fpoke better French than I, and was thoroughly
acquainted with the beft French books.   I was
lamenting to him my leaving Italy, without having ever been able to enter into the meafure, the
energy, and the harmony of Italian poetry. " The
" like reproach," anfwered he, " lies againft me
                                    " with

" with regard to French poetry : Chapelain's,
" Brebeuf's, Racine's, Rousseau's verses, those
" of *La Pucelle, Zara,* &c. are all alike to my
" ear ; not the least difference does it perceive in
" them. To me it is only so much rhyming
" prose."

During our stay at Florence, the Arno, swelled
by rains and the waters of the Chiana, which
the old Romans divided between the Arno and
the Tiber, overflowed up to the first story of some
of the houses. It was a general desolation : the
bale goods in the custom-house, and in many ware-
houses, floated ; boats were dispatched with pro-
visions to those parts which had been surprised by
the inundation : yet such damages were but slight,
in comparison to what the country suffered ; dung-
hills, cattle, trees, and wrecks of houses, driving down the Arno. On the ebbing away of the
waters, the lower streets, and the courts of the
houses in them, were covered with an ochreous
sediment three or four inches deep. Florence, we
were told, is subject to this calamity about once
in twenty years ; though, in all ages, a thousand
projects have been proposed for preventing or di-
minishing it. The only certain remedy is, to
deepen the Arno's bed along the whole course of
it, from Florence to the sea: its bed has risen above
six feet since the dispute in Tiberius's time, between
the inhabitants of Rome and those of Tuscany ;
the subject, particulars, and result of which, may
be seen in M. Fontenelle's Elogium of Viviani.

This inundation occasioned great repairs to be
made in the damaged houses, without respecting
the coarse red crosses with which the socle towards

the

the ftreet, of almoft all the buildings in Florence, is daubed. The only drift of thefe croffes is, to reftrain paffengers in a city, where the air is no lefs diuretic than it is anodyne at Naples. This old cuftom at Florence clears up Aretine's jeft in his comedy del Marefcalco : *Che un Cavaliere fenza entrata, è un muro fenza croci, fcompifciato da ognuno.* " That a gentleman without a fortune is, " like a wall without a crofs, piffed upon by every " body." And this joke he repeats in a letter to the bifhop of Vaifon, September 17, 1530.

In Leandro Alberti's Account of Illuftrious Florentines, I was furprifed at his fedulity to introduce a great number of Thomifts, Scotifts, and the like, doctors now quite forgotten; and yet not a fingle word for the *venerable* and *learned Boccaccio,* as Brantome ftyles him. He has been more mindful of Machiavel, whom he mentions as author of the Hiftory of Florence, of the Life of Caftruccio, of the Prince, *con molte altre degne opere* ; " with many other excellent works." But the fame Brantome ufed ironically to call him the *venerable preceptor of princes and men in power.* Some particulars of his life, which I collected at Florence, are as follow.

He was born in that city on the 3d of May, 1469. His father was Bernardo, doctor of laws; and Barthclomea, daughter of Stephen Nelli, his mother. He loft his father in his feventeenth year. The greater part of his youth he fpent as clerk under Marcello Vergilio Adriani, fecretary to the republic of Florence. He was at Nantz in Britany in 1501, and in the following year married Marietta Corfini, Lewis's daughter, by whom he had
feveral

several children. In 1520, he succeeded Adriani as secretary to the republic. In 1527, he was dismissed from this post, and died the twenty-second of June the same year. His *Prince*, which was published at Rome in 1515, under the inspection and privilege of Leo X. and dedicated to Laurence de Medicis duke of Urbino, was not put into the *Index Expurgatorius* till the pontificate of Clement VIII. His other works were posthumous. The comedy of *La Sporta*, which appeared in Gelli's name, is attributed to him. M. Nelli told me he had some *discorsi* of Machiavel's on Cæsar's Commentaries, after the manner of those written by him on Livy. Both Machiavel and Boccace are the less to be omitted among illustrious Florentines, the Florentine disposition being a mixture of those two authors.

To Galileo, a Florentine, Europe owes the renewal of that philosophy, the first tracks of which had been opened to the Greeks of Ionia and Italy by Thales and Pythagoras; and, like those sages, he became the head of a school, which at present obtains in all the scientifical academies. It was concentrated, during twenty years, in the society formed in 1650 by the great duke Ferdinand, and which afterwards was modelled into the academy *del Cimento*, instituted in 1657, by cardinal Leopold de Medicis. The works and discoveries of this academy are known among all the learned world. It originally consisted of seven members, most of them Galileo's pupils.

Paul del Buono, president of the imperial mint, was the author of the experiments on the compressibility of water, and introduced into Tuscany the

Egyptian

Egyptian manner of hatching chickens by means of artificial and graduated heat.

Candido del Buono his brother, prieſt of Stephen's at Campoli, invented the air-pump, and another machine for meaſuring and comparing the evaporations of various fluids.

Alexander Marſigli, profeſſor of philoſophy in the univerſity of Piſa.

Vincent Viviani, a panegyric of whom may be ſeen among thoſe of the Academy of Sciences at Paris, ſpoken by M. Fontenelle.

Francis Redi, known by ſeveral volumes of great erudition, employed himſelf chiefly in extracting ſalts from the aſhes of vegetables.

Count Lorenzo Magalotti, ſecretary to the academy.

Abbé Antony Oliva, a Calabrian, quitted Florence, and went to Rome, where he practiſed phyſic, and became firſt phyſician to Clement IX. but being afterwards implicated in Monſignor Gabrieli's affair, he was apprehended by the Holy Office, and died in priſon.

John Alfonſo Borelli, a Neapolitan, known by his works, and diſputes with Viviani, and among theſe who laboured moſt for the improvement and honour of the academy.

Count Charles Rinaldini, of Ancona.

With thoſe who had a ſhare in the labours of this ſociety may be claſſed Dominic Caſſini, Nicholas Stenon, and M. Auzout; whom attachment to the higher ſciences drew from France, and detained a long time in Italy.

The inquiries and diſcoveries of Don Benedetto Caſtelli, Evangeliſta Torricelli, and Nicholas
Aggiunti,

Aggiunti, Galileo's firft pupils, belong in fome meafure to this fociety, in the labours of which they would have affifted along with their acquaintance and fellow-pupils, had not their death been prior to its eftablifhment.

This account of the academy *del Cimento* I owe to Mr. Nelli, who has fince publifhed it himfelf in a quarto pamphlet of one hundred and forty pages, called *Saggio di Storia Litteraria Fiorentina nel fecolo* xvii. He it was who erected to Galileo the monument of which I have given an account. He is poffeffed of a prodigious quantity of letters and fmall pieces of that great man, not yet printed, and which he intends to publifh with his life, digefted from the information contained in that philofopher's works, and his correfpondence with all the learned of his time. Such a collection may well excite impatience for its publication.

Without the moft remote intention to derogate from Galileo's reputation, as efteemed the Thales of the philofophic fchool of Florence, I take the liberty to fay that he would poffibly be only its Anaxagoras, were the origin of it carried up to the firft of thofe two Pauls, of whom I have fpoken from Landini, concerning the meridian of Florence cathedral: this gnomon, which fixed the attention, and foon raifed the admiration, of fuch a judge as M. de la Condamine, who declared it the greateft performance of the kind at prefent in Europe, befpeaks, in him who undertook and executed it, a judgment, knowledge, and talents, the more wonderful, as far fuperior to the age in which he lived: *exortus uti æthereus fol.* If fuch a man has traced the various fciences implied in fuch a

work,

work, up to their fource ; if of himfelf he has fupplied the inftructions of antiquity, which in his
time lay ftill buried; if he has anticipated the
experiments which have led after-ages to proceffes
demanding no lefs genius than precifion ; if he
has left works, if he has formed difciples (and all
this Landini affures us he has done) ; he muft, as
prior to Galileo, be acknowledged the head of
the Florentine philofophic fchool.

Few are fo well qualified as M. Nelli to make
the Florentines acquainted with the difciples, the
labours, and difcoveries, of their illuftrious countryman. Galileo's glory will not be in the leaft
obfcured by fharing Paul's ; and that of Florence
will receive a new irradiation.

In my account of the foregoing particulars, I
cannot be chargeable with any breach of the efteem,
refpect, and veneration, which a view of them
infpires ; yet am I far from having come up to the
fentiments of the Florentines for whatever belongs
to their country. In this they are downright Athenians : Florence, in their eftimate, is to Europe
what Ifocrates, in his famous panegyric, makes
Athens to the reft of Greece. The fineft performances of all kinds they fee• in their city; what
other parts afford is mere aukwardnefs and barbarifm : they have created, they have invented, contrived, difcovered, and made every thing. In their
anceftors this was a commendable pride, as the
principle of their many beautiful and grand performances.

Among other inftances of foreign barbarifm,
they make themfelves very merry with the behaviour of Don Carlos's confeffor at the door of the
Medicean

Medicean library. This confeffor, a Cordelier, attended the young prince when he went to take poffeffion of the Tufcan dominions. Being the only perfon in the fuite, the cut of whofe vefture promifed fome fcholarfhip, the librarians concluding he muft long to fee one of the moft fplendid monuments, which the munificence of princes has dedicated to literature, immediately waited on him with a very refpectful invitation. He received the compliment tolerably well, and a day was fixed. The director had got together all the moft eminent fcholars in the city ; and the confeffor, after partaking of a very genteel collation, moved towards the library, followed by fuch a refpectable company. On coming to the door, he ftopped, and gazing round the ample falon, he called out to the director, " Mr. librarian, have you got the " book of the Seven Trumpets here ?" The director made anfwer in the negative ; and the whole company owned, with fome confufion, that they knew nothing of fuch book. " Well, then," faid the confeffor, turning back, " your whole library is " not worth a pipe of tobacco." No time was loft to get an account of this book, which was found to be a collection of pious ftories, all manifeftly apocryphal, and put into Spanifh by a Francifcan, for the ufe of the very loweft people.

It is from an attachment to all the traditions of their anceftors, that the Florentines ftill retain the guttural pronunciation, changing C into an H ftrongly afpirated, and which was fo peculiar to Florence, even in Dante's time, that he faid the people in the other world knew him to be a Florentine by the rattling in his throat. To judge of

this

this affectation from the rules laid down by Cicero*
for pronunciation, one readily perceives in it
thofe *fonos afperos, anhelatos, vaftos, hiulcos,* which,
fays he, *quofdam deleÆant, quo magis antiquitatem
retinere videantur.* The Roman pronunciation, to
which Cicero was for having the orator form himfelf, had even in thofe days the *fuavitatem pref-
fam, æquabilem, lenem, in qua nihil offendi, nihil
difplicere, nihil animadverti poterat, nihil fonare aut
olere peregrinum.* Thefe paffages may ferve as a
comment to the trite proverb, *Lingua Tofcana in
bocca Romana.*

The trade at Florence is at prefent reduced to
an extreme low ebb, in comparifon to what it was
formerly. *L'arte della lana,* or the woollen ma-
nufactory, to which Florence owes the greater
part of its opulence and fplendor, now fcarcely
fupplies the common people. As to all the apparel
for ornament or fervice, that is intirely Englifh
cloth.

Of filk Tufcany produces an immenfe quantity,
which, though of fuch an excellent quality, was
exported raw. The regency however, to keep
fuch a valuable commodity at Florence, and thus
encourage induftry, has prohibited that exportation. Accordingly, former manufactures are
revived, and new ones fet up. All exports of this
kind, as fattins, damafks, velvets, &c. are well
wrought, the colours fine, and the patterns in a
good tafte.

Jewelry and porcelaine, the manufactories of
which have continued in Tufcany from the ancient
Etrufcans, together with intagliatas, employ a great

* De Orat. L. iii.

many

many hands, though they cannot be accounted considerable branches of trade.

Dying was formerly the more considerable, as the territory of Tuscany produces a plant said to be a good substitute to indigo, and which might easily be multiplied, so as to supply all home wants, and at the same time furnish considerable exports.

The wine in the neighbourhood of Florence has a great run all over Italy. It is both stomachic and light, and thus unites the *generosum & lene,* which recommended a wine to the bottle-men of antiquity. This must be a very considerable article in trade, the price of it being pretty low at Florence.

The Jews have a *ghetto* for the rascality of that nation; and they who are able to keep a house in town, are on a footing with the other citizens; intermixed in the different classes of trade; capable of municipal offices with other merchants and dealers; and distinguishing themselves by punctuality, candour and probity; in a word, by sentiments from which they seem to think themselves dispensed, in those countries were they are treated with oppression and ignominy. The great dukes admitted them to settle at Florence, without subjecting them to those opprobrious marks, which in most other places distinguish them from Christians. In short, they are at Florence, what the Roman-catholics are in England, and the Calvinists in France, citizens contributing to the population, the wealth, and splendor of the state.

The actors, singers, and dancers, of both sexes, at the play-houses in Florence, instead of being
useless

uſeleſs members to ſociety, ſtumbling-blocks and
ſtones of offence, follow trades, the play-houſes
being open only at certain times in the year; and
this, not affording a ſubſiſtence, is conſidered only
as a bye advantage to them, and not a fixed engagement to idleneſs. Their dramatic talents
likewiſe improve by this twofold charaƈter, aƈting
as much on their own account as that of the
public, and not being forced, by mere neceſſity,
to expoſe themſelves by taking on them a part
for which they are not qualified. The harlequin, for inſtance, one of the beſt and moſt entertaining aƈtors I ever ſaw of the kind, kept a
very well-accuſtomed ſhop, with a warehouſe handſomely ſtocked. I have ſeen his books, and they
were kept with all the exaƈtneſs of the *complete
tradeſman.*

Bookſelling was once a capital branch of the
Florentine trade: all librarians are acquainted with
the Torrentius and Giuntos editions, and will
hardly, I believe, agree with the charaƈter given
of the head of the latter houſe by one of his countrymen, and his cotemporary*. *Thomaſo Giunta
non meno avaro que ricco, era unicamente occupato ne'
groſſi guadagni della ſua, piu toſto utile, che onore-
vole ſtamperia,* i. e. "Thomas Giunto, being no
"leſs covetous than rich, minded nothing but
"the great gains accruing to him from his printing,
"which, if uſeful, was not very honourable."
The preſent Giunto is a French bookſeller, of the
name of Boucharde. The former Florentine
book-trade turned almoſt entirely on the Florentine produƈtions. There are, beſides the writings

* Varchi Hiſt. Flor. L. ii.

of

of poets, artifts, lawyers, &c. about a hundred works written by Florentines, and printed at Florence, within the fixteenth and feventeenth centuries, on the general and particular hiftory of Florence.

Among thefe hiftorians Varchi claims a particular diftinction. His work makes a folio of fix hundred and forty pages, though the fubject of it be only the Hiftory of Florence under the Pontificate of Clement VII. that is, a relation of what that city performed and fuffered at that time, in defence of its liberty. The Greek hiftorians of the beft ages never produced any thing more engaging, or better written; and to this muft be added the very rare merit of impartiality and truth (d).

At Florence we got fcent of a ftrange object of trade, the management and particulars of which, however, we could never come at. The mafter of our inn was gone to Rome with a youth, whom he had brought up from his childhood to mufic, after caufing him to undergo the operation ufual in fuch cafes. Whether he had taken him from fome hofpital of foundlings, with the formalities obferved in thofe houfes on the difpofal of the baftards and orphans committed to their care; whether he had bought him of his parents; whe-

(d) The fpeeches which Varchi has interfperfed in his hiftory, may be juftified by the rules made ufe of by Mr. d'Ablancourt to juftify thofe of Thucydides: "When," fays he, "the dignity and importance of the fubject fixes you, "you hate whatever breaks the thread of it; but when it con-"tains only common matter, you have recourfe to other en-"tertainments, and, as it were, refting-places in a long "journey."

ther he was going to fell him at Rome, or only procure him a place, bargaining for a fhare of the emoluments, to the amount of his difburfe-ments, and a profit anfwerable to the hazard he had run ; thefe were circumftances we could not difcover : but we heard enough to fill us with afto-nifhment and horror, that fuch a trade was car-ried on in a chriftian country !

Among the multitude of mafter-pieces of art, and fuch excellent regulations which owe either their birth or improvement to Florence, I have omitted financing; the importance and advantages of which muft be eftimated by the brilliant and folid fortunes gained by it, and not from the cala-mity of the countries which have been the theatre of its fpeculations, inquiries and operations.

This fcience, with which our northern countries are little acquainted, was for a long time cultivated by the Florentines, who managed it with all that dexterity, addrefs, and fagacity, for which they were diftinguifhed in trade. It was one of the principal refources in their laft ftruggles for their liberty, in the years 1530 and 1531. Thofe who followed the fortune of Catharine de Medicis into France, *finding the country fallow, began tilling it with financing*; which lafted till part of the reign of Lewis XIII. The chief contractors were Flo-rentines, either fuch as had quitted their country, or ftill kept houfe at Florence : the very terms in financing fpeak the place of its origin : moft of thefe terms, and the facramental words, are bor-rowed from the Italian.

The Florentines complain in their turn of being *tilled* by thofe who have availed themfelves of their inftructions;

inftructions; but the remembrance of what is paft
fhould be fome alleviation to them under any prefent grievances. Financing may perhaps fare as
other fciences, ruined and loft by being extended.

P I˛S A.

Though we were in the middle of December,
the fky was fo clear, and the air fo mild, that we
hired a boat, which carried us from Florenee to
Pifa down the Arno; as pleafant, and nearly as fhort
a way, as by land, and without any thing of the
fatigue of the other.

Pifa, though much handfomer, is as thinly inhabited as Ferrara; and it is only in its bridges and
public edifices, that it retains any appearance of
its fplendor in the twelfth century. The Arno,
which is at leaft as broad as the Seine, running
through the middle of this place, gives its fituation pretty much the air of that of Paris.

Its northern part, like that of Paris, has been
built on a marfh, the laxity of which is the only
caufe of the phænomenon of the leaning tower fo
much talked of in all travels. Nicolas de Pifa, an
architect of the thirteenth century, to whom Pifa
owes many of the moft ftately edifices with which
it is ftill adorned, having, by the mifcarriages of
his predeceffors, perceived the badnefs of the
ground on which he was to build, made, fays Vafari in his panegyric on him, the foundations of
his buildings the chief object of his attention: befides, caufing piles to be driven, and carefully in-
fpecting the mafonry work in its daily progrefs, he
counterabutted it, on the Arno fide, by fpurs, and
fuch other armatures as have fecured its ftability.

Thefe

Thefe precautions have unhappily been overlooked in the building erected for the univerſity
by Cofmo III. and of which a tower for aſtrono-
mical obſervations is a part. M. Purelli, who is
at the head of thefe obſervations, aſſured me,
that the tower's progreſſive divergency towards the
Arno was become an article in his calculations,
after leading him into miſreckonings, which at
firſt he could by no means account for; but that
now the real cauſe was clear to him beyond all
doubt.

The damp, heavy, and ſickly air at Piſa, is
doubtleſs owing both to this quaggy ſoil, and to
a hill, which, covering Piſa towards the north in
a circular form, reverberates, down into the bottom, where this city ſtands, all the vapours wafted
againſt it by the ſoutherly winds : the want of inhabitants, likewiſe, has no ſmall ſhare in this inconveniency. The chamber in which I lay at the
poſt-houſe, was lofty, in the Italian manner ; that
is, walled and arched. Awaking in the night, I
found myſelf as in a bath, owing to the moiſture
tranſpiring from the walls and the arch. On this
I roſe, and ſpent the remainder of the night by
the fire ſide, in the common hall. The unwhole-
ſomeneſs of baths exuding from walls, built of a
light and very porous ſtone, which pumps up the
water from the foundations, is eaſily conceived.

The ancient Piſans, both from a principle of
magnificence, and that their ſtately ſtructures
might not be injured by this pernicious humidity,
made uſe of marble only, for which the neighbourhood of Carrara was a great conveniency. But
ancient Greece afforded them ſtill a greater advantage,

tage, in marble ready wrought to their hands.
Their continual voyages and expeditions to the
Levant, where their imports greatly exceeded their
exports, gave them an opportunity of bringing
home pieces of the ruins of all thofe wonderful
edifices, which were the admiration of antiquity,
and the untimely demolition of which this commerce greatly haftened.

From Greece came thofe feventy majeftic columns, which fupport the nave of the cathedral;
thence that multitude of columns of every module,
diftributed in the many periftyles of the leaning
tower, of the baptiftery, of the Auguftins fteeple,
&c. thence was brought that grand antique
vafe in the cathedral's fouth porch; thence all
thofe ftones lining its outfide in unequal courfes,
and of which many ftill fhew fragments of ancient
infcriptions: thence thofe exquifite baffo relievos
on the tomb of Beatrix, mother to the famous
countefs Matilda, among which a moft beautiful
Meleager's hunt, and which were the firft models
for Nicholas de Pifa, an artift to whom Italy partly
owes the reftoration of fculpture: laftly, from
Greece came one of the porphyry columns which
adorn the great altar in St. Stephen's church; a
piece the more ineftimable, as the original artift
of it has, on the fhaft where it joins the bafe, en-
graven in Greek characters, that it is nine feet in
length. Before the pillar was fet up in the place
where it now ftands, this infcription was obferved
by Mr. Nelli, who on examination concludes the
Greek foot to have been a little under what Bofius
makes it in 1561, and a little above Scamozzi's
eftimate of it in his Treatife of Architecture.

Among the monuments of the former magnificence of the Pifans, and their elegant tafte in the midft of barbarian rudenefs, the greateft of their three bridges is not to be omitted, being intirely of marble.

This magnificence influenced even fuch religious obfervances, which feemed the moft alien from it. Such is the famous burial-place, likewife built of marble, on the plan of that which I fince faw in France at Orleans. The ground in the open part of this church-yard, is intirely of earth brought by the Pifans, in 1224, from the valley of Jehofhaphat, near Jerufalem, in the fleet which they had fitted out for Frederic Barbaroffa's expedition. This earth ftill retains the virtue of totally confuming a corpfe in the fpace of twenty-four hours. The grave-digger affirmed, that this he very well knew from repeated inftances on multitudes of Germans, who died at Pifa in the war in 1733. *La terra,* faid he to me, *logoravagli con le loro groffe pancie, in termine di duoi giorni,* i. e. " The ground " within two days made an end of them and their " tun bellies."

Among the near and remote caufes of the depopulation of Pifa, may be reckoned the vicinity of Florence and Leghorn:

Mantua væ miferæ nimium vicina Cremonæ!

In order to remedy this evil as far as poffible, the great dukes have continued its univerfity, and made it the ftated refidence of the knights of the order of St. Stephen, inftituted by Cofmo I. in 1561, in imitation of thofe of Malta.

Among the univerfity profeffors are M. Parelli, who fills Galileo's roftrum with the moft eminent diftinction;

diſtinction ; and the fathers, Berti, Friſi and Cor-
ſini. This ſuffices to give an idea of its proſperity.
I was preſent at father Berti's lectures on eccleſiaſtical hiſtory. Theſe lectures (and it is the ſame all
over Italy) are not taken up with dictating, writing, and frivolous argumentations ; but form connected diſcourſes on points of hiſtory, divinity,
mathematics, &c. the ſeries of which makes the
profeſſor's annual courſe. They are in Latin, and
laſt an hour. The profeſſor afterwards takes a
walk for half an hour under the colonnade round
the college-court, when the ſtudents lay before
him in Italian any doubts and difficulties they
may have, which he reſolves in the ſame language.

It was not without ſome difficulty that I could
keep up with the Latin of the Tuſcan profeſſors.
In all the words ending in conſonants, as *dominum,
amant, gloriantur, ut,* they double the final con-
ſonant, and add to it an open E, pronouncing the
words above, *dominummé, amantté, gloriannurré,
utté:* yet is not this pronunciation to be declared
faulty, till we preciſely know how the ancient Romans pronounced their language. Our northern
pronunciation of the final *us* in maſculine ſubſtantives is contradicted by all Italy, Spain, and the
ſouthern parts of France, where this ſyllable is
ſounded *ous :* the Italians even aſſert that, agreeably to the energy of this articulation, *um,* the laſt
ſyllable of the accuſative ſingular of thoſe very
ſubſtantives, ſhould not in our mouths have the
ſound which we give it, like that of the word
homme, but that of the third perſon ſingular of
the preſent tenſe of the verb *humer.*

The chief of the order of St. Stephen, in ſpiri-

tuals, is Monfignor Cerati ; and as fuch he is invefted with part of the epifcopal prerogatives. I
had recommendations to him from France, Rome,
and Florence ; and never had I any of greater ufe :
they procured me the friendfhip and intimacy of
an aged gentleman, equally refpectable for his
ftation, his extenfive and well-digefted erudition,
and the moft amiable temper, with all the Lombard franknefs and Florentine amenity.

Animam qualem neque candidiorem
 Terra tulit.

In him I met with all the care, all the attention,
all the readinefs, and all the anticipations which
politenefs enjoins towards thofe to whom we are
under obligations; but which, from him to me, were
purely effufions of an ingenuous mind and a good
heart. He entertained me with a leifurely view
of whatever was curious in Pifa, and procured me
every acquaintance which he thought would fuit
me ; but none fuited me fo much as his : after
my firft acquaintance with this worthy prelate, I
never thought Pifa lonely.

He had with him his brother, who, like many
Lombards in eafy circumftances, ufed to come
and fpend the winter at Pifa, as being more tem-
perate than in Lombardy. By this inviting mildnefs, Pifa gets fome addition of inhabitants, and
lets houfes, which otherwife would ftand empty.

The baths, which are but a quarter of a league
off, between the city and the hill which inclofes it
towards the north, will likewife bring fome inhabitants when the great buildings juft finifhed, and
all the elegant conveniences making for the ba-
thers, fhall have brought them again into vogue.

Beyond

Beyond the great bridge, and on the left bank of the Arno, I faw, with fome aftonifhment, a large infcription on marble, in golden letters, containing an extract of the emperor's edict as great duke of Florence, ordering, that in 1746, as well as I can recollect, the year fhould begin in Tufcany on the firft of January, and fo to continue. By way of explanation I was informed, that till then the civil year of the Tufcans did not begin till the 25th of March, not fo much by reafon of the equinox, as of the feftival of the Annunciation, which they celebrate under the name of the *Conception of our Lord.* The knowledge of this ancient cuftom is neceffary for tracing down to 1746 the dates of the hiftories and chronicles of Florence, in which the three firft months in each year, computed according to the Roman ftyle, belong to the preceding year.

At the foot of the faid bridge is a vaft manfion-houfe, built in the fineft tafte of architecture by Cofmo I. Another ftory has been raifed on it, but little agreeing with the original building.

Along the fame bank is a fmall church, or old chapel, intirely of marble; the ornaments and pillars finely executed, but the infide far beneath fuch a beautiful appearance. I went in: it was mafs time; and there I faw a young perfon in the flower of her age, and of fuch beauty that I do not remember to have feen her equal in all Italy: fhe was efcorted by an old man in a very odd garb from head to foot, her father or guardian; not her hufband, I hope.

In the fquare before St. Stephen's church ftands a very fine ftatue of Cofmo I.

On

On the quays along the Arno are feveral palaces, which do great honour to Florentine architecture : that of Lanfranchi is accounted the fineft.

The bronze doors of the cathedral, embellifhed or rather loaded with baffo relievos, were one of the firft effays in this kind. They are of the twelfth century, and raife advantageous ideas of the efforts which the arts were even then making in Italy, to emerge from barbarifm.

In the fame point of view may be confidered the paintings on the infide of the large and fplendid burial-place above mentioned. The *Laft Judgment*, by Andrew Orgagna, fixes the eye, and exhibits the ideas which prevailed in Dante's time, The painter, not prefuming to determine Solomon's fate, has reprefented him between the elect and the damned, up to the middle in hell ; whilft the fate of all the others is feverally afcertained.

LEGHORN.

The country from Pifa to Leghorn is one vaft alluvion, of the quality of the Bourdeaux downs, as difficult, and may be as impoffible, to be improved. I have already mentioned fome trials for this purpofe. The rifings, and even the hills, on the eaft of this alluvion, are a congeftion of fand and fhells ; which has given rife to a no very profound differtation of Miffon concerning the formation of thefe foffils.

Certaldo ftands on the fummit of one of thefe hills. It is famous for having given birth to Boccaccio, who likewife fpent the laft years of his life there.

there. On his tomb is an epitaph, compofed by himfelf, in two diftichs ending with this verfe :

Patria Certaldum, ftudium fuit alma Poëfis.

It is fomething ftrange, that this writer fhould have characterifed himfelf by a talent, of which he had but a flender fhare, if we may judge of it by his remains in this kind ; that is, by the pieces at the clofe of each day in his *Decameron,* being fuch as fcarcely bear reading. He may perhaps have ufed the word *Poëfis* as a generical appellation of the entertaining fcience in which, to be fure, he was one of the moft confummate profeffors. The houfe he lived in ftill fubfifts, having been kept in repair from a regard to his memory : and over the door is an infcription on marble, beginning with this verfe,

Has olim exiguas coluit Boccacius ædes.

Leghorn is the work of the Medicis, who, on becoming fovereigns of Florence, made an exchange for this place, then of little confideration, with the Genoefe, of whofe dominions it was at that time a part. As a maritime town, it is at prefent no lefs an object of admiration than Florence. The Medicis, though in another kind, have fhewn in it the like magnificence as in the capital. It was the firft free port open in the Mediterranean. All nations, to the very Mahometans, have free accefs, and may fettle there without any diftinction of fect or religion. Thefe nations, which are divided into five bodies, make, as it were, fo many diftinct republics, of Englifh, Italians, Jews, Greeks, and French.

The emperor, as great duke of Tufcany, had

lately

lately confulted them on the caufes of the decay
of trade at Leghorn, and the means of reftoring it,
I have feen the memoirs in anfwer to this confultation : each of the five nations fets forth its ideas
relatively to its particular concern; and both the
caufes and remedies of the evil were laid open with
a force, a perfpicuity, and a freedom, feldom met
with in fuch compofitions.

The Englifh have a fpacious burial-place behind the harbour; in the city, the Jews have a very
fine fynagogue, and the Greeks likewife a church
according to their rite : thefe laft, who are almoft univerfally taylors, or falesmen, trading to
the Levant, and fupplying the Mediterranean
failors, make the leaft wealthy nation of the five.
The Jews are the richeft, which I fhould have
little imagined from the drefs and the whole appearance of that nation's fyndic, when I accidentally faw him at the French conful's, to whom he
came to fhew his nation's memorial in anfwer to
the emperor's queftion.

Leghorn harbour, near which ftands a very
beautiful pedeftrian ftatue of duke Ferdinand I.
who conftructed the greater part of it, was full of
fhips from the north, and chiefly Englifh. On the
left of this harbour is a *lazaretto* infulated on
every fide, and furrounded by wide ditches of running water. Here curiofity led me into an accident,
which might have been of very bad confequence.
The general communication of Leghorn with all
the places of the Levant and Africa, which are feldom free from the plague, often brings hither veffels actually infected, or ftrongly fufpected to be
fo. The crews, when only fufpected, are confined

fine dwithin the firft clofe of the *lazaretto:* the fecond is for thofe who are feifed with the infection,
who have already fome fymptoms; laftly, for thofe in
whom fuch fymptoms declare themfelves during
the courfe of quarentine ; fo that this fecond clofe
is a real peft-houfe. To all this I was a ftranger
when I went to the *lazaretto*; and I did not reach
it without a great deal of trouble, through a laby-
rinth of ditches and fortifications. In the firft
clofe I met people, fome of whom made bows to
me, drawing back, and making figns not to come
near them. I got into the firft yard of the fecond
clofe without any obftacle, the wicket, which is
always ftrictly guarded, happening not to be fo
then. As I was going up to the fecond wicket, I
found there a centinel, who called out for me
to keep off, and on feeing me coming on, fell a
fkipping, and making gefticulations like an ideot,
or one who is tickled. On my offering him a
buona mancia, his gefticulations were more extravagant than before; fo that, thinking the poor
fellow was really out of his fenfes, and I could not
fet him to rights, I left the place ; and being that
night at an entertainment in one of the capital
houfes of Leghorn, I related my difappointment.
The whole company fhuddered ; and I was given
to underftand, that, had my clothes in the leaft
touched the wicket, or thofe of the centinel, I muft,
ipfo facto, have been put into one of the cells of
the laft ward, and there performed quarentine
along with the infected, of whom it is the receptacle ; and that, if I had broke loofe from the
centinel, who would have collared me, and had I
betaken myfelf to my heels, his orders were to fire

at

at me, hitting me wherever he could beſt. This is ſaid by way of information againſt a precipitate curioſity.

There is no giving a complete idea of the preſent ſtate of the Leghorn trade, without abridging the memorials above mentioned, and of which we procured copies; but an extract would only whet the curioſity of the mercantile claſs, to ſee the originals.

At Leghorn we hired a bark for Genoa, ex-preſsly ſtipulating with the maſter, that it ſhould be wholly for ourſelves. But the water *Vetturini* are like their land-brethren: after incumbering us with what goods he could get, he gave us for fellow travellers, ſome ſhipwrights belonging to Toulon dock, with their overſeer; Breton ſailors, who were returning from England by the way of Venice; a Spaniſh Dominican, who was on his way home; with a female companion, whom the good father had picked up at Civita Vecchia.

PORTO-FINO.

We left Leghorn on Chriſtmas eve; and a very hard gale of wind, in which our poltron maſter and his men fell to wringing their hands, and ma-king more uſe of their chaplets than their oars, obliged us to put into Porto-Fino.

The day following, we were to have continued our courſe; but our honeſt maſter had other thoughts: Porto-Fino was the very place to which he, and the greater part of his crew, belonged; and it turned to better account with him to ſpend Chriſtmas holidays at home, than in Genoa har-

bour,

bour, where things are not fo cheap. We however obliged him to fet fail; but, by defigned mifmanagement in working the bark, there was a neceflity of putting back; and then faid he, " we " fhall avoid being both laughed at and blamed, " if we were loft in going to fea on Chriftmas day."

The Dominican, who had been fix weeks on his way from Civita-Vecchia, was the more pleafed with our putting back, having a point of intereft to fettle with the parifh prieft of Porto-Fino. Before faying his three maffes the preceding night, he had afked the prieft whether he had any *intentions* for him; which, in the phrafeology of the Italian clergy, fignifies afking a mafs with a defign of paying for it. The prieft had afked two; but inftead of the gratuity which the father expected, he had fignified to him, that a great many poor people had died in his parifh without the means of having maffes faid for them, and that his two fhould be applied to thefe forlorn fouls. This difpofition the Spaniard could not digeft, and was determined to avail himfelf of this opportunity to right himfelf. He was a comely man, raw-boned, choleric, and always clinching an enormous cane, which he brandifhed about with every gefture. He had already brought himfelf into feveral fcrapes, fince his leaving Civita Vecchia: for inftance, he had the prefumption to collar the governor of a fmall place for being, as he thought, wanting in refpect to the cloth, and who, from regard to St. Dominic's gown, could obtain no farther fatisfaction for fuch an outrage, than condemning him to perform quarentine, as coming from a fufpected country. He was in no great

hurry

hurry to reach Spain; for coming away without leave, with a view to follicit a licence at Rome to change his order, fix months imprifonment on bread and water was the leaft he could expect.

Returning in the evening from an excurfion we had made to the heights which overlook Porto-Fino, we found him on the pier, with his hat thruft over his eyes, brandifhing his cane, and fhewing in his countenance and carriage that he was on fome great fcheme. We afked how matters ftood with the prieft : *Adeffo, adeffo,* i. e. " Now " for it, now for it," anfwered he, haftening towards the church. The prieft being bufy in confeffing, he beckoned to him, faying in the Italian way, *Una, una.* The prieft not anfwering, he went up to the confeffional ; at which the prieft came out, and propofed going into the veftry. They were no fooner in, than the Dominican bolting the door, and flapping his cane on the table, renewed his demand with fuch emphafis, that the poor prieft gave him all the money he had in his pocket. He returned to the inn with the money in his hand, and related to us, with all the heat of the action itfelf, how he had brought the prieft to a compliance : he treated our domeftics, his female companion, and a Piedmontefe pilgrim, who was going to Rome to obtain abfolution for freedoms with a female coufin-german of his. It was the Dominican habit which drew from the pilgrim fuch a confeffion ; and, in return to his confidence, he let him into fome meafures for getting his abfolution at the cheapeft rate.

Porto-Fino is fheltered by an enormous rock, which forms a promontory battered on every fide

by

by the agitations of the fea. It is a full mile perpendicular above the water's edge. Having clam-
bered up this promontory, we walked all over its
fummit, which goes round the harbour. From
thence we had, on the right, a view of the city of
Genoa and its two *rivierás*, forming, as it were, the
two parts of an arch, and the city the centre; and
on the left, a fimilar arch terminating the point
of Spezzia bay. This whole cape * is one continued compound, formed of pebbles, bound by a
natural cement hard as any ftone. Time however,
and the waves, have made fome impreffion on it.
Some parts of this mafs, which have been loofened
by the corrofive water, and thus funk down perpendicularly, look perfectly like a wall made by
the hand of man : others, being excavated beneath, hang in the air, and fhew thofe arched
chafms fo frequent in Callot's prints.

We were abfolutely to put to fea the day after
Chriftmas day; but our fkipper, who minded his
fecret defigns more than our impatience, came to
tell us that the wind was againft us; that there was
no keeping the fea; and, in a word, he would not
ftir. Concluding that the next day we fhould hear
the fame ftory, I afked him if he had any commands for Genoa; and away I went, by the only
carriage to be had at Porto-Fino, that is, on foot,
with my domeftic carrying a bundle of clean linen
at the handle of his dagger. We had full fix
leagues to go; but from the cape, Genoa feemed
at fo fmall a diftance; and the fea, being but flightly
agitated, afforded fo chearful a profpect, the weather alfo was fo fine, the air fo clear and temper-

* See the article of MOLA.

ate,

ate, and the whole coaft fo charmingly difplayed all the beauties of fpring, that I ventured on the expedition, with a pleafure which received an additional relifh from the joy of feeing myfelf out of the prifon of Porto-Fino.

We had the cape to clamber up a fecond time; then to traverfe the long level, by which it joins to the coaft; afterwards, a fteep declivity; and all this by ways, with which the goats are beft acquainted; the path, in fome places between parallel rocks, being only a fhoe's breadth, fo that there was no moving forward for fome paces, but by fliding the fore-foot and bringing the other after.

From thence I had a view of a charming valley along a bay, covered to the fouth-weft by the prominence of the cape. In the centre of this bay lies a village called Santa Maria, the diverfity of the fcattered dwellings of which feems as if intended for the delight of the profpect.

All the level ground is formed by a road along the flope of the cape, the repair of which is owing to marfhal Richelieu in his expedition to Genoa; but the ground, on the fide in which it is in a great meafure cut, having fince given way in feveral places, is now practicable only to foot-travellers.

This way is a continued feries of towns, villages, and feats, both of a pretty conftruction, and delightfully fituated. Along the villages, and near the houfes, it is paved with bricks of feveral colours, placed in compartments like Hungary point. The orange-trees, of which this coaft is full, were loaded with fruit and bloffoms: jeffamine, thyme, myrtle, all the odorous herbs and plants, covering the uncultivable places, were in full bloom; as likewife

wife peas, which were fet in little fpots of a better foil: the birds, in fprightly ftrains, hailed
the fpring: but, as in thofe inchanted tracts with
which romances are decorated, here was no inn,
fo that I had much ado to get a drop of wine, and
fome very indifferent bread; thus I reached Genoa
both very tired and very hungry.

It was the next evening before I had the pleafure of feeing my fellow traveller. The mafter,
finding that I was really gone, had got under way
about noon; and having with fome difficulty wea-
thered the cape, he defignedly loft ground, and
hampered himfelf in the firft road, but fignified
to the paffengers that he would get out to fea on
the firft appearance of fair weather, though in his
own mind he determined to fpend the night, and as
much as he could of the day following, in a place
which he knew, and where provifions were cheaper
than at Genoa; fo that all my companion got by
his ftay was being toffed about all night in the
dark, amidft a very harfh grating clatter, like that
of large chains, caufed by the rolling and colli-
fion of fragments, great and fmall, detached from
the rock, whilft the mafter and his men lay fnug in
their beds afhore.

As I came to Genoa on foot, the reception I
met with at the inn was that of a foot paffenger. I
indeed afked for an apartment for two; but all I
could get was a fmall chamber with a very indifferent bed, in which, however, the journey procured
me a good night's reft: but many compliments
being fent me, the day following, by perfons to
whom I was recommended, the innkeeper made

very humble apologies, and aſſured me of his future good behaviour.

G E N O A.

One of the moſt judicious modern hiſtorians ſees,
in the croiſades, the origin of maritime powers;
the firſt of which were Venice, Genoa, and Piſa;
and likewiſe the eſtabliſhment of maritime commerce in Europe, which, till then, had been in
the hands of the Greeks and Arabs. The conqueſts, and the jealouſy of the conquering republics, and the wars which this jealouſy raiſed among
them, fill up the picture of this firſt epocha.

Genoa figures in it with pre-eminence: among its
conqueſts and ſettlements, acquired partly by fair,
and partly by foul means, were the iſles of Majorca,
Minorca, Candia, Sardinia, Corſica, Negrepont,
Malta, Leſbos, Scio, Smyrna in Aſia Minor,
Theodoſia, and ſeveral important places on the
Black Sea, and even the very ſuburbs of Conſtantinople. Such extenſive conqueſts, ſettlements,
and poſſeſſions, were what weakened it to ſuch a
degree, that, unable to defend its own territory,
it made a ſurrender of itſelf to Charles VI. king of
France, within a century after this formidable appearance. At the revolution, which cloſed the
reign of that prince, it re-aſſumed its liberty; but
labouring ſtill under its former debility, it was for
throwing itſelf into the arms of Lewis XI. who,
from an opinion that diſtant poſſeſſions would be
of no real advantage to France, rejected its offers,
which however were accepted by Lewis XII.
and

and Francis I. Andrea Doria, quitting the French
service, for that of the emperor Charles V. stipu-
lated with that prince for the freedom of his country, and gave his fellow citizens laws, which not
only settled that freedom, but has maintained it,
down to the present time, against both domestic
encroachments and foreign attacks. Such is the
power of a good head and a good heart united!
Genoa is full of monuments of gratitude towards this illustrious patriot. There is a marble
statue of him at the gate of the palace, in the great
council-hall, and in St. George's bank, with the
title of *Restitutor Libertatis.* In the centre of a
fountain in the garden of Doria palace stands
a colossal statue of this hero, with Neptune's
attributes. Lastly, in St. Matthew's church,
which was built by his ancestors, and repaired
by himself, is his tomb; the apposite ornaments
and inscription of which, majestically declare
him the Restorer of his Country.
All Europe beheld with admiration the bold and
successful effort made in 1746, by the commonalty of Genoa, to retrieve their freedom, against an
armed enemy, then master of the city, and of all
the republic's forces ; a noble instance of what
the love of one's country can still perform, and
related with an energy worthy of the subject, in
the Latin history of the last war in Italy, written
by M. Bonamici, an officer in the Neapolitan
service.
I have collected some anecdotes relating to this
great event, which had escaped the historian's
knowledge. Five months after the revolution,
money began to be wanting in support of it ; and

the leffer council were going to raife it by an additional impoft. The day they were to meet for drawing up the edict, M. Grillo, a perfon of high birth and very rich, but who was fomething fingular in many of his ways, came early into the antichamber of the council, and ftrewing it with pieces of cord about two feet long, went his way. Every counfellor, on coming in, afked how thofe ropes came there, and being anfwered, that it was M. Grillo's doings, gave a fhrug, and paffed along. The deliberation being entered on, in comes M. Grillo, who was immediately afked what he meant by thofe ropes: he made anfwer, that ever fince the taking up arms, the continual fervice for the defence of the republic having obliged the people to quit their daily occupations, by which they had before fupported their families, it would be an act of juftice and humanity, to give thofe pieces of rope among the people to hang themfelves, rather than faddle them with new impofts, which would drive them to defpair, and bring in nothing to the ftate. " But money muft be had," replied the council, " and where to get it ?" " Where it " is," anfwered he; and going away, foon returned, followed by porters with bags of gold and filver, to the amount of four or five hundred thoufand livres, and immediately poured them out in the middle of the hall : " Let every one of you do " the like," added M. Grillo, going away, " and " then the money will be made up." This example took ; the impoft was dropped, the nobility contributed in proportion to their abilities, and Genoa was faved. I was concerned to hear, that the fame nobility, departing from M. Grillo's

patriotic

patriotic views, were about continuing extraordinary impofts, to get back from the people what they had then up for given their own prefervation.

The nobility had not openly joined in the revolution, which, for fome time, was even a matter of confternation among them: the people in arms tumultuoufly infifted on their declaring themfelves, or laying down the government; which occafioned a moft tragical fcene, excellently defcribed by M. Bonamici. Though the fenate, the council, and the nobility, did not act in a body and openly, they affifted underhand, individuals mingling themfelves among the commonalty, who, that they might not be brought into any danger, called them among themfelves *Colliers*; at the fame time paying them the greateft deference and refpect.

But the boldeft champions were plebeians; and among thefe one Epingletta, a common fhoemaker, and till then known only for his facetioufnefs and acute fayings; but he foon diftinguifhed himfelf by very bold ftrokes: it was feen, both in his attacking and defending feveral pofts, which accidentally fell in his way, that his head was of a piece with his heart: the people ftrove who fhould fight under him. He was killed, fomething unexpectedly, towards the end of the fiege, at the head of two thoufand men whom he commanded, in an expedition where there was but little blood fhed. He had been one of the warmeft fticklers againft the nobility. I could not hear what the fenate has done for his widow and children.

I happened to be in the fenate at the *eftratto* of new members for one of the colleges, which form the fecret council of the ftate. The halls of

Z z
the

the palace were crowded with people of all ranks, and all feemed deeply concerned about this ceremony. I was informed, that this *eftratto* was exactly like the drawing of the lottery lately paffed in France, under the name of *Lotterie de l'Ecole Royale & Militaire*. The Genoefe, being mighty calculators, have invented this lottery ; and the ftate, from political views, countenances it. A citizen concerns himfelf about the *eftratto* of fuch a fenator, no farther than as having put into the lottery in his name, on a conceit that it will prove more lucky to him than any other.

This *eftratto*, or drawing, is performed with great folemnity. A foundling boy, very beautiful and richly dreffed, being, after many careffes from all the fenators, placed ftanding on a ftool between the doge's legs ; a velvet purfe, containing, in pieces of paper rolled up, the names of the fenators elected into the great council, was delivered to his ferenity. The doge having fhaken the purfe, the boy put in his hand, and drew out two tickets, which, being read by the firft fenator, were whifpered round among the whole affembly.

The palace in which this ceremony was tranf-acted, is the doge's manfion-houfe, as likewife of fome fenators who clofely keep him company. And, farther, here are held the feveral courts of law. It makes no great appearance outwardly ; but fome of the pieces within are magnificence itfelf, as the great and leffer council-chambers. In the laft are frefcos by Solimene, whofe light and brilliant pencil, far from obfcuring the room (a difadvantage ufually

ufually confequential to painting) feems to make it more chearful and lightfome.

The defigns of the great council probably are an imitation of Verfailles gallery. The roof and walls difplay the moft remarkable battles and victories of the Genoefe in their former wars with the Venetians, the Pifans, and Florentines, painted by Franchefchini, but with more art than fpirit. In the piers facing the fquare, and in the correfpondent piers, are niches with marble ftatues, bigger than life, of the republic's chief benefactors, the laft being marfhal Richelieu. Thofe ftatues are not executed fuitably to the place they ftand in. As for that of the marfhal Richelieu, in the habit of the order of the Holy Ghoft, the eye, in all the various particulars of that habiliment, fees only a turgid affemblage of puffs and curls, quite difproportionate to the head.

The monuments of this kind in the palace of St. George's bank are by better hands. To this bank, the æra of which is fo far back as the beginning of the fifteenth century, are appropriated two thirds of the republic's ordinary revenue. All money and paper affairs at Genoa are tranfacted in bills of this bank. At the head of it are eight directors : it has large funds and eftates, quite diftinct from thofe of the republic; and the only rub its credit ever met with, was at the revolution in 1746 : at the peace, its fafety was the firft thing attended to both by the nobility and people; the latter are particularly concerned to fupport an eftablifhment, which, taking the finews of the ftate out of the government's hands, forms a powerful counterpoife to its authority.

At Genoa, the ftate has the monopoly of bread, wine, and oil. The bakers, in the feveral parts of the city, muft fetch all they fell from the republic's ovens, which are in one building, containing every conveniency for the feveral operations required in fuch a large fupply. The republic's cellars are no lefs furprifing in another kind, being large barks in the bafon or dock, and thus expofed all fummer to the heat of the fun, the intenfenefs of which is increafed by being reflected from the buildings round thefe floating cellars : accordingly, the wine and oil are fuch as might be expected from fuch a ftaple.

As to the magnificence of the city's buildings, which have gained it the title of *Superba*, all Genoa is in the *Strada Nuova*; the palaces of which are indeed fuperb, and moftly built from plans of Galeazzi of Perugia. Among thofe palaces, the Jefuits have a houfe, the lefs inferior to them in magnificence, as its whole inward decoration, being open to the ftreet, prefents a pleafing and well-difpofed affemblage of fteps, flights of ftairs, periftyles, baluftrades, orange-trees and a fhrubbery, beautifully intermingling nature with art.

The furniture of the palaces of Strada Nuova vies with the grandeur of the architecture. Several have ineftimable collections of paintings. In that of Brignole is a fuit of filk, gold and filver hangings, reprefenting the Triumphs of Scipio, from Julio Romano's cartons. The owner of this palace being doge when I happened to be in Genoa, as a mark of this dignity the gates of his palace had been taken down, and only a rough wooden bar fixed at each end, acrofs the entrance, at the height of fix feet.

Doria

Doria palace, in the whole detail, anfwers the reputation of the famous Andrea Doria, who built it. Thofe parts which are ufually neglected, ftill fhine with paintings, ornaments, and grotefques, by Pordenone, Beccafami, and the beft mafters of thofe times. Here is fhewn the table, at which Charles V. Francis I. and Clement VII. were attended by Andrea Doria.

The churches of Genoa, likewife, contain a great number of pieces, which are admired even by thofe who conclude their view of Italy with this city. The Annunciada, St. Cyr, St. Philip de Neri, the Carignan church, all built by fome eminent family at Genoa, exhibit a ftriking affemblage of productions in the three arts, fubordinate to defign. In the latter are two admirable ftatues; St. Sebaftian, a nudity; the other, a bifhop in his cope, by the famous Puget. A hofpital, and our Lady of the Vines, have alfo two not inferior pieces of this mafter, who, enflaved by his talents, placing his whole ambition in the perfection of his art, and like the famous Le Gros being above courting either panegyrifts or patrons, was fcarce known in his own country, and had no other employment befides ornamenting the ftems of galleys and merchant veffels. His *Milo*, which he ventured to expofe for fale, a piece to which the emperor Auguftus would have affigned one of the firft places in the Palatine gallery, could meet with no better reception at Verfailles, than to be put in the gardens.

The facred edifices at Genoa, like thofe of Naples, are full of funerary infcriptions, but generally as plain as thofe of Naples are turgid and

far-

far-fetched. They have commonly annexed to them fome moral or prudential maxims for the ufe of the *viator*, who, in compliance with the invitation of moft of thefe infcriptions, has ftopped to read them. On the frieze of the magnificent tomb of one of the name of Spinola, is the following, in very large characters.

QUOD PER TE FACERE POTES,
ALTERI NE COMMISERIS.

In fome public places are infcriptions of another kind, alfo confecrated to pofterity, but perpetuating the infamous memory of fuch who have injured the ftate, and whofe names are fet up in the chief places of the Genoefe territories. I could hardly reconcile perpetuating monuments of this kind with the humane maxim, *Gratiæ ampliandæ, odia reftringenda.*

The whole learning of Genoa is confined to the Jefuits college. The Genoefe, being all naturally intended for trade, think themfelves difpenfed from any ftudy and fcience, which has not an immediate reference to that fupreme object.

Pueri longis rationibus affem
Difcant in partes centum diducere.

Yet I have been told, that natural hiftory was known and cultivated there, even in the laft century, as a matter both of curiofity and commerce : which confirms what Mr. Addifon fays of his having, in the year 1688, feen a collection of fhells at M. Miconi's in Genoa ; and he fpeaks of it as the moft complete collection in Europe. And I muft
not.

not forget the famous emerald veſſel, which,
ſuppoſing it inconteſtable, would be the moſt capital piece of natural hiſtory in the univerſe.

According to Andrea Doria's original laws, the
government of Genoa was to be in the hands of
the ancient nobility, excluſively of the new : but
by a regulation between thoſe two bodies in 1576,
the partition wall was broken down, and both
were made equally capable of the higheſt employments : being, however, ſtill diſtinguiſhed into
Porto Vecchio and *Porto Nuovo*, they not only
meet in ſeparate places, but have diſtinct intereſts.
The Porto Vecchio, where the old nobility
meet, is an open place, along the great ſtreet : in
it are always ſome old elbow-chairs of crimſon velvet, on which only the old nobility can ſit : a new
nobleman, on paſſing near this place, makes
a very low bow to thoſe who are met there, and
which they are ſure to return very careleſsly ; nay,
they often beckon to him, at which he goes up,
and reſpectively attends to what is ſaid to him.
The new nobility have no other meeting-places
but the little marble ſeats, round the Banchi houſe,
and without any of the formality and diſtinctions of
the Porto Vecchio.

The nobility, both new and old, join in ex-
ploding that prejudice which holds trade incompatible with nobility : they always have concerned themſelves in banking and commerce ; both
which at Genoa, being not only conſiderable, but
well conducted, are very lucrative. Manufactures
indeed have been great ſufferers by the laſt revolution, but are in a fair way of ſoon ſeeing themſelves
on their former footing. Leghorn was the ſtaple
of

of all Italy for Dutch and Spanish tobacco, till,
by the clogs which the emperor's farmers were
imprudently for forcing on this trade, it has taken
its flight to Genoa, which, I should before have
obferved, has likewife been made a free port. England, in confequence of doing more bufinefs than
France with Genoa, in its oranges and lemons, its
dried and preferved fruits, improves this connexion
for vending at Genoa great quantities of grain and
manufactures.

Both fexes at Genoa are in general perfonable
and handfome, and affect the French drefs to the
utmoft extent of the fumptuary laws, by which
men are allowed only to wear black with a fhort
fattin cloak, and their fedans coarfely varnifhed
with black. The fame laws prohibit women from
pearls, diamonds, and laces. Their carriage is
the fame as that of men ; and all their light, after dark, is a forry lantern on one of the poles of
the leading chairman. The only perfons difpenfed
from thefe rigid laws are the *fpofe*, or fuch as are
promifed in marriage ; and this for fix weeks before and after their nuptials. In this happy interval their love of finery has its full range : they go
in gilded chairs fplendidly glafed, with white wax
flambeaux before and behind ; and in the richeft
full dreffes, glittering with jewels and laces.
During this tranfient period, it is the fame with
them as with young women who are about taking
the veil, and who are led to the parifh-church in
all the pomp and glitter which their family can
furnifh.

The disfavourable and energetic portrait of the
Genoefe, with which Dante concludes the thirty-
third

third canto of his *Hell*, is unqueftionably owing to the frequent wars, the rivalry and commercial jealoufy, which have ever fubfifted between that people and his countrymen the Tufcans :

> *Ahi Genovefi, uomini diverfi*
> *D'ogni coftume e più d'ogni magagna,*
> *Perche non fiete voi del mondo fperfi ?*
> *Che col peggiore fpirto di Romagna*
> *Trovai un tal di voi, che per fu' opra,*
> *In anima in Cocyto gia fi bagna,*
> *Ed in corpo par ancor vivo difaprà.*

It is from the fame national rancour, that Landini, in his commentary on that piece, roundly fays, *Degna e ben collocata efclamazione, per molti rifpetti ! i quali, per non ufar invettiva, contra mia confuetudine, al prefente non pongo, ma fono noti quafi à tutti.* " A very juft exclamation, and per-" fectly appofite in many refpects, but which, from " my known averfion to invective and obloquy, I " fhall not particularife."

A retrofpect on more remote times fhews us Virgil, a true Lombard, faying, in the fecond book of his Georgics,

> *Affuetumque malo Ligurem.*

And the like prejudice fuggefts to him Camilla's reproaches to a vapouring boafter :

> *Haud Ligurum extremus, dum fallere fata finebant :*
> *Vane Ligur,* (fays Camilla to him) *fruftraque animis*
>   *elate fuperbis,*
> *Nequicquam patrias tentafti lubricas artes.*

But

But all, who have a right way of thinking, know what ſtreſs to lay on theſe national criminations.

We hired a felucca at Genoa, which brought us back to France, with our Toulon ſhipwrights and our Breton ſailors, who had kept us company from Leghorn. The Genoeſe ſeamen, whom we had an opportunity of knowing in theſe two voyages, that is, the inhabitants of the two *rivierás* of Genoa, were for a long time, both from incli-nation and intereſt, in the French ſervice ; whereas they now prefer that of Spain. They enter only for a year, will be well paid, are robuſt, ſober, very laborious, but faint-hearted in danger.

They and the Provençals, for their reciprocal ſecurity, make an exchange of their fiſheries. Whilſt we were on this coaſt, it ſwarmed with Provençals down as far as the ſeas of Sicily, leaving Martigues and the coaſt of Provence to the Genoeſe.

Our return was not without ſome riſque. Two Engliſh cruiſers lay off Villa-Franca harbour : our maſter, getting intelligence of this at St. Remo, acquainted us with the difficulty ; on which calling a council, we determined to leave the felucca with only one ſervant on board, and foot it to Nice along the coaſt. The experience I had acquired from Porto-Fino to Genoa, qualified me for keeping up our company's ſpirits ; and accordingly they all owned me their conductor. The appearance of the ſky, the country, and the ſea, was indeed perfectly vernal ; but we had enormous mountains to paſs over, and the deſcents not leſs difficult and toilſome than the acclivities. We breakfaſted

at

at Bordiguerra, where our bill, being a monſtrous exaction, was ſettled by the commandant of Ventimiglia. We dined at Turbia with a Swiſs officer, who commanded ſome invalids there. This poſt conſiſts of a diſmal houſe, ſerving both for inn and corps-de-garde ; and the remains of a tower built by Cæſar on mount Turbia, to ſecure the paſs in his return from Gaul into Italy. It is this edifice which Virgil alludes to in the following verſe in the ſixth book of the Æneid :

Aggeribus ſocer Alpinis atque arce Monæci
Deſcendens.

From the top of Turbia you ſee Monaco directly under you, down an amazing depth ; yet it ſtands on a rock, at a great height above the water's edge.

We diſcovered at ſea, off Ventimiglia, a large tartan : as it was paſſing by, one of the Engliſh frigates immediately got under ſail, gave it chace, and fired ſeveral ſhot ; and the tartan making a running fight of it, at length got clear. Our view of this engagement was like ſeeing the dramatic battles from the upper regions in the operahouſe ; but it gave us much more pleaſure to ſee our ſkipper, who had taken the very inſtant of the frigate's putting to ſea, paſs without moleſtation by the mouth of the harbour, and row away into that of Nice.

The latter is a work of the king of Sardinia, having been made by his orders under the cannon, or rather the rubbiſh, of Nice fort, which was totally demoliſhed by marſhal Catinat in the ſucceſſion-war.

All I obſerved at Nice, was an inſcription in
white

white marble over the door of the clock-tower.
It animadverts, in very fine Latin, but in very free
terms, on the alliance of the French with the
Turks in their joint expedition againſt Nice under
Francis I. I am ſurpriſed that the French, having
been maſters of this city for ſeveral years under the
marſhals Catinat, Maillebois, and Belleiſle, ſhould
have let ſuch a monument ſtand, which was
daily before their eyes, in the principal ſquare of
Nice.

The acquaintance, whoſe memoirs I have mentioned in the article of PLACENTIA, had in his paſſage to Nice an adventure which I ſhall here tran-
ſcribe: it may ſerve for the hiſtory of noxious in-
ſects. " In 1745, in a fine evening in July, as I was
" walking alone towards La Trinitá, in the narrow
" cultivated ſpace along the Paglion, I perceived,
" a little up the hill, a lofty fig-tree with a fig
" hanging on it, which had been overlooked by
" the people who had ſtripped the tree: it was ſo
" tempting, that ſtanding a tip-toe on my right
" foot, I plucked it; but, recovering myſelf on
" my heel, I felt my inſtep pricked in two places,
" as if lacerated by two ſmall ruſty files. The
" pain was ſo ſharp, that I own it made me cry
" out; and away flew my ſhoe, without my un-
" buckling it: afterwards looking down, I ſaw
" ſcuttling away an inſect, in ſhape and ſize very
" much like a chaffer, but ſhorter and thicker:
" its coat was of a changeable green yellow; and
" its head terminated in two ſtrong *antennæ*, bend-
" ing inwards like thoſe of the beetle. I thought
" that it had dropped from the fig-tree into the
" hollow made between my foot and the ſhoe by
" my

" my motion to reach the fig, and that, feeling
" itſelf ſqueezed, it had ſtung me in its own de-
" fence; ſo that I forbore revenging myſelf. The
" pain in the mean time continued, and feeling
" my foot ſwell, I pulled of my ſtocking: then
" acroſs the inſtep were two parallel marks, about
" three lines in length, and two lines diſtant one
" from the other. After a fruitleſs endeavour to
" ſqueeze blood from them, I went back towards
" the city; but the pain had pervaded all the
" nerves of my foot, ſo that I was ſcarcely able to
" ſtand. Pulling off my ſtocking a ſecond time,
" I perceived round the two marks a black circle,
" which (it being the only remedy at hand) I
" bathed copiouſly with urine; then making free
" with the firſt wine-prop I met, and putting on
" my ſhoe ſo as not to bear on the wound, I reached
" Nice, and went into the firſt apothecary's ſhop.
" Having given him an account of the accident and
" the inſect, he told me they called it *tavan*, and
" very ſeriouſly checked me for not having killed
" it, purſuant to the axiom, *the venom dies*
" *with the beaſt.* He applied a bolſter of cam-
" phirated brandy, adviſed me to eat no ſupper,
" and, if I could, to ſleep, promiſing to call on me
" the next morning. He came, and was very
" much ſurpriſed at my having had ſo very good
" a night, told me that he reckoned he ſhould have
" found me feveriſh, and attributed the fair way I
" was in to the natural topic, which I had made
" uſe of on the ſpot. In the night time, my in-
" ſtep was grown black, and the pain ſtill very
" acute. Some camphirated brandy, however,
" and a few days reſt, completed the cure.

" L

" I refer to naturalifts the inquiry into what " affinity there may be between the *tavan* and the " tarantula, and the effects of the ftinging of " one, with that of the other."

Thefe are the obfervations we have collected concerning Italy, and the *difpofitions, humours, and ways,* of the Italians, during the year we fpent in *rubbing and filing our brain againft theirs**. They connect objects which we have feen, or thought we faw ; facts received from the affurance of perfons, moft of them intelligent, and in no wife concerned to impofe on us ; confequences, in the juftnefs of which we may have erred, and which we pretend not to vindicate. Truth was our capital view, without flattering or offending any country or perfon whatever, and without extending our praifes or our remarks to every thing which might have afforded matter.

The character of the Italians in general fhould naturally come in here, as the conclufive corollary of our obfervations. The principal ftrokes of it, if not exhibited in formal words, are virtually reprefented in many parts of thefe volumes : as to combining them, that we leave to the reader's fagacity. It is only with a view of guarding the public againft the judgments which ftrangers are apt to make, concerning every nation whatever, that we fhall here fet down feveral decifions, given at different times on the Italians, by authors of the middle age, and others more modern ; but which we adopt no farther than as they agree with our obfervations. That we may not be charged with

* Mont. L. i. c. 29.

any

any falſification, we ſhall give them *verbatim* in the terms of the reſpective authors.

Gregory of Tours, the father of the Hiſtory of France, ſpeaking of the Italians being threatened with an invaſion of the Lombards before the fall of the Grecian empire in Italy, gives this character of them : *Eſt omnis populus infidelis, per-juriis deditus, furtis obnoxius, in homicidiis promp-tus, à quibus nullus juſtitiæ fructus ullatenus gliſcit, non decimæ dantur, non pauper alitur, non tegitur nudus, non peregrinus hoſpitio excipitur.*[*]

Ditmar, an hiſtorian of the eleventh century, quoted by Muratori, exclaims, *Multæ ſunt, proh dolor ! in Romania, atque in Longobardia, inſidiæ. Cunctis huc advenientibus exigua patet caritas. Omne ibi venale eſt, et hoc cum dolo ; multique toxi-cati cibo pereunt.*[†]

Innocent II. was for providing a young French abbé with a biſhoprick in Italy : St. Bernard, to diſ-ſuade him from it, made uſe of a reaſon, which for this long time has loſt its weight: *Inſolentia Longo-bardorum,* ſays he to the pope, *& inquietudo eorum, cui non eſt nota ? aut cui magis quàm vobis ? Quid putamus eſſe facturum juvenem, viribus corporis frac-tum, et quieti eremi aſſuetum, in populo barbaro, tumultuoſo, procelloſo ?*[‡]

Whether riches and plenty had in the following age wrought a happy change in the manners of the Italians, or whether James de Vitry had con-ſidered them better, or with a more favourable eye, he draws the following picture of the Genoeſe and the Piſans, whom he muſt have thoroughly

---

[*] Hiſt. L. i. c. 6.   [†] Diſſ. xxiii.   [‡] Epiſt. clv.

known, as living along with them in the expedition of which he has given us the hiftory : *Homines
Italici*, fays he[*], *et graviores, et maturi, et pru-
dentes, et compofiti, in cibo parci, in potu fobrii, in
verbis ornati et prolixi, in confiliis circumfpecti, in
republica procuranda diligentes et ftudiofi, tenaces
et fibi in pofterum providentes, aliis fubjici renuentes,
ante omnia libertatem fibi defendentes, jura, leges et
inftituta fibi dictantes et firmiter obfervantes. Terræ
Sanctæ valdè funt neceffarii, non folùm in præliando,
fed in navali exercitio, in mercimoniis peregrinis et
victualibus deportandis. Quoniam in potu et cibo
modefti funt, diutiùs in Orientali regione vivunt,
quàm aliæ Occidentales nationes.*

This picture, by a French hand, greatly mol-
lifies the irony on the Italians, which John of Salifbury puts in the mouth of the French : *Æmilia-
nos et Ligures*, fays this fatirical writer[†], *Galli de-
rident, dicentes eos teftamenta conficere, viciniam
convocare, armorum implorare præfidia, fi finibus
eorum teftudo immineat quam oporteat oppugnari :*
a paffage which might have ferved Rabelais for a
motto to his *Poltronifmus rerum Italicarum*.

The learned Barclay, in his *Icon Animorum*, after
eftimating the pre-eminence of Italy above other
European countries, and after weighing the reafons and motives of the general prepoffeffion in
favour of that country, fpeaks of the Italians in
the following manner : *Nihil autem eft tam arduum
fedulitati humanæ, ad quod Italici acuminis præ-
ftantia non tollatur. Ab ultima etiam forte vulgi
non paucos quotidie in nomen atque opes felix induftria
producit. Nullum curarum genus quod divitias pro-*

[*] C. 66.   [†] De Nug. cur. L. i. c. 4.

mittat,

mittat, aut, fi opus eft, humilitatis fpecimen, afpernantur: longi quoque laboris fpeique patientes, quorum alterum faftus Hifpaniæ, alterum fubita atque præceps vis Gallorum non toleret. Aliæ, et ad rerumpublicarum gubernationem validæ mentes, ad omnem fortunam idoneæ, frugi homines, intentique ad futura.

Latinè fcribere inter illos haud pauci, non utique loqui nôrunt. Linguam quoque, quâ vulgò utuntur, quanquam nihil eft aliud quàm cum corruptâ latinitate barbarorum mixtura verborum, quantum poffunt ab originis fuæ veftigiis, loquendo, fcribendoque, avertunt, &c.

Tamen amœnitas ftudiorum in Italiâ non exigua, maximè eæ partes ad quas vivax naturæ lepiditas invitat. Teftis gentilitii carminis pulchra, et ad vicinorum invidiam gravis ubertas, quæ nomina poetarum, tot amorum ignibus ad fupplicii celebritatem fiðis ardentia, facravit. Nec enim intereft, fuâ an antiquorum linguâ locuti fint; cum fit ejufdem virtutis impetus, qui tenerum et opulentum ingenium in popularem, quique in veterem facundiam, laxat. Nam et Græci quæ intelligeret populus, fcribebant; et Romani Græcos mimos, et Atticæ eloquentiæ efficax robur, ad fui vulgi aures accommodaverunt.

Jam quid de Italicis hiftoriæ fcriptoribus dicam? Iftis quidem fincera prudentia victuris, illis autem tantum nimia eloquentia et partium favore peccantibus? Sed et fapientia cœleftis, et humanæ prudentiæ difciplina, cæteraque omnia quæ in Mufarum tutela funt, nunquam parum illius populi ingeniis debuerunt. Ad extremum non alibi fanðiorum virtutum exempla, pejorumve facinorum, quam in Italicis animis cernas; et quod quidam de Atticâ dicebat, nullibi

libi vel atrocior cicuta est, vel suavius apes exsuctis digestisque floribus cellas implent. See the sixth chapter throughout.

Instead of presuming to comment on the different parts of this animated picture, I shall only observe, concerning the article of arts and sciences, that Italy first cultivated several branches of study, which, in many countries where they have succesively come into vogue, are imagined to be new.

What author, for instance, can natural history produce, who had laboured for it with such firmness, extent, success, and so little profit to himself, as the celebrated Aldrovandi? On œconomics and agronomy, with all their appurtenances, Italy had excellent works, both in verse and prose, so early as the sixteenth century. Luigi Allamanni's poem *della Coltivazione*, of which Robert Stephens published the first edition in 1546, is universally known. The same subject, in all its particulars, had been discussed by Peter Crescenzi, so far back as 1473; and about the same time the Greek and Latin authors *de Re Rustica* were translated into Italian. The most eminent scholars and artists did not disdain to lay out their talents on that subject. Palladius was translated by Sansovino: the learned Peter Victorius, or Vettori, published a treatise on the culture of olive-trees; and to Soderini and Davanzati the Tuscans are obliged for excellent dissertations on the best manner of cultivating their vines and fruit-trees. The same century and the following produced a multitude of treatises on music, several good performances on tactics and every particular of the art

of

of war *(f)*, the firſt principles of which were laid down by the Italians. As to the higher ſciences, how well Galileo, the academy *del Cimento*, Caſſini, and ſeveral ingenious men whom the chief academies in Europe are proud to enrol among their members, have deſerved of them, is well known.

In the entertaining kinds, France owed tales to Boccacio and other Italians, whoſe talents in this manner of writing gained univerſal applauſe : Voiture's letters, with many others, were owing to thoſe of Annibal Caro, Aretin, and Tolomei : the burleſque kind had its riſe from the imitation of Berni, and other famous writers ; the ingenious criticiſm intitled *Guerre des Auteurs*, and *Reforme du Parnaſſe*, ſprung from the ſprightly criticiſms of Boccalini, and from Herrico's piece called *delle Guerre di Parnaſo*, printed in 1643. Laſtly, the *Chef-d'Oeuvre d'un Inconnu* is but a flat imitation of the famous *Commento di ſer Agreſto ſopra la ficcta del Padre Ciceo (g)*. If

(f) Such compoſitions were in no great eſteem with a famous Italian : *Libri*, ſays he, with a warmth ſuitable to the ſubject, *che altro non hanno in ſe che parole, non poſſono inſegnare i fatti ad altrui. Campi ſono ſcuole ; gli eſſerciti diſcepoli, e l'armi penne, le quali intinte nel ſangue inimico, ſcrivono l'arte Militare in la carne. Onde biſogna rivolgere e notare ſi fatte coſe in le guerre, e non in le camere, chi vuole imparare à vincere et a glorificarſi come buon Cavaliero e gran Duce.* Aretin, Letter 342, L. viii. i. e. "Books, as conſiſting merely of words, "cannot teach actions. Camps are the ſchools, armies the "ſcholars, weapons the pens, with which, dipped in the "enemy's blood, the art of war is to be written on the fleſh. "It is among theſe, and not in a ſtudy, that he who aſpires to "military glory, and the reputation of a great commander, muſt "make his remarks on tranſactions in war."

(g) M. d. Floncel, royal cenſor at Paris, has in his library all the beſt Italian productions in the ſeveral kinds above mentioned, to the amount of better than ten thouſand volumes,

If we take a view of the dramatic kind, what a multitude of tragedies and comedies, written with great regularity and real beauty, do we not meet with in Italy, before any other nation had so much as thought of trying its talents this way!

Thus, on a confideration of what arts, literature, and fcience, owe to the Italians, the advice of Pliny the younger to his friend Maximus, who was going governor of Achaia, may be extended to every gentleman of the north on his fetting out for Italy. *Cogita te peregrinum veniffe in eam regionem ubi humanitas et litteræ inventæ funt; ad homines qui jus à natura datum virtute, meritis, amicitia, foedere denique et religione tenuerunt. Reverere conditores Deos, reverere gloriam veterem et hanc ipfam fenectutem quæ in homine venerabilis, in urbibus facra. Sit apud te honor antiquitati, fit ingentibus factis, fit fabulis quoque. Habe ante oculos hanc effe terram quæ nobis miferit jura, que leges non victa acceperit, fed petentibus dederit. Recordare quid quæque civitas fuerit, non ut defpicias quod effe defierit. Qua magis nitendum eft ne rudis et incognitus, quam exploratus, probatufque, humanior, melior, peritior, fuiffe videaris*.*

* Lib. viii. Epift. ult.

The E N D.

COMPARATIVE HISTORY

OF THE

ITALIAN and FRENCH MUSIC.

EDITOR's PREFACE.

WHILST I was printing the preceding OBSERVATIONS ON ITALY, &c. this ESSAY fell into my hands.

From its fubject, and the manner in which it is handled, I conceived it would be no improper Appendix to the faid Obfervations. It contains feveral ancient and modern facts, equally relating both to Italians and French, and to the Art of which it gives the hiftory.

If this Effay does not prove a final decifion, at leaft it may ferve for a voucher in the controverfy, which for thefe twelve years has been on foot between the French and the Italian mufic, affigning fixed points, and giving a body to a conteft, which from its origin is, in moft mouths and pens, only a wrangle about words.

COMPARATIVE HISTORY

OF THE

ITALIAN and FRENCH MUSIC.

THE love of fong, which nature has annexed to the human organifation, was, according to the poets, what firft formed focieties :

Sylveſtres homines, &c.

The firft lifpings of melody, as directed by philofophy, enthuſiafm, or the paſſions, were the firft vehicle of laws, tenets, and foft emotions *(a).*

To follow ancient muſic through its developments and progreſſes, in a nation whoſe heart and organs were open to every object of fenſibility, does not belong to my fubject : befides, nothing can be added to the feveral details on this head given by M. Burette. Let me only be permitted to defire, that fome capable perfon, equally con-

(a) *Quis ignorat Muſicam tantum jam in illis antiquis temporibus, non ſtudii modo, verùm etiam venerationis habuiſſe, ut iidem Muſici et Vates et Sapientes judicarentur ?* Quintil. L. i. c. 10,

verfant

verfant with Greek and the theory of mufic, would, from the lights fcattered in the Memoirs of the Academy of Infcriptions, in the didactic treatifes of Greek muficians, and in the learned Meibomius's commentaries on thofe treatifes, compofe a connected hiftory of ancient mufic : fuch a work would be highly acceptable to the fcholar and the harmonift, as it may open frefh views ; and though it be, partly, no more than picking from the above monuments, yet it is a picking which requires a mafterly hand.

From Plutarch's Treatife, and M. Burette's comment on it, I fhall produce fome facts which belong to my fubject, and are preparative to it.

In the country which the Greeks and their firft colonies occupied, each tribe being equally enamoured with the Beautiful, and the harmony from which it refults, ftruck out different ways in the purfuit and attainment of it. Hence that difference of dialects in pronouncing one common language, which they enriched in varying it; hence that variety in the orders, the ftandards of architectonic beauty ; hence likewife that diverfity of modes, into which mufical melody was modelled.

Whether this diverfity be attributed to the climate, or the different conformation of the organs ; whether it be accounted the mere effect of chance, or the force of habit; it muft difpofe us to fee, without aftonifhment, what is doing among us and among our neighbours. Let us therefore not be furprifed, that the fame tafte for finging does not unite nations, of an extent far beyond the narrow limits of Greece;

nations

nations fpeaking different languages ; in a word,
nations no lefs difcordant in their manner of
feeling, than in their way of feeing and thinking.

It is natural that each nation fhould impart to
its finging and mufic the ftamp of that national
characteriftic, which diftinguifhes its genius,
manners, ufages, and cuftoms : it is natural,
from the analogy of relations and conformities
between fpeaking and finging, (the latter being
only pronunciation more varied, and more ftrongly
articulated) that, the fpeech of thefe nations being
different, their finging fhould likewife be different:
laftly, it is natural, that each nation, being
as jealous of its mufic as of its language, fhould
have an exclufive efteem for it, preferve it with
like care, and oppofe any too fudden and ftriking innovations.

Mufic, which for a long time had, among
the Greeks, been confined to the worfhip of the
gods, and to education, no fooner began to ftep
out of the circle to which the primitive artifts
had limited it, than a general outcry was raifed
againft the innovators. Auftere Sparta banifhed
Therpander for having added two ftrings to the
lyre ; the Argians impofed penalties on thofe
who fhould prefume to go about the like attempts; and, purfuant to the notion that mufic
had a direct influence on the manners and the
government, moft of the Greek republics loudly
declared againft every appearance of raifing it
from that mafculine and vigorous fimplicity, to
which tradition attributed its ftrongeft impreffions.

Thefe meafures failed of their effect, when
Greece,

Greece, inebriated with its profperity *(c)*, was carried away by a paffion for fhows. Mufic having got poffeffion of the theatre, Poetry, by which it had before been ruled, became the mufician's mercenary flave : words were facrificed to founds; energy, to extravagant modulations; the pleafure of the foul, to the aftonifhment of the ear; in fhort, Mufic, which till then had flowed like a gentle ftream between fixed banks, gradually became a torrent without banks, and without bottom.

Plato, who was himfelf a great mufician, ftrenuoufly oppofed the torrent, but in vain ; and to as little effect was he feconded by Ariftotle. The difciples of thofe two great mafters, unable to do any more than lament the depravation of the mufical art, confined their endeavours in its behalf, to difquifitions on the caufes and the degrees of this depravation.

The theatre fided with them. We owe to Plutarch the fragment of a comedy of Pherecrates, where *Mufic*, all in rags, and beaten to mummy, comes before the magiftrates with a complaint, againft one Menalippides, for beginning to enervate it ; againft Cynefias the Athenian, who had disfigured it by ftrained prolongations of the voice, without either expreffion or harmony; againft Phrynicus, who, with his arbitrary ftrains, paffages, and diminutions, had made it

(b) Ut primùm pofitis nugari Græcia bellis
    Cæpit, &c.   Hor. Ep. II. L. i.

  Si difciplina civitatis laboravit, et fe in delicias dedit, argumentum eft luxuriæ publicæ, orationis & cantûs lafcivia. Senec. Ep. 94.

    Luxuriant animi rebus plerumque fecundis.

quite unnatural; laftly, againft Timotheus, who by his mincings and hafhings had reduced it to extravagant quavers. Philoxenes had efcaped this cenfure; but that of Ariftophanes fell the heavier on him, charging him with *having made mufic more flabby, more flexile, more rumpled than a cabbage-fprout, fuperfeding melody with a fqueaking, fit only for low-lived ears.* " All the other " comic poets," adds Plutarch, " joined with " the general outcry."

The revolution which occafioned it, dates its æra from Greece's fine age; from that age, when Eloquence, Poetry, and all the polite arts, had been brought to perfection, by efforts and innovations, which were juftified in the confequences, gradually leading artifts to the exact imitation of fair nature, whilft the fantaftic efforts of the muficians threw them at a greater diftance from it.

Had the general outcry caufed by the latter, been the outcry of temporary jealoufy, it would not have impofed on the fagacious equity of pofterity; whereas Plutarch, together with moft of the Greek muficians who have reached us, and who were pofterior to the age in queftion, form as it were a perpetual concert of praife on ancient mufic, of threnodies on its depravation, and of complaints againft the innovators.

From whence it feems to follow, that objects of tafte, as mufic, have a point, *quod ultra citraque nequit confiftere rectum*; that the fame love of novelty, which leads to it, hinders one from ftopping at it, infenfibly leading on to deviations; that

posterity

pofterity is the only competent judge of the fuccefs or mifcarriage of artifts; in a word, that, as to arts, every age may be compared to a paffenger in a boat, who often imagines he is going forward, when in reality he is lofing ground.

By the light of ancient facts, and of maxims refulting from them, we fhall illuftrate fome particulars relating to the French and Italian mufic.

Long before the French name made any figure in Europe, the Gauls, our anceftors, had a national mufic, which, like that of the Greeks, was connected with their religion and politics; and the more intimately, being performed exclufively by a clafs of that fingular order of priefts, who, having wormed themfelves into the feveral branches of government, had infenfibly got into their hands the higheft prerogatives of the fovereignty. The hiftory of the Gaulifh nation throws no light on the beginning, nor confequent-ly on the duration, of this phænomenon: all we know is, that the authority of this body, the whole force of which lay in the clofe union of its members, was founded on ignorance and fuperftition; that is, on the exclufive poffeffion* it had affumed of literature, the fciences, and religion; on an intolerance with fword in hand; laftly, on their horrid facrifices, as the choice of the human victims was eafily made to fall on thofe who had prefumed to give the order

* *Avara et fœneratoria Gallorum philofophia,* Val. Max. Lib. ii. c. 6.

any

any umbrage or offence *(k)*. The Bards, a claſs incorporated with the Druids, were the poets and the muſicians of the nation. Their labours in both kinds, being ſubordinate to the intereſt, and directed by the views of the fraternity, precluded all the improvements, to which the rivalry of artiſts, the deſire of pleaſing, the love of novelty, &c. give birth.

Theſe poetical muſicians were poſted at the head of armies, and in the heat of battle ſang the proweſſes of the nation's demi-gods. To judge of their muſic from the account which the Romans have left us of this martial chanting, every circumſtance in it favours of barbariſm : ſome, comparing it to the bellowing of enraged elephants, called it *barritum* :* the emperor Julian compares it to the diſmal cry of owls and ſcreech-owls ; παραπλήσια ταῖς κλαγγαῖς τῶν ταχὺ βοώντων ὀρνίθων : Marcellinus, to the noiſe of an agitated ſea daſhing againſt the rocks.

The conqueſt of the Gauls by the Romans, the

(k) " The Druids," ſays Dion Chryſoſtom, Diſc. 49. " ruled in the Gauls, where the kings, amidſt all the ſplen- " dor of regality, are in fact no more than the miniſters " and executors of the good pleaſure of the prieſts :" ὧν ἄνευ τοις Βασιλευσιν ᵒδὲν εξῆν πρατlειν ᵒδὲ Θελευεσθαι. ὥϛε τὸ μὲν ἀληθὲς, εκείνᵒς ἄρχειν, τᵒς δὲ Βασιλεας αὐτῶν ὑπηρέτας ᵡ διακόνᵒς γίγνεσθαι της γνώμης, εν θρόνοις χρυσοῖς καθημένᵒς, ᵡ ᵒικίας μεγάλας ᵒικᵒντας, ᵡ πολυτιμῶς εὐωχᵒμένᵒς.

This paſſage has been overlooked by Dom Bouquet, in whoſe collection it ſhould have been inſerted; and likewiſe by Mr. Du Clos, who in his learned Memoir on the Druids lays down, as the leading fact, an ariſtocracy excluſive of all monarchy.

* In Antioch. Lib. ii.

downfall of Druidifm, which followed it, the
forced trade of the Gauls with their new mafters,
had but little affected their mufic, at leaft that of
the northern Gauls ; for, near four hundred years
after that conqueft, the emperor Julian, bantering
with a friend of his on a compofition which he
was fending to him from the fartheft part of Gaul,
faid, comparing it to thofe of the mufical poets of
this country, Ταῦτά σοι Γαλλικὴ κ̀ Βάρβαρος Μῦσα
προσπαίζει.

Two of Theodoric's letters,* written by Caf-
fiodorus, among whofe works they are to be
read, inform us, that the Gaulifh mufic continued ftill the fame at the time of the conqueft of the Gauls by Clovis. This prince, in-
tending to retain muficians in his palace, *qui
poteſtatis fuæ gloriam oblectarent*, had defired
Theodoric, *magno opere, magnis precibus*, to fend
him one of the fingers belonging to his chamber-
band. In the firft of the above-cited letters,
Theodoric orders one of his beft performers to
be felected, *qui cum dulci fono gentilium corda
domet* ; and, in the fecond, he acquaints Clovis
with the artift's being fet out.

The gravity of the Chriftian religion†, for a
long time allowed, in public worfhip, only a
pfalmody which differed but little from common
fpeech (*m*). After the converfion of Conftantine

to

* Epift. 40. et 41. Lib. ii. † Bona de Divin. Pfalmod.

(*m*) The finging of hymns, however, we meet with in
the earlieft antiquity of the church. St. Paul recommends
it to the Chriftians. Pliny certifies it to have been the
cuftom of the primitive Chriftians. Clement of Alexandria
has preferved one of the moft ancient teftimonies. The
Therapeutæ

to chriftianity, St. Athanafius had excluded
from the church of Alexandria the chanting which
was getting'footing there: St. Ambrofe afterwa:ds
countenanced it in the church of Milan, fancti-
fying, among the profane tunes of paganifm,
fuch as had folemn graces comporting with the
dignity of divine worfhip.

This regulation, being juftified by the tears
which the ambrofial mode of finging drew from
St. Auguftine*, foon fpread throughout the church.
St. Gregory devoted part of the cares of his
pontificate in introducing into the Roman church
the finging known by the name of the *Gregorian chant.*

The Gallican church, authorifed by general
example, gradually adapted to public worfhip
many of its ancient national tunes, which tradition had preferved. In the latter times of
the Roman empire, the entertaining arts, with
which mufic may unqueftionably be claffed,

Therapeutes, who by many learned men are placed among
the firft Chriftians, paffed the nights of folemnities in finging, in two choirs, (one of men, the other of women)
hymns of different meafures, and different tunes, partly
alternately moving the arms, the hands, and all the body,
advancing, ftopping, turning from the right to the left,
and from the left to the right; the mixture of the men's
voice with the fhrill voice of the women, producing a
fymphony, by the meafure of which that of the choirs
was regulated. This was likewife the practice of Pagan
Greece, in finging odes intermixed with epodes, ftrophes,
and anti-ftrophes. See Philo in the Treatife on a *Contem-
plative Life,* publifhed by P. Monfaucon.

* Aug. Confeff. Lib. x.

being

being driven out of Europe by the incurfions of the Barbarians, now exifted only in remembrance, tradition, and a rote that could furnifh nothing new to the performances which this revolution in the difcipline of the church required.

Rome was the beft provided ; for St. Gregory, collecting the remains of tafte which Rome ftill retained under its ruins, and borrowing from the Greek, and the principal Latin churches, the airs which he thought moft fuitable to the office of the church, compofed and pricked down, with his own hand, the antiphonary which on that account he called *Antiphonarium centonem*, and by which the finging of the Roman church is to this day regulated.

This antiphonary contained only the fubftance of the finging, and that indicated rather for recollecting than learning it. In order to fettle and perpetuate this modulation, St. Gregory founded a fchool of fingers, as a nurfery for this part of the ecclefiaftical office, and of which he himfelf was the firft mafter.

What St. Gregory did for Rome, Claudian Mamert, brother to the bifhop of Vienne, who inftituted the Rogation days, had already done for part of the Gauls, at leaft, according to the epitaph confecrated to his memory by Sidonius Apollinaris.

PSALMORUM HIC MODULATOR ET PHONASCUS
ANTE ALTARE, GRATULANTE FRATRE,
INSTRUCTAS DOCUIT SONARE CLASSES.

Hiftory gives us no infight into the ftate of the Gallican finging till the eight or ninth centuries.

Abbé

Abbé Lebeuf conceives, that in that early epocha it had borrowed certain modulations from the Roman finging, which likewife had borrowed from the Gallican. But fome it had of its own growth, abfolutely peculiar to itfelf, and of which not a few are tranfmitted down to our times : fuch are the *melodies, triomphes, tropes,* or *laudes,* ftill fung in fome French cathedrals, before the epiftle, on the great feftivals. In fome places they are called *laudes epifcopi,* and fung by regular canons, who, we may be fure, formerly fhone in this part of the finging : their gratuities for this performance are paid by the bifhop.

It would be quite needlefs to inform the reader, that the premiffes relate only to plain church finging.* Mufic in parts, if the Romans and Greeks were at all acquainted with it, had been buried with the fine arts under the ruins of the empire. Its birth or revival, call it which you pleafe, is of a much later date than the time we are fpeaking of. So early as the ninth century, the Roman fingers, according to abbé Lebeuf, had taught the Gaulifh fingers. The multiplication of the concords, their feveral combinations, the organifations *in duplo, in triplo, in quadruplo,* the *faux-bourdon,* the *dechant,* and the *counter-point,* at length, after four centuries of trials, feelings, and endeavours, produced our prefent mufic. By means of the diatonic fcale, invented in the twelfth century by an Italian monk, it became a particular language, independent of all national idioms, and in which harmonifts could

* See Pere Kircher's *Mufurgia.*

B b 3

fix their ideas, revife them, communicate them to others, and tranfmit them to pofterity.

A learned Roman prelate has proved, that the arts depending on defign are indebted to the Chriftian religion for the prefervation of their manual practice, and their revival in Europe (*n*); and if we apply the fame kind of proofs to mufic, it would be ftill more eafy to demonftrate that it owes all it is to that fame religion.

On a retrofpect to the ftate of it in Europe, before the ninth century, we find it eftablifhed in the Roman and Gallican church, but with all the different modulations naturally arifing from the different genius of the two nations, the difference of language and organs, the ancient Roman urbanity, and the prejudice of a nation, which, after the moft vigorous refiftance againft the Roman yoke, defended its mufic as it had defended its liberty.

The Merovingian kings, not having Clovis's tafte for mufic, were obliged, even for their chamber, to make ufe of church-finging performed by priefts and clerks. Gregory of Tours * relates, that being, in 585, at king Gontran's court, that prince defired, at dinner, that the Gradual might be repeated by the deacon who had fung it at the mafs in the morning; and that, being much delighted with it, he immediately caufed the fame pfalm to be fung out, in a full chorus, by all the priefts and clergy who had attended their bifhop to court.

(*n*) Monfignor Francis Carrara, in his fpeech at the Capitol, on the 18th of September, 1758, on the diftribution of the prizes given for the three arts, by the academy of St. Luke. See the *Obfervations*, in the article of ROME.

* Greg. Tur. Lib. viii. N. 3.

Under

Under thefe kings of the firft race, the popes had only a very remote influence, even in the church-affairs of the French nation; till mutual fervices connecting the firft Carlovingian kings with the court of Rome, the popes took advantage of thefe connexions to extend to ecclefiaftical concerns, that immediate influence which had been lately given to them in one of the moft important ftate affairs. They endeavoured to introduce the Gregorian finging, inftead of the old Gallican moods, and in this were effectually feconded by Pepin and Charlemagne, who, having been feveral times at Rome, were become prepoffeffed in favour of the Roman finging.

Towards the middle of the eighth century,* Pepin had already fent to Rome fome monks to be inftructed in the Gregorian chant, in St. Gregory's fchool, under the infpection of pope Paul I. " In " 787†, on the celebration of Eafter at Rome " before Charlemagne, the fingers of his chapel " were for finging in the choir with the fingers " of the pope's chapel; *et ecce orta eft con-* " *tentio !* the French affirmed they fang the beft " and moft correctly; the Romans, on the other " hand, claimed the whole advantage to be on " their fide, and charged the French with being " utterly ignorant of the way of hitting a note, " befides their rude enunciation. The difpute " being laid before the emperor, and the French " making themfelves fure of his protection, grew " more vehement in afferting their fuperiority.

* Epift. Pauli ad Pepin.

† Monach. Engolifm. in D. Bouquet's Coll. T. v. p. 185.

" The

" The Romans, proud of their profound know-
" ledge and their regular ftudies in this kind,
" called the French, clowns, dunces, affes (o).
" The monarch, having decided the conteft in
" favour of the Romans, defired of the pope
" twelve chorifters of his chapel, whom he diftri-
" buted in France to teach the Roman note, or
" the Gregorian chant."

Whether it was malignity, or the want of fkill
in them, or obftinacy in the French, thefe inftructions, far from anfwering the end defired, fpread
in feveral parts of France a mode of finging, fo
ridiculoufly mottleyed, as to be neither Roman nor
Gallican. On Charlemagne's complaints, Adrian II.
recalled thofe chorifters, punifhed their mifbeha-
viour with imprifonment, and prevailed on the
emperor to leave two of his fingers at Rome,
whofe inftruction he himfelf would take care of.
When they were become mafters of the Roman
mood, he fent them back to Charlemagne, who
kept one for his chapel, and fent the other to his
fon Drogon, bifhop of Metz.

The inftructions of thefe two men*, backed by the
emperor's repeated orders, at length eftablifhed
the *Roman chant* in France : the French, whofe

(o) *Dicebant Galli fe melius cantare et pulchrius quàm Romani :
Dicebant fe Romani cantilenas ecclefiæ proferre, ficut docti fuerant
à S. Gregorio papa ; Gallos corruptè cantare, et cantilenam fanam
deftruendo dilacerare. Quæ contentio ante D. regem Carolum
pervenit. Galli, propter fecuritatem regis Caroli, valde expro-
brabant cantoribus Romanis : Romani vero, propter autoritatem
magnæ doctrinæ, eos ftultos, rufticos, et indoctos, veiut bruta
animalia, affirmabant, et doctrinam fuam præferebant rufticitati
eorum.*

* Monach. Engolif. *fuprà*.

name has fince been given to this note,* expreffed it tolerably well, efpecially at Metz, except the *diæfis*, the B flat, and the cadences, which the ftiffnefs of their organs *(p)* turned into a kind of braying.

This ingenuous confeffion of a French writer, to the difadvantage of his nation, John, deacon of the church of Rome, aggravates in unfeemly terms in his Life of St. Gregory :† " Thefe fep- " tentrional throats," fays he, " can exprefs only " the explofions of thunder, and the roar of " ftorms : when their rigor aims to bring itfelf to " any agreeable modulation, inftead of the ca- " dences, the trills, and diminutions, required in " fuch a modulation, you hear the rumble of " heavy carts jolting down a rugged flope ; and " thus, inftead of pleafing, they deafen the " ear *(q)*." National prejudice furnifhed the co- lourings of this picture. John was for revenging his nation of the reproaches caft on it by the French, that they had fpoiled finging by loading

* Capitul. Carol. M. *paffim.*

(p) Omnes cantores didicerunt notam Romanam quam vocant Francifcam, excepto quod tremulas vel tinnulas, five collifibiles vel fecabiles voces in cantu non poterant perfectè exprimere Franci, naturali voce barbarica, frangentes voces in gutture, potiùs quam exprimentes.

† Lib. ii. c. 7.

(q) Vocum fuarum tonitruis altifone perftrepentes, fufceptæ mo- dulationis dulcedinem proprie non refultant, quia bibuli gutturis barbara groffitas, dum inflectionibus et repercuffionibus mitem niti- tur reddere cantilenam, naturali quodam fragore, quafi plauftra per gradus confufè fonantia, rigidas voces jactat ; ficque audien- tium animos quos mulcere debuerat, exafperando magis ac obftre- pendo conturbat.

it with primneffes and puerilities *(r)*; and his re-crimination he concludes with this reflection, fug-gefted by the like odious principle: *Hæc retulerim ne indifcuffam Gallorum levitatem videar præter-mififfe.*

Amidft thefe endeavours for introducing the Gregorian chant into France, Charlemagne had greatly at heart the retaining fome pieces of the Gallic finging, which tradition had preferved in old military fongs : he was even a compofer in this kind ; and certainly no man in his whole kingdom more capable, if, as abbé Lebeuf affirms, though without quoting any authority, both the mufic and the words of *Veni Creator* are his.

Italy, in thofe early times, had *joculatores*, or poetical muficians, fince known in France by the names of *Trouveres*, *Miniftrels*, &c. Father Le Brun, and M. Du Clos (in his Memoir on the Scenic Games) have collected feveral articles of the capitularies and canons of councils held in France in the ninth century, againft priefts, ab-bots, and clerks, countenancing by their prefence the buffooneries *(joca obfcena, verba turpia)* of the jongleurs (joculatores) or who even bore a part in them. Suppofing thefe laws to have been general, it would follow, that the fhows pointed at prevailed not only in France, but even in Germany, as well as Italy.

Charlemagne*, coming down the Alps into Lombardy, in 774, was met by a Lombard poet,

(r) *Gallorum procacitas cantum à noftratibus quibufdam Næniis argumentabatur effe corruptum.*

* Apud Murat. Rer. Ital. T. i. P. 2. Lib. v. c. 10.

who fang to him a copy of verfes which he had compofed in his praife (s).

The troubles during and fubfequent to the reign of Lewis the Debonnaire, the wars in which both the empire and the French fceptre were wrefted from the houfe of Charlemagne, deprived the Mufes of the neceffary leifure and quiet for carrying on their labours with any fuccefs. Befides the general evils in which France and Italy became involved, the former fuffered extremely from the inroads and depredations of the Normans. Thefe calamitous times caufed, in the hiftory of the mufic of the two nations, a void of between two and three centuries, in which nothing relating to mufie fhews itfelf, but a few endeavours of the clergy and monks for preferving the old church-mufic from thofe adulterations, which an ignorant love of novelty was introducing.

This void throws us back to the twelfth century: the cities of Italy, availing themfelves of the anarchy in which the public misfortunes had left the Italians and French, fet up the ftandard of liberty, and erecting themfelves into independent ftates, rofe by agriculture, arts, trade, a numerous population, and all the advantages of which liberty, directed by good laws, is productive, to a very flourifhing degree of profperity.

The fine arts caught the ardour of thefe revolutions. About the beginning of the twelfth century, Guy Aretin having opened a way for carrying mufic to perfection, the Italians came into it

(s) Ad Carolum venit jocalator Lombardus, et cantiunculam à fe compofiiam de eodem, ore rotunde in confpectu fuorum cantavit.

iu

in crowds, whilft the French declared for the ancient method.

Abbé Lebeuf, * on the contrary, thinks that it does not appear in hiftory, that Aretin's method met with any oppofition, and that the worth of it was not perceived: but Du Cange, in the word *Nota*, quotes a paffage of Letald, whom he makes cotemporary with Guy Aretin, *(qui eodem fæculo vixit)*. In this paffage, which is taken from the Life of St. Julian, bifhop of Mans, Letald, the author of his Life, mentions the office of that fame faint, the words and mufic of which he had compofed, and concerning which he gives to underftand, that he has preferred the ancient method to the new, the firft effays of which were but little agreeable to French ears *(barbaram et inexpertam)*. " For my part," adds the French monk, " thefe novelties are my averfion, their only merit " being a deviation from our ancient mafters *(t)*."

Inftead of taking on me to fettle thefe clafhings of authorities, I fhall only mention the perplexity in which their oppofition leaves me.

This perplexity would be removed, were the paffage, in which John of Salifbury complains of the new mufic being introduced into the churches, applicable to the churches of England and France: that new mufic, according to his defcription of it, differs but little from the moft laboured mufic of

* Tr. du Ch. Greg. p. 4.

(t) Neque omnino alienari voluimus à fimilitudine veteris ritûs, ne barbaram et inexpertam, uti perhibetur, melodiam fingeremus; non enim mihi placet quorundam muficorum novitas, qui tantâ diffimilitudine utuntur, ut veteres fequi omnino dedignentur autores.

the

the prefent times; which looks as if he had in his eye the country where this mufic had but recently made its appearance; that is, Italy *(u)*.

On this paffage of John of Salifbury, the abbé grounds two affertions*. 1. That this finging, very different from the Gregorian chant, and adapted for private ufe, or profane affemblies, is not admitted into the church: 2. That its admiffion is very late.

The former little agrees with the Englifh writer's complaints of that finging being introduced *in confpectum Domini, in ipfis penetralibus fanctuarii.* The fecond, for which one may rely on the abbé Lebeuf's particular knowledge in the rites and the rubricks of the churches of France, is a direct proof, that John of Salifbury in this paffage meant only Italy, whither he had travelled.

From the churches it fpread among the people, and foon became the foul and band of thofe fchools and focieties of the *mirthful fcience,* to which both the Italians and the French equally owe their language, their poetry, and their mufic.

(u) Ipfum cultum religionis inceftat quod ante confpectum Domini, in ipfis penetralibus fanctuarii, vocis lafcivientis luxu, quadam oftentatione fui, muliebribus notis, notarum articulorumque cæfuris, ftupentes animulas emollire niuntur, cum precinentium et fuccinentium, canentium et definentium, intercinentium, et occinentium præmolles modulationes audieris, fyrenum cantus audire credas.... Ea fi quidem eft afcendendi defcendendique facilitas, ea fectio vel geminatio notularum, et replicatio articulorum, fingulorumque confolidatio: fic acuta vel acutiffima, gravibus vel fubgravibus temperantur, ut auribus fui judicii fubtrahatur autoritas. Cum hæc ita modum excefferint lumborum pruriginem, quam devotionem mentis poterunt citiùs excitare. Policrat. Lib. i. c. 6.

* Ch. Greg. p. 72.

Provence

Provence was the nurſery of theſe ſchools for both nations : the pure air of this charming country ; the fire of the men, and the ſoft livelineſs of its females ; the neighbourhood of the many polite courts in South France ; an hereditary taſte for arts, in a houſe which for a long time held the ſovereignty of Provence ; the reſidence of the popes at Avignon ; the love of pleaſure, which affluence had fomented among the Italians ; the munificent rewards which they beſtowed on the inſtruments of their pleaſures, concurred to promote a ſcience, in which modern Italy, and afterwards France, rivalled ancient Greece. The following ages were ſo far convinced of the obligation they were under to Provence, as to imagine that Charlemagne, in the diviſion of his dominions, had given up the intire property of it to the poets, jeſters, minſtrels, and other members of the *mirthful ſcience*.

The learned Muratori, in his twenty-ninth diſſertation on the Antiquities of Italy in the middle age, makes mention, from cotemporary monuments, of the *plenary courts* very frequently held by the princes and ſtates of Italy, and at which there never failed to be companies of minſtrels, mimes, jeſters, buffoons, mountebanks, &c. Under the generical name of *Court-men (Uomini di corte)* theſe people, joining their talents, improved the merriments of the jocund ſeaſons, which ſometimes laſted a whole month. During all this time, they were handſomely boarded, and, agreebly to a cuſtom of which ſome adumbrations are to be met with in Ariſtophanes*, Martial, and St.

* Ariſtoph. Comed. of the Clouds.

Auguſtine,

Auguſtine*, each on his diſmiſſion had a ſuit of
cloaths given to him; and it was nothing uncom-
mon for the top performers of each kind to be pre-
ſented with chains of ſilver, and even of gold,
horſes with rich capariſons, &c.† At the wedding
of Antony De la Scala, a liſt was taken of above
two hundred of theſe virtuoſos, *qui ſinguli perce-
perunt indumenta valoris ad minas decem ducatorum
pro quoque.*‡ That of Galeazzo Viſconti drew together ſuch a number, that the gratuities amounted
to *pluſquam ſeptem millia pannorum bonorum*§. Laſtly,
above fifteen hundred were preſent at à plenary
court held by the Malateſtas at Rimini.

Theſe largeſſes encouraged, ſupported, and
perpetuated the pleaſureable arts, which thus amply partook of the riches with which Italy at that
time abounded. They had not ſuch a good time
of it in other countries, where œconomy ſeconded
the anathemas which the church uſed frequently
to fulminate againſt thoſe profane amuſements.
The emperor Henry II. on his marriage with
Agnes de Poitiers, ſent away, without the leaſt
entertainment or reward, an infinite multitude of
virtuoſos, whom the confident expectation of another kind of treatment had drawn to that ſolem-
nity *(x)*. The princes and nobility, in order to
rid themſelves of ſuch expence, and at the ſame

* Auguſt. in Johan. Tr. 100. c. 2.
† Pulci Hiſt. Vicentina.
‡ Guill. Ventura Chron.
§ Chron. di Ceſena.

*(x) Infinitam multitudinem Hiſtrionum & Joculatorum ſine cibo
& muneribus vacuam et mœrentem dimiſit.* Chron. Virzi-
burg.

time to be revenged of thofe fulminations which curtailed their diverfions, would fometimes let loofe the virtuofos on the clergy, empowering them to levy contributions for their reward; a licence which, in a council held at Ravenna,* in 1286, was condemned as *importunita abufiva*.

At this very epocha the Italians had regular plays, whilft the French knew nothing beyond farces, half burlefque and half religious, fuch as the *Simple Mother*, the *Afs*, with exhibitions of the Paffion, and the Myfteries, and this only in holiday times, fottifhly imagining, that thus acting the Saints, the Bleffed Virgin, and God himfelf, were acts of exalted devotion: whereas, in Italy, the *Corti bandite*, or feftive companies, who reforted to thefe feftivals, of which public notice was given fome time before the celebration, compofed among themfelves plays ftrictly conformable to the rules of *drama*, and animated by a judicious combination of all the feveral powers of Poetry, Mufic, and Dancing; together with ballets relative to the main action.

" The ftage-players," fays an old Milanefe chronicle, " ufed to fing the feats of Rowland and Oliver; " and thefe fongs were intermixed with, and fol-" lowed by, dances accompanied with mufic, " performed by buffoons and mimes in various " evolutions, equally grave and graceful." (y)

Donifon the monk, in the firft book of his poem on the famous countefs Matilda, has in a fingle line, not indeed very harmonious, fummed up the

* See Father Labbeus's councils.

(y) *Cantabant Hiftriones de Rolando et Oliviero. Finito cantu, Bufoni et Mimi in cycharis pulfabant, & decenti corporis motu fe circumvolvebant.*

feveral

feveral inftruments which formed the orcheftras of thofe fpectacles :

Tympana cum cytaris, ftivifque (z) lyrifque fonant hæc.

Spectacles of this fort had likewife their decorations and machines, which indeed were the main part in that exhibition defcribed in the following manner by John Villani :

" The citizens," fays he*, " of St. Friano's
" quarter at Florence, had an old cuftom of
" giving every year an exhibition, the fcheme of
" which was always new, and ftrikingly fingular.
" In the beginning of the year 1304, that jocund
" body gave notice, that whoever was for know-
" ing news from the other world (*faper novelle*
" *de l'altro mondo*) fhould repair, on the firft of
" May, to the bridge which divides the city of
" Florence. On the day appointed, the bed of
" the Arno was found covered with machines,
" reprefenting dens and caverns of various forms,
" in which, amidft fire, flames, fhrieks, ejula-
" tions, and howlings, were feen the tortures
" which devils, under a thoufand hideous forms,
" were bufy in inflicting on the damned ; when,
" lo ! in the height of the fhow, the bridge being
" then only of wood, part of it gave way under
" the croud !"

In thofe ages of darknefs I have met with only one act of hoftility between Italy and France,

C c

relating

(z) The word *ftiva* occurs indeed in Du Cange ; but Donifon's line is the only voucher quoted for it. Should it not rather be *pivis*, from *piva*, a very old Tufcan word, and fynonymous with *cornamufa*, but indeed more fuitable to poetry ?

* Lib. viii. c. 10.

relating to mufic; and that is, in a decree of
the republic of Bologna, which Ghirardacci,
in his hiftory of that republic, places in the year
1288. That decree orders, *Ut cantores Franci-*
genorum in plateis communis ad cantandum omnino
morari non poffent.

I know of no monument, from which any fure
judgment may be formed of the ftate of Italian
mufic during thofe times: it may only be fuppofed, that the opportunities of diftinguifhing itfelf at the feftivals and exhibitions, which were
infinitely more frequent in Italy than in France;
the kind reception which entertaining talents every
where met with, together with the rewards beftowed on the *Coryphæi* of thofe arts, muft of
courfe have powerfully improved and ftimulated
the natural difpofitions of thofe numerous companies, which devoted themfelves to mufic, as
their fettled bufinefs.

I had made myfelf fure of finding fome information, concerning the ftate and the refpective
claims of the Italian and the French mufic, in
that letter of Petrarch's, where he lays before
Urban V. the feveral reafons, which in his
opinion intitled Italy and the Italians to that pontiff's preference above France and the French:
whereas in this, and all the articles of mere pleafure, he feems to give the fuperiority to the
French, but referves the folid and effential qualities for his own countrymen: *De moribus vulga-*
ribus, fays he, *fateor Gallos et facetos homines, et*
geftuum verborumque levium, qui libenter ludunt,
lauté cænant, crebrò bibunt, avidè convivantur:
vera autem gravitas et realis moralitas apud Italos
femper fuit. Epift. Genil. lib. ix. ep. i.

As

As to the remaining monuments of French music under the same epochas, they have all passed through abbé Lebeuf's hands: the most ancient are of the eleventh century. He has seen some of the two following centuries: he has perused the old French ballad-makers; he has examined the count De Champaign's famous ballads, with Danz Gauthier's songs and lamentations; and in all these compositions, even those of the twelfth and thirteenth centuries, he could see only " tunes " with little or no melody; tunes, in which many " graces were left to be supplied by the singers; " tunes, which were mere Gregorian singing, and " that of the *seventh mood*, of all others the most " dull and disagreeable, and at the same time the " most difficult: but," adds the judicious censor, " the ears of that time probably were accustomed " to them, so that those tunes seemed fine, and " affected them accordingly."

It must be added, that Italy, in the composition of musical dramas, was some centuries beforehand with France; and that *those aukward groupes of pilgrims**, who opened the first theatre in Paris with representations of the Passion, brought the first notion of them from Italy.

Indeed, we find from the ancient Italian chronicles,† that such representations of the Passion and other mysteries, prevailed in Italy, so early as the thirteenth century. The grand jubilee in the following century, drawing numberless crowds of pilgrims from all parts of Europe to Rome, this put them on the design of introducing into their several countries the imita-

C c 2

tions

---

* Boileau.   † See Muratori.

tions of fhows, which from their novelty, and their agreement with the tafte of the times, could not fail of having a great run.

As to dramatic compofitions in mufic, on fubjects either taken from pagan mythology, or purely allegorical, the mufical improvements of the Italians qualified them to fhine in this kind, long before other nations were in any wife capable of fuch performances. The æra of them was from the year 1480. The firft effay was exhibited by cardinal Riari, to the pope his uncle, and the whole Roman court, in an opera entitled *Pomponiano**. The Medicean family foon gave into this fplendid kind, and difplayed that tafte and munificence, for which every branch of the fine arts was fo highly indebted to it.

From Florence thefe reprefentations quickly fpread into all the Italian ftates that were able to fupport the great expences of decorations, dreffes, and machines, which even then were a part of thefe performances.

John Antony Baïf, who had been brought up among thefe fhows, during the embaffy of his father (the celebrated Lazarus Baïf) at Venice, was the firft who introduced the tafte for them into France. He turned his houfe into an academy of mufic, which was frequented with applaufe both by the court and city; but this academy died with its founder. †

Amidft all the fondnefs of Catharine de Medicis, and the Italians in her fuite, for their country exhibitions, all that the annals of French mufic

* Sulpitius in Epift. dedic. ad. Notas in Vitruvium.
† Papir. Maffon, in Elog. Baïffiorum.

mufic mention of this fpecies, is only a kind of opera, acted in 1582, at the rejoicings of the famous nuptials of the duke de Joyeufe and the princefs of Vaudemont.

I had hopes of finding fome infight into the ftate and the refpective claims of both mufics, towards the clofe of the fifteenth century, in the poem by Jean le Maire de Belges, called The Reconciliation of the Two Languages. The poet's fcope in it was, *to bring about a thorough peace and agreement between two nations feparated by the Alps, and ftill more by the difference of the climate, of manners and cuftom, as to action; and by accents, geftures, and pronunciation, as to fpeech.*

The author of this poem, which for the moft part confifts of triplets, after the Italian manner, places about Venus a mufic *loofe and wanton like herfelf*; and the inftrumental part of which was quite in a new tafte; the old pfalterions, dulci-mers, and pipes, being thrown afide for harps and monochords.

Whether the poet meant to indicate the Italian improvements in inftrumental mufic, or had his eye on fome efforts of the French in that kind, fcarcely could the latter fupport them, even under the reign of Francis I. though that prince was eminent for munificence to the fine arts, and his wars laid open a communication between France and Italy.

The Louvre collection of ordinances has one of Charles VI. dated the 24th of April, 1407, in favour of the fcience of *Minftrelifm*, and its practitioners, the chief of whom was ftyled King. In the fame collection there is even a memoir concerning a like ordinance, iffued by king John, in favour of the Paris minftrels. However emi-

C c 3

nent

nent we may fuppofe thefe hands to have been,
Francis I. thought fit to bring back, and to procure from Italy, feveral virtuofi in this kind. One
of the moſt diſtinguiſhed was Mercer Albert. (b)
Aretin, in a letter of the 16th of June, 1538,
compliments him on his excelling in an art, di che,
fays he to him, ſiete lume, e vi ha fatto sí caro a ſua
maeſtá e al mondo, i. e. " of which you are the
" luminary, and which has fo endeared you to his
" majefty, and to the world." He concludes with
defiring him to deliver to the king a letter which
he had written to him.

Whether thefe muficians had gone retrograde;
whether (which is little probable) Henry II. and
Catharine de Medicis had, on the deceafe of Francis I, fent them back to their own country; or whether, during their ftay in France, the art had been prodigiouſly improved in Italy; Brantome, in his Life
of Marſhal Briffac, tells us, " that this nobleman,
" who was for a long time Henry the IId's general
" in Piedmont, had the beft band of violins in all
" Italy, and paid them very handfomely. The late
" king, Henry II. and his queen, hearing great com-
" mendations of them, afked them of the marſhal,
" to teach their band, who were good for nothing,
" and no more than as little Scotch rebecks in com-
" parifon of them. They were immediately fent,
" the head performers being Jacques Marie and
" Baltazarin : the latter, coming afterwards to
" be valet-de-chambre to the queen, was named
" M. de Beaux-Joyeux."

If

(b) He is mentioned by feveral poets, and acquired a handfome fortune.

If the ftate of mufic in the country deferves to
come into account, I might mention, that in 1672,
Lewis XIV. paffing through the capital of a province neareft to Paris, that city, which now has
regularly two concerts a week, could give the
king no other mufical entertainment than a concert in the manner of that in Scarron's comic
opera, that is, of eight choir-boys, two of whom
fang, two played on the top of a bafs viol, and
the four others were hanged to four violoncellos,
under the direction of the mafter of the chorifters.
This the proprietor of the houfe where the
king had taken up his lodgings, accounted
an event fit to be tranfmitted to pofterity in a
picture; and from the very picture have I taken
this defcription.

On the fecond revival of the fine arts in France,
under M. Colbert's miniftry, to whom it owed
that of mufic is well known. Some zealous
Frenchmen will have it, that Lully acquired his
whole fkill and knowledge on this fide the Alps;
yet for the fymphonies of his firft opera he could
find only *forry rebecks*, the faintnefs of which for
a long time fhackled a genius, whofe fublimity
and fire was not known till it met with inftruments capable of keeping pace with it.

A writer, both cotemporary with that renova-
tion, and an excellent judge, has fpoken of it
with equal truth and impartiality. " M. Lully,"
fays he, " has enriched our mufical reprefentations
" with the moft happy productions of art, know-
" ledge, genius and experience, combined. Born in
" the country of fine productions, and on the other
" hand habituated to our ways by living long in

France,

" France, he has, from the difpofition of his
" nation blended with ours, made that mafterly
" mixture of one and the other, which pleafes,
" which affects, which ravifhes, and in a word,
" inftead of leaving any thing in Italy for us to
" envy, enables us to fet it copies."

The Italians who are moft able to form an
eftimate, have the fame thoughts of Lully, and
likewife of Rameau and Mondonville; nay, the
ftandard by which they judge of their own mufic,
is the melody which thefe French harmonifts have
hit on, and which they complain is often wanting
in the productions of their modern compofers.

Perfevering in the contraft between them and
the French, they have retained the ancient fimplicity in the accompaniments, and ftill more
ftrictly in their touch of the organ. Every note
is diftinctly heard, and the mafculine gravity of
their play anfwers to the majefty of the places,
where this inftrument is peculiarly admitted. It
commonly executes the thorough-bafs of the pfalmody, and afterwards performs its part *piano*, without lengthening or fetting it off with futile trills,
even in thofe pieces where it is left to its own liberty.
They who have heard, at Rome and Naples,
fome of the pieces which the organ plays at the
Elevation, mention them as pieces compofed and
executed in that noble fimplicity, which charac-
terifes and ever accompanies the Sublime.

In all other compofitions, the prefent Italian
mufic is a continual ftruggle againft difficulties
arifing one from the other. When no more difficulties fhall remain to overcome, when the glory
of getting the better of them fhall ceafe, when
they

they shall be smoothed to all symphonists, the love of change will necessarily bring back music to simplicity; and a melody, disincumbered from the noise which drowns it, will be felt by every ear.

This revolution perhaps is not far off; all instruments are carried in Italy to a point which seems a *ne plus ultra:* but the most brilliant execution there cannot deceive the ears of eminent connoisseurs; with them, the noise which astonishes the sensitive organs, is very different from the melody which should speak to the soul.

Naples has, for a long time, been the school and seminary of the best violins; yet they question their skill till they have been tried by the renowned Tartini, so that they flock to Padua purely to court his approbation. Tartini coolly hears them; and, after very attentively listening to what they propose to execute, " That's fine," says he, or " that is very difficult; that is bril-" liantly executed; but," adds he, putting his finger to his breast, " *it did not reach hither (b).*"

Father Martini Vallotti of Padua, an intimate friend of Tartini, and of the same taste in music, has formed a scheme for bringing the art and artists to true principles; and it is carried on by himself, Tartini, monsignori Giustiniani, and Marcello, Venetian nobles. This scheme comprehends the book of Psalms translated into Italian verse, as literally as could be without injuring the poetry, and set to a music as simple as Lully's plainest composition. I have seen the first production of this scheme, in two volumes excellently engraved.

(b) This exactly agrees with the *Observations*. See vol. II. p. 138.

graved. This mufic at firft fight appears to be common church-mufic.

Whilft the Italians are clofely furling the fails of mufic, France fpreads them all, and improves every wind to forward its courfe through the rocks, fands, and dangers, of a fea noted for wrecks. That which it feems to defy, would perhaps be rather advantageous than hurtful to it; as thereby it would only lofe the refufe of the Italian ware-houfes, of which it has haftily made up its cargo.

To fpeak plainly, when the revolution in Italy, of which the endeavours above mentioned feem a commencement, fhall be accomplifhed; when Italy, excluding from mufic thofe *concetti*, which its prefent poets and orators are no lefs careful to avoid, than thofe of the laft century were ftudious to affect; the French, notwithftanding their language, will be found hampered in all the bellowings, of which the Italians have rid themfelves, and which France will likewife lay afide in time, either from reflection or fatiety.

Of this the confequence will be, that two nations, fo like one another in fo many amiable qualities, will for a long time greatly differ with regard to mufic; that the endeavours of the French to clofe with the Italians may only widen the difference; and laftly, that thofe two nations, though running the fame race, may perhaps never meet at the goal.

The E N D.

I N D E X.

INDEX.

I N D E X.

Flo-

INDEX.

I N D E X.

INDEX.

Stu-

INDEX.

INDEX.